双语名著无障碍阅读丛书
·第三级·

珊瑚岛

The Coral Island

［英国］R.M.巴兰坦 著

沈忆文 沈忆辉 译

中国出版集团
中译出版社

图书在版编目（CIP）数据

珊瑚岛：英汉对照/（英）巴兰坦（Ballantyne, R.M.）著；沈忆文，沈忆辉译. —北京：中译出版社，2012.7（2017.3重印）

（双语名著无障碍阅读丛书）

ISBN 978-7-5001-3443-5

I.①珊… II.①巴… ②沈… ③沈… III.①英语—汉语—对照读物 ②儿童文学—长篇小说—英国—近代 IV.①H319.4：I

中国版本图书馆CIP数据核字（2012）第149775号

出版发行 / 中译出版社
地　　址 / 北京市西城区车公庄大街甲4号物华大厦六层
电　　话 / （010）68359827； 68359303（发行部）； 53601537（编辑部）
邮　　编 / 100044
传　　真 / （010）68357870
电子邮箱 / book@ctph.com.cn
网　　址 / http://www.ctph.com.cn

出版策划 / 张高里
策划编辑 / 胡晓凯
责任编辑 / 胡晓凯　范祥镇
封面设计 / 潘　峰

排　　版 / 陈　彬
印　　刷 / 保定市中画美凯印刷有限公司
经　　销 / 新华书店

规　　格 / 710毫米×1000毫米　1/16
印　　张 / 16
字　　数 / 200千
版　　次 / 2012年7月第一版
印　　次 / 2017年3月第四次

ISBN 978-7-5001-3443-5　　　　定价：22.50元

版权所有　侵权必究
中译出版社

出版前言

多年以来，中译出版社有限公司（原中国对外翻译出版有限公司）凭借国内一流的翻译和出版实力及资源，精心策划、出版了大批双语读物，在海内外读者中和业界内产生了良好、深远的影响，形成了自己鲜明的出版特色。

二十世纪八九十年代出版的英汉（汉英）对照"一百丛书"，声名远扬，成为一套最权威、最有特色且又实用的双语读物，影响了一代又一代英语学习者和中华传统文化研究者、爱好者；还有"英若诚名剧译丛""中华传统文化精粹丛书""美丽英文书系"，这些优秀的双语读物，有的畅销，有的常销不衰反复再版，有的被选为大学英语阅读教材，受到广大读者的喜爱，获得了良好的社会效益和经济效益。

"双语名著无障碍阅读丛书"是中译专门为中学生和英语学习者精心打造的又一品牌，是一个新的双语读物系列，具有以下特点：

选题创新——该系列图书是国内第一套为中小学生量身打造的双语名著读物，所选篇目均为教育部颁布的语文新课标必读书目，或为中学生以及同等文化水平的社会读者喜闻乐见的世界名著，重新编译为英汉（汉英）对照的双语读本。这些书既给青少年读者提供了成长过程中不可或缺的精神食粮，又让他们领略到原著的精髓和魅力，对他们更好地学习英文大有裨益；同时，丛书中入选的《论语》《茶馆》《家》等汉英对照读物，亦是热爱中国传统文化的中外读者所共知的经典名篇，能使读者充分享受阅读经典的无限乐趣。

无障碍阅读——中学生阅读世界文学名著的原著会遇到很多生词和文化难点。针对这一情况，我们给每一本读物原文中的较难词汇和不易理解之处都加上了注释，在内文的版式设计上也采取英汉（或汉英）对照方式，扫清了学生阅读时的障碍。

优良品质——中译双语读物多年来在读者中享有良好口碑，这得益于作者和出版者对于图书质量的不懈追求。"双语名著无障碍阅读丛书"继承了中译双语读物的优良传统——精选的篇目、优秀的译文、方便实用的注解，秉承着对每一个读者负责的精神，竭力打造精品图书。

愿这套丛书成为广大读者的良师益友，愿读者在英语学习和传统文化学习两方面都取得新的突破。

译 序

《珊瑚岛》(1885年)是英国著名作家罗伯特·迈克尔·巴兰坦的成名之作，流传甚广，被列为经典著作之列。本书所采用的删节本，自1931年问世以来，已再版数十次。

小说描写了三少年在南太平洋珊瑚岛上的经历。主人公拉尔夫从小热爱大自然，特别向往遥远神秘的珊瑚岛。他十五岁时征得父亲的同意，乘船周游世界。船遇暴风雨失事后，他和两个好友杰克和彼得金漂到珊瑚岛上，开始了一段难忘的历险生活。

岛上奇特的生物景观、美妙的热带风光迷住了三个孩子，但他们很快就发现生活并不像表面那么和平宁静，食人者的暴行使他们深感震惊和愤怒，他们不惜一切代价，勇敢机智地向受害者伸出了救援之手。最后他们终于找到机会，踏上了归乡之途。

三少年热爱生活、勇于探索、乐于助人的精神风貌在书中得到了充分展现，给人留下了很深的印象。

值得一提的是：本书是专门为学习英语的读者准备的，小说经过删节后词汇量不超过两千，而且几乎都是英文最常见的词汇。本书语言简单、生动、地道，保持了原著的风格,不失为学习英语的一本理想读物。

  巴兰坦是苏格兰人,生于1825年4月24日,卒于1894年2月8日,另著有《雪光和日光》(1855年)。

译 者

目录
CONTENTS

Chapter 1　The Storm ·················· 002
　　　　　暴风雨

Chapter 2　The Coral Island ·················· 010
　　　　　珊瑚岛

Chapter 3　Coconuts and Other Things ·················· 018
　　　　　椰子和别的东西

Chapter 4　At the Bottom of the Lagoon ·················· 034
　　　　　在环礁湖底

Chapter 5　We Look at the Island ·················· 044
　　　　　查看海岛

Chapter 6　A Shark ·················· 058
　　　　　鲨鱼

Chapter 7　A Garden, Some Nuts and Other Things ··· 072
　　　　　花园、坚果及其他

Chapter 8　Strange Clouds ·················· 094
　　　　　奇怪的水雾

Chapter 9　The Second Day of Our Journey ·········· 104
　　　　　我们旅行的第二天

目录 CONTENTS

Chapter 10　Back to Our House ·············· 120
　回家

Chapter 11　Diamond Cave ·············· 130
　钻石洞

Chapter 12　Pig Sticking ·············· 150
　杀猪

Chapter 13　We Build a Boat ·············· 158
　我们造了一条船

Chapter 14　We Examine the Lagoon ·············· 168
　我们查看环礁湖

Chapter 15　Penguin Island ·············· 180
　企鹅岛

Chapter 16　Another Storm ·············· 194
　另一场暴风雨

Chapter 17　A Battle ·············· 208
　一场战斗

Chapter 18　Alone Again ·············· 230
　再陷孤独

Chapter 19　Good-bye to the Coral Island ·············· 240
　告别珊瑚岛

Robert Michael Ballantyne

Chapter 1
The Storm

Wandering has always been, and still is, what I love to do, the joy of my heart, the very sunshine of my life. As a child, as a boy, and as a man, I have been a wanderer throughout the length and **breadth**① of the wide, wide world.

My father had been a captain, and when I was about twelve years of age I went to sea. For some years I was happy in visiting the seaports, and in coasting along the shores of England. But, while **engaged**② in the coasting trade, I met with many seamen who had travelled to almost every quarter of the globe. Of all the places of which they told me, none pleased my thoughts so much as the Coral Islands of the Southern Seas. They told me of thousands of beautiful islands that had been formed by a very small creature called the coral animal; islands where summer **reigned**③ nearly all the year round; yet where, strange to say, men were wild, **bloodthirsty**④ **savages**⑤. These accounts had so great an effect upon my mind that, when I reached the age of fifteen, I **resolved**⑥ to make a journey to the South Seas myself.

I had much difficulty in persuading my parents to let me go; but

1
暴风雨

① breadth /bredθ/ n. 宽度

② engaged /ɪnˈɡeɪdʒd/ a. 忙碌的,使用中的

③ reign /reɪn/ v. 当政,统治,占有优势
④ bloodthirsty /ˈblʌdˌθɜːstɪ/ a. 嗜杀的,残忍的
⑤ savage /ˈsævɪdʒ/ n. 野蛮人,野人,残酷之人
⑥ resolve /rɪˈzɒlv/ v. 决定,解决,决心

  周游世界,无论过去还是现在,一直都是我最喜欢的事情,它使我心中充满欢乐,是我生命中的阳光。从童年,少年,一直到成年,我都是一个旅行家,漫游整个广阔无垠的世界。

  我的父亲曾是位船长,在我十二岁时带我出海。那以后的几年里我曾有幸到过许多港口,并沿着英国海岸线航行。当我们在沿海做贸易的时候,我遇到了许多水手,他们几乎到过地球的各个角落。在他们讲给我听的所有地方中,我最感兴趣的是南海的珊瑚岛。他们给我讲述了那数以千计的由一种名叫珊瑚虫的小生物构成的美丽岛屿,岛上几乎四季如夏,然而说来奇怪,那里的人反倒成了嗜血成性的野蛮人。这些话在我心里留下了深刻的印象,在我十五岁的时候,决定离开父母漫游南海!

  说服我的父母让我独自旅行,是件相当不容易的事情。但是我极力强调如果父亲只满足于在沿海做做贸易,就永远不能成为一个伟大的船长。他认

The Coral Island

when I urged on my father that he would never have become a great captain if he had remained in the coasting trade, he saw the truth of what I said, and gave his consent. My father placed me under the charge of an old friend of his, a **merchant**① captain, who was about to sail to the South Seas in his own ship, the Arrow.

It was a bright, beautiful, warm day when our ship spread her sails to the wind and sailed for the regions of the south. The captain shouted; the men ran to **obey**②; the noble ship bent over to the wind, and the shore gradually **faded**③ from my view, while I stood looking on with a kind of feeling that the whole scene was a **delightful**④ dream.

There were a number of boys in the ship, but two of them were my special favourites, Jack Martin was a tall, broad-shouldered youth of eighteen, with a handsome, pleasant, firm face. He had been to a good school and was clever and lion-like in his actions, but **mild**⑤ and quiet by nature. Jack was a general favourite, and had a special **fondness**⑥ for me. My other **companion**⑦ was Peterkin Gay. He was little, quick, funny, and about fourteen years old. But Peterkin's fun was almost always harmless, else he could not have been so much liked as he was.

"Hallo, young man!" cried Jack Martin, touching me on the shoulder the day I joined the ship. "Come below, and I'll show you your bed. You and I are to be companions, and I think we shall be good friends, for I like the look of you."

Jack was right. He and I and Peterkin afterwards became the best and truest friends that ever sailed together on the stormy waves.

I shall say little about the first part of our voyage. We had the usual amount of **rough**⑧ weather and calm; also we saw many strange fish **rolling**⑨ in the sea, and I was greatly delighted one day by seeing a number of flying fish come out of the water and fly through the air about a foot above the surface.

① merchant /'mɜːtʃənt/ a. 商业的

② obey /ə'beɪ/ v. 服从, 听从

③ fade /feɪd/ v. 褪色, 消失, 凋谢

④ delightful /dɪ'laɪtfʊl/ a. 令人愉快的, 可喜的

⑤ mild /maɪld/ a. 轻微的, 温柔的, 文雅的

⑥ fondness /'fɒndnɪs/ n. 友好, 溺爱

⑦ companion /kəm'pænjən/ n. 同伴, 同事

⑧ rough /rʌf/ a. 粗野的, 粗暴的

⑨ roll /rəʊl/ v. 滚, 使…转动, 摇摆

为我说得对，就同意了，并把我托付给他的一位老朋友。他是一艘商船的船长，将开着自己的船——"箭号"——到南海去。

在一个温和而晴朗的日子里，我们的船在微风中扬帆起航，驶向南方。水手们认真地执行着船长的命令。我们的大船乘风破浪。陆地渐渐地消失在我的视野中。当我站在那里注视着这些的时候，突然有一种感觉，就仿佛这一切都是一个欢乐的梦。

船上还有另外几个男孩子，其中有两个成了我的好朋友。杰克·马丁是个高个子宽肩膀的十八岁男孩儿，有着一张英俊的脸，看起来意志坚强而又惹人喜爱。他受过良好的教育，聪明，有着狮子般敏捷的动作，但是天性却安静平和，他很有人缘，大家都很喜欢他，并且他和我特别好。我的另一位朋友是彼得金·盖伊。他个子小小的，十四岁左右，动作敏捷，爱开玩笑。但是彼得金的玩笑是没有恶意的，否则的话我们也就不会像现在这样喜欢他。

"你好！哥们儿！"在我第一天上船的时候，杰克·马丁一边拍着我的肩膀一边同我打招呼，"跟我下去，我带你去看你的床。你和我现在是同伴了，我挺喜欢你的，我想我们一定能成为好朋友！"

杰克是对的。在狂风暴雨的海上，他和我还有彼得金后来成了一起航行过的最要好、最可信赖的朋友。

起初一切都很顺利，无论是狂风暴雨还是风和日丽，我们都习以为常。我们还看到了许多从没见过的鱼在海里游弋。有一天我还惊奇地发现有许多飞鱼从水里跃出，在离开水面将近一英尺的空中滑翔。

The Coral Island

At last we came among the **coral**① islands of the Pacific, and I shall never forget the delight with which I gazed — when we chanced to pass one — at the pure white shores, and the green **palm**② trees, which looked bright and beautiful in the sunshine. And often did we three wish to be landed on one, thinking that we should certainly find perfect happiness there! Our wish was granted sooner than we expected.

A Wreck③

One night, soon after we entered the **tropics**④, an awful storm **burst**⑤ upon our ship. For five days the storm continued in all its force. Everything was swept off the decks except one small boat, and we all thought ourselves lost. The captain said that he had no idea where we were, as we had been blown far out of our course; and we were much afraid that we might get amongst the dangerous coral reefs, of which there are so many in the Pacific.

At **daybreak**⑥ on the sixth morning of the storm we saw land in front of us. It was an island circled by a **reef**⑦ of coral, on which the waves broke with great force. There was calm water within this reef, but we could only see one narrow opening into it. This opening we tried to reach, but before we reached it a great wave broke over the back of the ship, damaged it, and thus left us at the mercy of the waves.

"That's the end of us now!" said the captain to the men. "Get the boat ready, we shall be on the rocks in less than half an hour."

The men obeyed in silence, for they felt that there was little hope for so small a boat in such a sea.

"Come, boys," said Jack Martin, in a grave tone, to me and Peterkin as we stood on the **deck**⑧ awaiting our fate. "Come, boys; we three shall **stick**⑨ together. You see. it is impossible that the little boat

① coral /ˈkɒrəl/ n. 珊瑚

② palm /pɑːm/ n. 棕榈树

③ wreck /ˈtrɒpɪk/ n. 失事，破坏
④ tropic /ˈtrɒpɪk/ n. 回归线，热带
⑤ burst /bɜːst/ v. 爆裂，突发

⑥ daybreak /ˈdeɪbreɪk/ n. 黎明，拂晓
⑦ reef /riːf/ n. 暗礁

⑧ deck /dek/ n. 甲板
⑨ stick /stɪk/ v. 钉住，粘贴，坚持

最后我们来到了太平洋珊瑚岛附近的海域，最让我难忘的是，当我们碰巧驶过一座珊瑚岛时，那洁白的海岸和翠绿色的棕榈树，在阳光的照耀下是那么明媚美丽，让我欣喜万分。我们三个经常渴望能够登上一座珊瑚岛，心想那里肯定能找到完美的幸福！然而，不久我们的梦想就成为现实，比我们预想的要快得多。

失　事

我们刚刚进入热带地区的一天晚上，一场可怕的暴风雨袭击了我们的船。这场暴风雨一连肆虐了五天。狂风席卷了甲板上所有的东西，只留下一只小艇。而且在风中我们迷了航。船长也不知道我们现在的方位，因为我们被吹得远离了航线。更令人担心的是，在太平洋中到处是危险的珊瑚暗礁，我们或许正身处其中。

这场暴风雨中的第六个黎明到来的时候，我们的前方出现了一块陆地。那是一座被珊瑚礁环抱的小岛，狂风掀起的巨浪拍打着礁石，而珊瑚礁内却风平浪静。我们发现只有一条狭窄的水道通向那里。我们试着靠近这个开口。就在我们快要到达的时候，一个巨浪打在我们船尾，船毁了，我们只能任凭风浪的摆布了。

"我们完了！"船长对大家说，"把小艇准备好，也许在半小时之内我们的船就沉了。"

水手们默默地执行着命令，因为他们知道在这样的大海里，这艘小艇太小了，不能对它抱什么希望。

"嗨，小伙子们，"当我和彼得金站在甲板上听天由命的时候，杰克·马丁用严肃的语气对我们说，

can reach the shore, crowded with men. It will be sure to turn over; so I mean rather to trust myself to a large **oar**①. I see through the **telescope**② that the ship will strike at the tail of the reef, where the **waves**③ break **into**④ the quiet water inside, so, if we manage to keep hold of the oar till it is driven over the waves, we may perhaps reach the shore. What say you, will you join me? "

We gladly agreed to follow Jack, although I knew by the sad tone of his voice that he had little hope; and indeed, when I looked at the white waves that broke on the reef and boiled against the rocks as if in anger, I felt that there was but a step between us and death.

The ship was now very near the rocks. The men were ready with the boat, and the captain beside them giving orders, when a great wave came towards us. We three ran forward to lay hold of our oar, and had only just reached it when the wave fell on the deck with a sound like **thunder**⑤. At the same moment the ship snuck, the **mast**⑥ **broke off**⑦ close to the deck and went over the side, carrying the boat and the men along with it. Jack seized an axe to cut our oar free, but, owing to the motion of the ship, he missed and struck the axe deep into the oar. Another wave, however, washed the oar free. We all seized hold of it. and the next instant we were in the wild sea. The last thing I saw was the boat turning over, and all the **sailors**⑧ in the angry waves. Then I lost my senses.

① oar /ɔː, ɒə/ *n.* 桨,橹
② telescope /ˈtelɪskəʊp/ *n.* 望远镜
③ wave /weɪv/ *n.* 波,波浪,波动
④ break into 闯入

⑤ thunder /ˈθʌndə/ *n.* 雷电,雷声
⑥ mast /mɑːst/ *n.* 船桅,旗杆
⑦ break off 折断(断绝,突然中断)

⑧ sailor /ˈseɪlə/ *n.* 海员,水手

"来吧，小伙子们，我们三人要齐心协力。很显然，这艘载着这么多人的小艇根本不可能到达岸边，肯定会翻船。所以我宁愿依靠一把大桨。我从望远镜里看到我们的船会撞在礁石的后部，从那开始海浪涌进环形珊瑚礁内，变成一片静水，因此只要我们设法紧紧抓住桨让它跟着浪走，我们就有可能上岸。你们说怎么样，跟我来么？"

虽然我从杰克近乎绝望的声调里听出他几乎不抱什么希望，但我们还是很乐意跟着他。实际上当我看到泛着白沫的巨浪疯狂地拍打着珊瑚礁和岩石的时候，我意识到我们和死亡之间只有一步之遥。

现在我们的船更接近岩石了。当一个大浪向我们砸来的时候，水手们在船长的指挥下已经将小艇准备好了。我们三个冲上去紧紧抓住我们的桨，就在这时一个巨浪带着雷鸣般的呼啸砸在甲板上，我们的船触礁了，断裂的主桅杆打在甲板上，带着甲板上的小船和水手滚到一边。杰克抓住一把斧子准备砍断系着桨的绳索，但是由于船的晃动，他砍偏了，斧子砍进了桨里。然而，又一个大浪冲过来，使桨脱离了大船。我们紧紧抓住桨，瞬间落入了白浪滔天的大海。我看到的最后一幕是小艇翻了，所有的人被抛向愤怒的浪涛之中。接下来我就失去了知觉。

Chapter 2
The Coral Island

On recovering my senses, I found myself lying on a bank of grass, under the **shelter**① of a rock, with Peterkin on his knees by my side, **tenderly**② washing my face with water, and trying to stop the blood that flowed from a **wound**③ in my head. I slowly recovered, and heard the voice of Peterkin asking whether I felt better. Little by little the roar of the waves became louder and clearer. I thought about being left on a distant island far, far away from my native land, and slowly opened my eyes to meet those of my companion, Jack, who was looking **anxiously**④ into my face. I now raised myself on my arm, and putting my hand to my head, found that it had been cut rather **severely**⑤, and that I had lost a good deal of blood.

"Come, come, Ralph," said Jack, **pressing**⑥ me gently back. "Lie down, my boy; you are not right yet. Wet your **lips**⑦ with this water, I got it from a spring close by. There now, don't say a word," said he, seeing me about to speak. "I'll tell you all about it, but you must not say a word till you have rested well."

"Oh! don't stop him from speaking, Jack," said Peterkin, who, now that his fears for my safety were removed, **busied**⑧ himself in

2
珊瑚岛

① shelter /'ʃeltə/ n. 庇护所,避难所,庇护
② tenderly /'tendəlɪ/ ad. 柔软地(温和地)
③ wound /wuːnd/ n. 创伤,伤害,苦痛

④ anxiously /'æŋkʃəslɪ/ ad. 忧虑地,不安地
⑤ severely /sɪ'vɪəlɪ/ ad. 严重地(艰难地,紧凑地,纯朴地)

⑥ press /pres/ v. 扫,压
⑦ lip /lɪp/ n. 嘴唇

⑧ busy /'bɪzɪ/ v. 使忙于

　　我苏醒过来的时候,发现自己躺在长着青草的岸上,一块岩石的下面。彼得金跪在我身边,正轻轻地用水擦拭着我的脸,并试图止住我头上的伤口流出的血。我慢慢地恢复了知觉,听见彼得金在问我是不是感觉好一点了。渐渐地,波涛的轰鸣声变得越来越响,越来越清晰,我意识到我这是在一座远离家乡的孤岛上。我慢慢地睁开眼睛,正好和我的同伴杰克的目光相遇,他正焦急地盯着我的脸看。我用胳膊撑起身体,把手放在头上,发现我的伤势相当严重,而且还流了好多血。

　　"听我说,拉尔夫,"杰克一边说着一边把我轻轻地往后按,"躺下,伙计,你现在还没完全好。这是我从附近泉眼里取来的水,用它湿一下你的嘴唇。好啦,别说话,"看到我想说话,他阻止我说,"我会告诉你一切的,但是得等完全休息好之后你才可以说话。"

　　"哎!杰克,别阻止他讲话。"彼得金说,看到我转危为安,他已经不那么担心了,现在正忙着用

· 011 ·

building a shelter of broken branches to protect me from the wind; which, however, was almost unnecessary, for the rock beside which I had been laid completely broke the **force**① of the wind. "Let him speak, Jack. It's a comfort to hear that he's alive, after lying there **stiff**② and white for a whole hour. I never saw such a **fellow**③ as you are, Ralph; you are always trying to be funny. You've almost knocked out all my teeth, and nearly killed me, and now you go trying to make us think that you are dead. It is very **wicked**④ of you; indeed it is."

While Peterkin was talking like this, my mind became quite clear again, and I began to understand what had happened.

"What do you mean by saying I've half-killed you, Peterkin?"

"What do I mean? Don't you speak English; or shall I say it in French? Don't you remember —"

"I remember nothing," said I, "after we were thrown into the sea."

"Be quiet, Peterkin," said Jack; "remember Ralph is not well. I'll explain it to you. You remember that after the ship struck, we three jumped over the side into the sea. Well, I noticed that the oar struck your head and gave you that cut, which made you lose your senses, so that you seized Peterkin round the neck without knowing what you were doing. In doing so you pushed the telescope — which you held on to as if it had been your life — against Peterkin's mouth —"

"Pushed it against his mouth!" cried Peterkin. "Say forced it down his **throat**⑤. Why, there's the mark of the edge on the back of my throat at this moment!"

"Well, well, be that as it may," continued Jack, "you held on to him, Ralph, till I feared you really would kill him; but I saw that he had a good hold of the oar, so I tried my hardest to push you towards the **shore**⑥, which by good **fortune**⑦ we reached without much trouble,

① force /fɔːs/ *n.* 力量

② stiff /stɪf/ *a.* 僵硬的

③ fellow /ˈfeləʊ/ *n.* 人，朋友

④ wicked /ˈwɪkɪd/ *a.* 坏的,邪恶的,缺德的

⑤ throat /θrəʊt/ *n.* 喉咙

⑥ shore /ʃɔː, ˌʃɒə/ *n.* 岸滨

⑦ fortune /ˈfɔːtʃən/ *n.* 财产,命运,运气

树枝为我搭起一个避风的地方。其实，这几乎没有必要，因为在我身边的这块岩石已经完全把海风挡住了。"让他说吧，杰克。他浑身僵硬，脸色苍白，在这里躺了整整一个小时，现在能听见他的声音真是令人欣慰。拉尔夫，我从来没见过像你这样的人，你真是滑稽透顶。你几乎敲掉了我所有的牙齿，还差点杀死我，可现在你又企图让我们相信你死了。你简直是个大坏蛋，真是太坏了。"

彼得金说这些的时候，我完全清醒了，开始记起来发生了什么事。

"彼得金，你说我差点杀了你，这话是什么意思？"

"我这话是什么意思？你难道听不懂英文吗？还是我应该用法语来告诉你？你难道不记得……"

"我们被抛进大海之后，我就什么都不记得了。"我说。

"别说了，彼得金，别忘了拉尔夫还没好，"杰克转向我说，"我会向你解释的；你还记得在船触礁之后我们三个就跳进了海里吧。对，后来我看到船桨打在你头上，你头上的伤口就是这么来的，这一下子让你失去了知觉。你一把抱住彼得金的脖子，而不知道自己在干什么。你还紧紧抓住一架望远镜，就好像它是你的命根子，你用它推彼得金的嘴……"

"用望远镜推嘴！"彼得金大叫，"不如说是强迫我吞下去。噢，直到现在我的喉咙里还觉得噎得慌。"

"好了，好了，事情也许是这样。"杰克接着说，"拉尔夫，你紧紧抓住他，连我都担心你会把彼得金勒死的，但是后来发现他牢牢地抓住桨，我就使

The Coral Island

for the water inside the reef is quite calm."

"But what has become of the ship, Jack?" said Peterkin. "I saw you climbing up the rocks there while I was watching Ralph. Did you say she had gone to pieces?"

"No, she has not gone to pieces, but she has gone to the **bottom**①," replied Jack.

What We Hope to Do

There was a long silence after Jack **ceased**② speaking, and I have no **doubt**③ that each was thinking of our strange case. For my part, I cannot say that my thoughts were very happy. I knew that we were on an island, for Jack had said so, but whether there were people on it or not, I did not know. If there should be people, I felt certain, from all I had heard of the South Sea Islanders, that we should be **roasted**④ alive and eaten. If it should turn out that there were no people on the island, I **fancied**⑤ that we should die of hunger. "Oh," thought I, "if the ship had only struck on the rocks, we might have done quite well, for we could have obtained food from her, and tools with which we could build a shelter; but now — alas! alas! we are lost!" These last words I spoke aloud.

"Lost, Ralph?" cried Jack, while a smile **spread**⑥ over his face. "Saved, you should have said."

"Do you know what I think?" said Peterkin. "I have made up my mind that it's fine — the best thing that ever happened to us, and the most **splendid**⑦ chance that ever lay before three young sailor-boys. We've got an island all to ourselves. We'll take possession **in the name of**⑧ the king; we'll go and enter the service of the black natives. Of

劲把你向岸上推。幸运的是,珊瑚礁里的水面相当平静,所以我们很容易就上了岸。"

"我们的船怎么样了,杰克?"彼得金问。"我照看拉尔夫的时候,看到你爬上了岩石,我们的船是不是已经成了碎片。"

"不,它没有被撞成碎片,而是沉了。"杰克答道。

我们希望什么

杰克说完后很久都没有人说话,我确信每个人都在回忆我们奇特的经历。对我来说,这些经历并不怎么愉快。正像杰克所说的那样,我们在一座孤岛上,但我不知道岛上是否有人。如果有的话,根据我听到的所有关于南海诸岛的土著人的传说,我敢肯定,我们会成为野人的一顿烤肉。如果这个岛是座荒岛,那我想我们就得饿死。"哦,"我想,"如果船仅仅撞在礁石上,我们的日子就可以过得相当不错。因为我们可以从船上找到现成的食物,我们还可以用船上的工具建一个栖身的地方。但是现在——天哪!天哪!我们完了!"最后的几个词我大声地说了出来。

"完了?"杰克叫道,同时一丝笑容浮现在他脸上,"拉尔夫,你应该说我们得救了。"

"你们知道我在想什么吗?"彼得金说,"我现在肯定这是件好事,对我们来说是件再好不过的事情了,一个绝好的机会正展现在三个年轻的水手面前。这个岛完全属于我们,我们可以代表国王占有这座岛,还可以参加土著黑人的祭祀。当然我们应

① bottom /ˈbɒtəm/ n. 底部

② cease /siːs/ v. 停止,终了
③ doubt /daʊt/ n. 怀疑,疑惑

④ roast /rəʊst/ v. 烤,烘焙
⑤ fancy /ˈfænsɪ/ v. 想像,设想

⑥ spread /spred/ v. 传播;散布

⑦ splendid /ˈsplendɪd/ a. 极好的
⑧ in the name of 以⋯的名义

course we'll rise to the top. You shall be the king, Jack, and Ralph, the chief minister, and I shall be —"

"But **suppose**① there are no natives?"

"Then we'll build a charming house, and plant a lovely garden round it, full of the finest tropical flowers, and we'll farm the land, plant, **sow**②, **reap**③, eat, sleep and be joyful."

"But to be serious," said Jack, with a **grave**④ face, checking Peterkin's way of making fun of everything, "we are really in rather an uncomfortable condition. If this is a **desert**⑤ island, we shall have to live very much like the wild **beasts**⑥, for we have not a tool of any kind — not even a knife."

"Yes, we have *that*," said Peterkin, putting his hand in his pocket, from which he drew forth a small pocket-knife with only one **blade**⑦, and that broken.

"Well, that's better than nothing. But come," said Jack, rising; "we are wasting our time in *talking* instead of *doing*. You seem well enough to walk now, Ralph. Let us see what we have got in our pockets, and then let us climb some hill and find out what sort of island we have been cast upon, for, whether good or bad, it seems likely to be our home for some time to come."

① suppose /sə'pəʊz/ v. 推想,假设

② sow /səʊ/ v. 播种,散布
③ reap /riːp/ v. 收获,获得
④ grave /greɪv/ a. 严肃的,庄重的,严重的
⑤ desert /'dezət/ a. 沙漠的,荒芜的
⑥ beast /biːst/ n. 畜生,野兽

⑦ blade /bleɪd/ n. 刀锋,刀刃

该是他们的首领。杰克,你将会成为国王;拉尔夫,你是首席大臣,而我将是……"

"但是假如这里没有土著人呢?"

"那么我们就建一所漂亮的房子,周围再开辟一座美丽的花园,里面种满了热带的奇花异草。而且我们还可以开垦一片土地,在上面播种、收割,这样我们有吃的住的,多快活。"

"但是还是现实一点,"杰克神态庄重地说,端正彼得金把任何事都当作儿戏的态度,"我们目前的状况确实相当恶劣。如果这是一座荒岛,我们就不得不像野兽一样活着,因为我们甚至连像小刀这样的工具都没有。"

"不,我们有,"彼得金说着,把手伸进口袋里,拿出一把折断了的、只有一个刃的小水果刀。

"不错,有一个总比没有强。来吧,"杰克说着站起来,"我们只说不做,是在浪费时间。拉尔夫,你看起来已经可以走路了。让我们翻翻口袋看看还有什么,然后爬到高处,看一看被抛到了一座什么样的岛上,无论好坏,看来在未来一段时间里,这个岛可能就是我们的家。"

Chapter 3
Coconuts and Other Things

We now seated ourselves upon a rock, and began to examine our things. When we reached the shore, after leaving the ship, my companions had taken off part of their clothes and spread them out in the sun to dry; for although the wind was **blowing**① **fiercely**② there was not a single cloud in the bright sky. They had also **stripped**③ off most of my wet clothes and spread them also on the rocks. Having put on our **garments**④, we now searched all our pockets with all possible care, and laid their contents out on a flat stone before us. Now that we fully understood our condition, it was with great anxiety that we turned our pockets inside out in order that nothing might escape us. When all was collected together, we found that our **worldly**⑤ goods consisted of the following:

First, a small pocket-knife with a single blade, broken off about the middle and very **worn**⑥, besides having two or three pieces out of its edge. (Peterkin said of this, with his usual fun, that it would do for a saw as well as a knife, which was a great advantage.) Second, an old **brass**⑦ pencil-case without any lead in it. Third, a piece of thin **rope**⑧

3
椰子和别的东西

① blow /bləʊ/ v. 吹,风吹
② fiercely /ˈfɪəslɪ/ ad. 猛烈地,厉害地
③ strip /strɪp/ v. 脱衣,被剥去,剥夺
④ garment /ˈɡɑːmənt/ n. 衣服

⑤ worldly /ˈwɜːldlɪ/ a. 世间的,世上的

⑥ worn /wɔːn/ a. 磨损的

⑦ brass /brɑːs/ n. 黄铜
⑧ rope /rəʊp/ n. 绳,索

  我们坐在一块大石头上,开始清理东西。在离船上岸后,我的伙伴已经脱掉了湿衣服,在太阳下摊开晒干。尽管风很大,晴朗的天空里却没有一丝云彩。他们也脱下了我的湿衣服晾在大石头上。穿好衣服后,我们把口袋翻过来仔仔细细地查找,把找到的东西放在面前一块平整的岩石上。因为每个人都很清楚我们当前的处境,所以才这样急于把口袋翻个底朝天,生怕漏掉任何东西。把所有的东西收集到一起后,我们看到全部财产有:

  一、一个单刃的小水果刀,很钝,而且中间折断了。刀刃上还缺了几块。(彼得金带着他惯有的幽默,说这样的好处是既可以当锯子,又可以当刀。)二、一个没有铅芯的黄铜做的旧铅笔套。三、一段大约六码长的细绳。四、一根织帆人用的针,细的那种。五、船上的望远镜。船沉的时候,这架望远镜刚好在我手里,落水以后我还一直紧紧地抓着它。在我躺在岸上昏迷不醒的时候,杰克费了很

about six yards long. Fourth, a **sailmaker's**① needle — a small one. Fifth, a ship's telescope, which I happened to have in my hand at the time the ship struck, and which I had held on to firmly all the time I was in the water. Indeed, it was with difficulty that Jack got it out of my hand when I was lying helpless on the shore. Sixth, a ring which Jack always wore on his little finger. In addition we had the clothes on our backs.

While we were examining these things and talking about them, Jack suddenly started and cried out:

"The oar! We have forgotten the oar!"

"What good will that do us?" said Peterkin. "There's wood enough on the island to make a thousand oars."

"Yes, Peterkin," replied Jack; "but there's a bit of iron at the end of it, and that may be of much use to us."

"Very true," said I, "let us go and **fetch**② it." And with that we all three rose and went quickly down to the beach. I still felt a little weak from loss of blood, so that my companions soon began to leave me behind; but Jack saw this, and, with his usual kindness, turned back to help me. The storm had suddenly **died away**③, just as if it had blown hard till it **dashed**④ our ship upon the rocks, and had nothing more to do after that.

The Island

The island on which we stood was **hilly**⑤, and covered almost everywhere with the most beautiful and richly coloured trees and **bushes**⑥, of none of which I knew the names at that time, except, indeed, the **coconut palms**⑦, which I knew at once from the many pictures that I had seen of them before I left home. A white, sandy

① sailmarker /ˈseɪlmeɪkə(r)/ n. 修帆工

② fetch /fetʃ/ v. 接来,取来,带来

③ die away 渐熄(减弱,消失)

④ dash /dæʃ/ v. 猛掷,泼溅,冲撞

⑤ hilly /ˈhɪli/ a. 多小山的,丘陵的

⑥ bush /bʊʃ/ n. 灌木,灌木丛

⑦ coconut palm 椰子树

大的劲儿才把它从我手里拿出来。六、杰克总是带在小指上的一个戒指。另外就只剩下我们身上穿的衣服了。

我们边清理边谈论着这些东西,杰克突然叫了起来:

"桨!我们忘了那条桨!"

"那能用来干什么呢?"彼得金问,"岛上有足够做一千条桨的木头。"

"没错,彼得金,"杰克回答说,"可那桨的一头有一小块铁,这对我们可能有大用处。"

"说得对,我们去把它取回来。"我说。随着话音,我们三个都站起来,向海滩跑去。因为失血过多,我仍然觉得有些虚弱,所以很快落在了同伴的后面。总是很关心人的杰克,注意到了这一点,就回来帮我。暴风雨已经突然停下来了,就好像它用尽了力气把我们的船吹到礁石上撞翻后,就无事可做了!

海　岛

我们脚下的海岛山丘起伏,长满了各种异常美丽、五颜六色的树和灌木。说真的,除了椰子树,我当时对其他植物的名字一无所知。因为在出发前我就见过许多椰子树的图片了,所以一眼就能认出它。白色的沙滩像一条银链环绕着翠绿的海岸,不时有细碎的海浪冲上来。这种情景很令我吃惊,因为我记得在家乡的时候,暴风雨过后,海上的巨浪要持续很久才会平息。但是当我向海里望去的时

The Coral Island

beach lined this bright green shore, and upon it there fell the little waves of the sea. This last surprised me, for I remembered that at home, the sea used to fall in huge waves on the shore long after a storm had **died down**①. But on my looking out to sea the cause was at once seen.

About a mile distant from the shore I saw the great waves of the ocean rolling like a green wall, and falling with a long, loud roar upon a low coral reef, where they were **dashed into**② white clouds of water. These clouds sometimes flew very high, and every here and there beautiful coloured **bands**③ were formed for a moment among the falling drops. We afterwards found that this coral reef **stretched**④ quite round the island, and broke the force of the waves before they reached the shore. Beyond this, the sea rose and **tossed**⑤ from the effects of the storm; but between the reef and the shore it was as calm and as smooth as a **pond**⑥.

A Lucky⑦ Find

While we thus gazed, we were surprised by a loud cry from Peterkin, and on looking towards the **edge**⑧ of the sea, we saw him dancing and jumping about, and ever and again pulling with all his **might**⑨ at something that lay upon the shore.

"What a funny fellow he is, to be sure!" said Jack, taking me by the arm and hurrying forward. "Come, let us go and see what it is."

"Here it is, boys; come along. Just what we want!" cried Peterkin as we drew near, still pulling with all his power. "First class!"

I might say that my companion, Peterkin, often used very strange words, and that I did not always know the meanings of them.

On coming up we found that Peterkin was trying to pull the axe out

① die down 渐渐消失，平息

② dash into 冲入，与…猛撞

③ band /bænd/ n. 带子
④ stretch /stretʃ/ v. 伸展，张开，延伸

⑤ toss /tɒs/ v. 投掷，摇荡，辗转

⑥ pond /pɒnd/ n. 池塘
⑦ lucky /ˈlʌkɪ/ a. 幸运的

⑧ edge /edʒ/ n. 边，边缘，优势
⑨ might /maɪt/ n. 力量

候，就立刻找到了答案。

在离岸边一英里以外的海里，巨浪像一堵绿色的墙，翻卷着冲向低矮的珊瑚礁，发出惊天动地的轰鸣声。海浪在礁石上撞得粉碎，形成了白色的水雾。这些水雾有时飞得很高，在很多地方能看到绚丽的彩虹。很快我们就发现岛的四周都被珊瑚礁包围着。在海浪到达海岛之前珊瑚礁削弱了它的力量。珊瑚礁以外的大海里，因为暴风雨的关系海浪汹涌澎湃，但是在珊瑚礁里的海水却像池水一样平静。

幸运的发现

正当我们凝神注视着远方的时候，被彼得金的大叫吓了一跳。我们向海边望去，看见他又蹦又跳，一次又一次地用尽力气企图把什么东西从海滩上拔出来。

"真的，他可真是奇怪，"杰克边说边扶着我的胳膊急匆匆向前走，"来吧，我们去看看到底是什么？"

"在这儿呢，伙计们，来啊，这正是我们要的。"我们走近时，他一边用力拔着，一边向我们嚷道，"头等货！"

我得说我们的伙伴彼得金经常用一些奇怪的词，有时连我都不能明白他的意思。

走到近前，我们发现彼得金正试图把嵌在桨里的斧子拔出来。还记得吧，船沉的时候，杰克想用这把斧子砍断系着桨的绳索，但斧子却嵌进桨里。

of the oar, into which, it will be remembered, Jack drove it while trying to cut the oar free when the ship struck. The axe had remained fast in the oar, and even now all Peterkin's strength could not draw it out.

"Ah! that is good **indeed**①!" cried Jack, at the same time **plucking**② the axe out of the wood. "What good luck this is! It will be of more value to us than a hundred knives, and the edge is quite new and **sharp**③."

"The **handle**④ certainly is strong!" cried Peterkin. "My arms are nearly **pulled off**⑤!"

We carried the oar up with us to the place where we had left the rest of our things, intending to burn the wood away from the **iron**⑥ at some other time.

"Now, boys," said Jack, after we had laid it on the stone which had on it all that we had, "let us go to the **tail of**⑦ the island, where the ship struck, which is only **a quarter of**⑧ a mile off, and see if anything else has been thrown on shore. I don't expect anything, but it is well to see. When we get back here it will be time to have our supper and prepare our beds."

"Agreed!" cried Peterkin and I together. We would have agreed to anything Jack had said, for he was older and much stronger and taller than either of us, and was a very clever fellow. I think he would have been chosen by people much older than himself for their leader, especially if they wished to be led on a **bold**⑨ **attempt**⑩.

Food

Now, as we hurried along the white beach, which shone so **brightly**⑪ in the rays of the setting sun that it quite hurt our eyes, the idea suddenly came into Peterkin's head that we had nothing to eat except the

① indeed /ɪnˈdiːd/ ad. 的确,真正地
② pluck /plʌk/ v. 摘,猛拉,拔
③ sharp /ʃɑːp/ a. 锋利的
④ handle /ˈhændl/ n. 柄,把手
⑤ pull off 扯下
⑥ iron /ˈaɪən/ n. 铁

⑦ tail /teɪl/ n. 尾部,后部
⑧ quarter /ˈkwɔːtə/ n. 四分之一

⑨ bold /bəʊld/ a. 大胆的
⑩ attempt /əˈtempt/ n. 企图,试图

⑪ brightly /ˈbraɪtlɪ/ ad. 明亮地,鲜明地

直至现在斧子依然深深地嵌在里面,彼得金使尽全身力气也无法将它拔出来。

"啊!这真是太好了,"杰克边说边将斧子从木头里拔了出来,"真是太幸运了!这比一百把刀子都管用,况且它的刀刃还很新,很锋利。"

"斧柄也挺结实的!我的胳膊都快被拔出来了。"彼得金也叫道。

我们把桨同其他东西放在一起,打算以后把木头烧掉,这样就可以把铁弄下来。

当我们把桨放在摆着我们全部财产的石头上后,杰克说:"小伙子们,岛的后面离我们只有大约四分之一英里远,咱们的船就是在那里沉的,我们去看看是不是还有什么其他东西被冲上岸了。我并不指望会找到什么,但也不妨去看看。等我们回来的时候,就该是吃晚饭和准备睡觉的时候了。"

"好的!"我和彼得金同时喊道。杰克说什么我们都会同意,因为他无论年龄,力气和个头都比我们要大得多,更何况他是个聪明绝顶的家伙。我想,即便是年龄比杰克大的人,也会选他当头儿的,特别是在他们期望有人能带领他们去冒险的时候。

食 物

我们在白色的沙滩上快步走着,落日的余晖在沙滩上强烈的反光把我们的眼睛弄得生疼。彼得金突然想到除了在四周到处生长的各种野果子外,我们什么可吃的东西都没有。

The Coral Island

wild fruits, many of which grew all round us.

"What shall we do, Jack?" said he, with a sad look. "Perhaps they may not be good to eat; they may kill us!"

"No fear of that," **replied**① Jack, "I have **observed**② that a few of them are like some of the fruits that grow wild on our own native hills. Besides, I saw one or two strange birds eating them just a few minutes ago, and what won't kill the birds won't kill us. But look up there, Peterkin," continued Jack, pointing to the head of a coconut palm. "There are **nuts**③ for us in all stages."

"So there are!" cried Peterkin, who, not being very **observant**④, had been thinking too much of other things to notice anything so high above his head as the fruit of a palm tree.

But whatever **faults**⑤ my young friend had, he could certainly move quickly. Indeed, the nuts had hardly been pointed out to him when he climbed up the tall **trunk**⑥ of the tree, and in a few minutes came down with three nuts, each as large as a man's hand.

"You had better keep them till we come back," said Jack.

"Let us finish our work before eating."

"So be it, **captain**⑦! Go ahead," cried Peterkin, putting the nuts into his pocket. "In fact, I don't want to eat just now, but I would give a good deal for a drink. Oh, that I could find some water! But I don't see the smallest sign of any about here. I say, Jack, how does it happen that you seem to know everything? You have told us the names of half a **dozen**⑧ trees already, and yet you say that you were never in the South Seas before."

"I don't know everything, Peterkin, as you'll find out before long," replied Jack, with a smile; "but I have been a great reader of books of travel all my life, and that has taught me a good many things that you, **perhaps**⑨ do not know."

① rely /rɪˈplaɪ/ v. 回答,答复

② observe /əbˈzɜːv/ v. 观察,注意到

③ nut /nʌt/ n. 坚果

④ observant /əbˈzɜːvənt/ a. 观察力敏锐的

⑤ fault /fɔːlt/ n. 缺点

⑥ trunk /trʌŋk/ n. 树干

⑦ captain /ˈkæptɪn/ n. 船长,首领

⑧ dozen /ˈdʌzn/ n. (一)打,十二个

⑨ perhaps /pəˈhæps/ ad. 也许,可能

"我们怎么办,杰克?"他伤心地说,"可能这些野果子都不能吃,我们会被毒死的!"

杰克回答说:"不用怕,我注意到一些野果和我们家乡山上的野果子很相像,况且几分钟前我还看到一两只从没见过的鸟儿吃了它们。鸟儿没被毒死,那我们也不会死的。再向上看,彼得金,"杰克用手指着椰子树的树冠接着说,"我们什么时候都会有这种果子吃。"

"太对了!"彼得金叫道,他是个观察力不够敏锐的孩子,头脑里又充满了其他的念头,所以根本没注意到像头顶上的棕榈树果子那样高的任何东西。

但是无论我的这位小朋友有什么样的小缺点,他的行动可算是十分敏捷。告诉他有果子吃的话音还没落,他已经爬上了高高的树干,几分钟后,手里拿着三个巴掌大小的果子又爬了下来。

杰克说:"现在最好先留着这几个果子,等我们回来吃。我们得先干完活再吃东西。"

"遵命,头儿。走吧。"彼得金大声回答,边说边把果子放进自己的口袋里。"说真的,我现在根本就不想吃东西,就是很渴,要是能找到水就好了。真遗憾,这儿连水的影子都没有。喂,杰克,你怎么什么都知道啊?你说你从来没到过南海,你怎么能说出这么多树的名字呢?"

杰克笑着回答:"你马上就能知道我并不是万事通,彼得金。我从小就非常喜欢读游记,从中我学到了许多你也许还不了解的东西。"

"噢!杰克,你说的这些可真没道理。如果你一

The Coral Island

"Oh, Jack, that's all **nonsense**①. If you begin to say you have learnt everything from books, I'll quite lose my opinion of you," cried Peterkin.

"Very well, Peterkin, we shall see," said Jack, stopping under the shade of a coconut tree. "You said you were **thirsty**② just a minute ago; now jump up that tree and bring down a nut — not a **ripe**③ one, bring a green, unripe one."

Peterkin looked surprised, but seeing that Jack was in **earnest**④, he **obeyed**⑤.

"Now cut a **hole**⑥ in it, and put it to your mouth, old fellow," said Jack.

Peterkin did as he was told, and we both **burst into**⑦ laughter at the changes that instantly passed over his **expressive**⑧ face. When he had put the nut to his mouth, and thrown back his head in order to catch what came out of it, his eyes opened to twice their usual size with surprise, while his throat moved quickly in the act of swallowing. Then a smile and look of great delight came over his face. At length he stopped, and, drawing a long breath, cried:

"Wonderful! Perfectly wonderful! I say, Jack, you're a Briton — the best fellow I ever met in my life. Only taste that!" said he, turning to me and holding the nut to my mouth.

I **immediately**⑨ drank, and certainly I was much surprised at the delightful drink that flowed down my throat. It was **extremely**⑩ cool, and had a sweet, but sharp, taste. I handed the nut to Jack, who, after tasting it, said:

"Now, Peterkin, you unbeliever, I never saw or tasted a coconut in my life before, except those sold in shops at home; but I once read that the green nuts **contained**⑪ that **stuff**⑫ and you see it is true!"

① nonsense /ˈnɒnsəns/ n. 胡说,荒谬的言行

② thirsty /ˈθɜːstɪ/ a. 口渴的
③ ripe /raɪp/ a. 成熟的

④ earnest /ˈɜːnɪst/ n. 诚挚,认真
⑤ obey /əˈbeɪ/ v. 服从,听从
⑥ hole /həʊl/ n. 孔,洞,穴

⑦ burst into 突然进入(某种状态)
⑧ expressive /ɪksˈpresɪv/ a. 表情丰富的

⑨ immediately /ɪˈmiːdjətlɪ/ ad. 立即
⑩ extremely /ɪksˈtriːmlɪ/ ad. 极其,非常

⑪ contain /kənˈteɪn/ v. 包含
⑫ stuff /stʌf/ n. 东西

开始就告诉我你所知道的一切都是从书本上学到的,我对你的看法可能会完全不同,"彼得金大声叫道。

"好的,彼得金,我们等着瞧吧,"杰克说着在一棵椰子树下站住,"你刚才不是说你渴了吗?现在你上树摘一个椰子下来,不要熟透了的,摘一个青的,不太熟的。"

彼得金很吃惊,但看到杰克认真的样子,只好听从了。

杰克又说:"现在,在椰子上挖一个洞,老伙计,把它凑近你的嘴巴。"

彼得金照着吩咐做了。看到他那极富表情的脸上瞬息间的变化,我们不禁笑出了声。他把椰子端到嘴边,仰起头喝着流出来的汁水,眼睛因吃惊而瞪得有平常的两个那么大,喉咙里不停地吞咽着,满意的微笑浮上了他的脸。最后他停下来深深地吸了一口气,叫道:

"太棒了!真是太棒了!哎,杰克,你是个好样的,是我这辈子见到的最棒的人。尝尝这个!"他说着把椰子送到我嘴边。

我马上喝了一口。的确,我也没有料到流入喉咙里的椰子汁是如此美妙,它特别清凉、甘甜,但又有些辣味。我把椰子递给杰克,他尝了尝,说:

"彼得金,你这个怀疑论者,除了在家乡商店里卖的,我从来没见过、也没尝过椰子。但我曾从书里读到过青椰子里有这玩艺儿,你瞧,这是真的。"

"请你告诉我,熟椰子里又有什么玩艺儿呢?"

"And **pray**①," asked Peterkin, "what sort of 'stuff' does the ripe nut contain?"

"A **hollow**② centre," answered Jack, "with something like milk in it; but it does not **satisfy**③ thirst so well. It is, however, very good food, I believe."

"Meat and drink on the same tree," cried Peterkin; "washing in the sea, **lodging**④ on the ground—and all for nothing! My dear boys, we're set up for life; it must be the ancient Garden of Eden—**hurrah**⑤!" And Peterkin tossed his **straw**⑥ hat in the air, and ran along the beach, shouting like a madman with delight.

We had now come to the point of rock on which the ship had struck, but did not find a single thing, although we searched carefully among the coral rocks, which at this place went out so far as nearly to join the reef round the island.

We Prepare for the Night

It was beginning to grow dark when we got back, so we **put off**⑦ our visit to the top of a hill till next day, and employed the light that yet remained to us in cutting down **a quantity of**⑧ branches and the broad leaves of a tree of which none of us knew the name. With these we **erected**⑨ a sort of house, in which we meant to pass the night. Having put leaves and dry grass all over the floor, we turned to thoughts of supper. But it now occurred to us, for the first time, that we had no way of making a fire.

"Now, there's a **fix**⑩! What shall we do?" said Peterkin, while we both turned our eyes to Jack, to whom we always looked in our difficulties.

Jack did not seem to know what to do.

① pray /preɪ/ v. 请问

② hollow /'hɒləʊ/ a. 空的
③ satisfy /'sætɪsfaɪ/ v. 使…满意

④ lodge /lɒdʒ/ v. 临时住宿,安顿
⑤ hurrah /hʊ'rɑː/ v. 欢呼,以欢呼迎接,呼万岁
⑥ straw /strɔː/ n. 稻草,麦秆

⑦ put off 推迟,拖延

⑧ a quantity of 大量

⑨ erect /ɪ'rekt/ v. 建立

⑩ fix /fɪks/ n. 〈口〉困境,窘境

珊瑚岛

彼得金问道。

杰克回答说:"它中间是空的,里面有些像奶汁似的东西,虽然不太解渴,但我相信它们是极好的食物。"

彼得金大声嚷道:"在同一棵树上既有好吃的又有好喝的,在海里洗澡,在岸上睡觉,所有这一切还都是免费的!我亲爱的伙伴们,我们生活中需要的一切都应有尽有。这里一定是古时候的伊甸园,好哇!"彼得金把他的草帽扔向天空,一边高兴地沿着岸边狂奔,一边像个疯子似的大叫着。

现在我们来到了船沉没的地方,这里的珊瑚礁一直向海里延伸,几乎和环岛的暗礁连在一起。尽管我们在珊瑚石中仔细地寻找,却一无所获。

我们准备过夜

我们回来的时候天已经快黑了,登山只能推迟到明天进行了。我们必须趁现在还看得见,从一棵不知名的树上砍下大量树枝和阔叶,用它们建起一间房子,准备在那里过夜。我们把树叶和干草都铺在地上以后,就准备吃饭了,但是直到这时我们才第一次意识到没法生火。

"噢,这可是个难题!我们怎么办?"彼得金说,我们俩都看着杰克。每当有困难的时候,我们总是看着他。

杰克好像也不知道该怎么做。

"在海滩上,倒是有足够多的石头,"他说,"但没有铁,光有石头也没用。"

The Coral Island

"There are stones enough, no doubt, on the beach," said he, "but they are of no use at all without a **steel**①."

"Oh, I have it!" Peterkin cried, starting up. "The telescope — the big glass at the end will light a fire!"

"You forget that we have no sun," said I.

Peterkin was **silent**②.

"All, boys, I've got it now!" cried Jack, rising and cutting a branch from a **neighbouring**③ bush, which he stripped of its leaves, "I remember seeing this done once at home. Hand me the bit of rope."

With the rope and branch Jack soon formed a **bow**④. Then he cut a piece, about three **inches**⑤ long, off the end of a dead branch, which he pointed at the two ends. Round this he passed the rope of the bow, and placed one end against his body, which was protected from its point by a piece of wood; the other point he placed against a bit of dry wood, and then began to saw hard with the bow. In a few seconds the dry wood began to smoke; in less than a minute it caught fire, and in less than a quarter of an hour we were eating and drinking coconuts round a fire that would have **roasted**⑥ an entire sheep, while the smoke and **flames**⑦ flew up among the broad leaves of the palm trees over our heads, and **cast**⑧ a warm glow upon our **leafy**⑨ house.

① steel /stiːl/ n. 钢，钢制品

② silent /ˈsaɪlənt/ a. 沉默的,无言的

③ neighbouring /ˈneɪbərɪŋ/ a. 附近的

④ bow /bəʊ/ n. 弓
⑤ inch /ɪntʃ/ n. 英寸

⑥ roast /rəʊst/ v. 烤,烘焙
⑦ flame /fleɪm/ n. 火焰,火舌,热情
⑧ cast /kɑːst/ v. 投,掷,抛
⑨ leafy /ˈliːfɪ/ a. 叶茂的

"噢！我有主意了。"彼得金叫着站了起来，"望远镜——那块大玻璃能点着火！"

"你忘了，太阳已经下山了。"我说。

彼得金沉默了。

"好了，伙计们，我想出来了！"杰克叫道。他站起来从旁边的一棵灌木上砍下一根树枝，把叶子都弄掉。"我记得在家乡时有一次看别人这么做过。给我一根绳子。"

杰克很快把绳子和树枝绑成一张弓。然后又从一个枯树枝的末端砍下大约三英寸长的一段，把两头都削尖。他把弓弦绕在这截枯枝上，在身上放一片木头做保护，再把短树枝的一端顶在木头上，另一端顶在一块干木头上，在干木头上用弓猛烈地来回锉动。只几秒钟，干木头就开始冒烟了。一分钟不到，它着起火来。又过了大约一刻钟的时间，我们就在能烤熟一头羊的火堆旁吃椰肉喝椰汁了。烟雾和火苗冲上我们头顶上的宽宽的棕榈树叶，把我们的草房照得异常温暖。

Chapter 4
At the Bottom of the Lagoon

What a joyful thing it is to **awaken**①, on a fresh, **glorious**② morning, and find the rising sun shining into your face! When I awoke on the morning after the ship struck, I found myself in this delightful condition. Just at that moment I caught sight of a very small **parrot**③. It was seated on a branch that **overhung**④ Peterkin's head, and I was quickly lost in **admiration**⑤ of its green and other brightly-coloured **feathers**⑥. While I looked I observed that the bird turned its head slowly from side to side, and looked downwards, first with one eye then with the other. On **glancing**⑦ downwards I observed that Peterkin's mouth was wide open, and that this **unusual**⑧ bird was looking into it.

Peterkin used to say that I had no fun whatever in my nature, and that I never could understand a funny saying. In regard to the **latter**⑨, perhaps he was right, yet I think that, when they were explained to me, I understood them as well as most people: but in regard to the former he must certainly have been wrong, for this bird seemed to me to be extremely funny; and I could not help thinking that, if it should happen to **faint**⑩, or **slip**⑪ its foot, and fall off the branch into Peterkin's mouth, he would perhaps think it funny too! Suddenly the parrot bent down its

4
在环礁湖底

① awaken /əˈweɪkən/ v. 唤醒,醒来,唤起
② glorious /ˈglɔːrɪəs/ a. 光荣的,辉煌的
③ parrot /ˈpærət/ n. 鹦鹉
④ overhung /ˌəʊvəˈhʌŋ/ v. 伸出
⑤ admiration /ˌædməˈreɪʃən/ n. 钦佩,赞赏
⑥ feather /ˈfeðə/ n. 羽毛
⑦ glance /glɑːns/ v. 瞥闪,瞥见
⑧ unusual /ʌnˈjuːʒʊəl/ a. 不平常的,异常的
⑨ latter /ˈlætə/ n. 后者
⑩ faint /feɪnt/ v. 昏倒
⑪ slip /slɪp/ v. 滑倒

　　早上,空气清新、天气晴朗,睁开眼,感到朝阳正照在脸上,这真是一件快乐的事情!在船触礁后的第一个清晨醒来,我发现自己正置身于这样一个美好的环境当中。我一睁开眼睛,就看到一只小鹦鹉,站在彼得金头顶的树枝上。它那五颜六色的羽毛让我看呆了。当我观察它的时候,发现这只鸟慢慢地把头从一边摆向另一边,向下望着,开始是用一只眼睛,后来就用上了另外一只,我往下一瞥,发现彼得金的嘴张得大大的。这只不寻常的鸟正向里面张望。
　　彼得金总是说我天性没有幽默感,而且从来也听不懂笑话,关于后面这一点,也许他是对的。但是我想,一旦人们向我解释这个笑话,我的理解力并不比别人差。至于前面那一点,他完全错了。比如这只鸟,在我看来就是一个绝好的玩笑,我禁不住想,如果它现在刚好晕倒,或者碰巧滑了一下,就有可能从树枝上直接掉到彼得金的嘴里,彼得金大概也一定会觉得这个很可笑。突然,鹦鹉低下头,冲着彼得金的脸大叫了一声。彼得金被吵醒

head and **uttered**① a loud cry in his face. This awoke him, and, with a cry of surprise, he sat up, while the **foolish**② bird flew quickly away.

"Oh, you wicked bird! " cried Peterkin, making a face at the bird. Then he **rubbed**③ his eyes, and asked what time it was.

I smiled at this question, and answered that, as our watches were at the bottom of the sea, I could not tell, but it was a little past sunrise.

Our Morning Swim

Peterkin now began to remember where we were. As he looked up into the bright sky, and drew in a **breath**④ of the fresh air, his eyes shone with delight, and he uttered a faint "Hurrah! "and rubbed his eyes again. Then he gazed slowly round, till observing the calm sea through an opening in the bushes, he jumped suddenly up, as if he had received a shock, uttered a loud shout, threw off his garments, and, rushing over the white sands, ran into the water.

The cry awoke Jack, who rose on his arm with a look of **grave**⑤ surprise; but this was followed by a quiet smile on seeing Peterkin in the water. Jack acted quickly only when he was moved, and on this **occasion**⑥ he jumped to his feet, threw off his clothes, shook back his hair, and, with a lion-like spring, dashed over the sands and into the sea, with such force as quite to cover Peterkin in a **shower**⑦ of water.

Jack was an extremely good swimmer and **diver**⑧, so that after he entered the water, we saw no sign of him for nearly a minute; after which he suddenly came up, a good many yards out from the shore.

My **spirits**⑨ were so much **raised**⑩ by seeing all this that I, too, **hastily**⑪ threw off my garments and tried to jump to my feet as Jack had done; but my foot caught on a branch and I fell to the ground; then I

① utter /ˈʌtə/ v. 发出，作声
② foolish /ˈfuːlɪʃ/ a. 愚蠢的
③ rub /rʌb/ v. 擦，搓，摩擦

④ breath /breθ/ n. 呼吸，气息

⑤ grave /greɪv/ a. 严重的
⑥ occasion /əˈkeɪʒən/ n. 场合

⑦ shower /ˈʃaʊə/ n. 阵雨，淋浴
⑧ diver /ˈdaɪvə/ n. 潜水员

⑨ spirit /ˈspɪrɪt/ n. 精神
⑩ raise /reɪz/ v. 升起，举起
⑪ hastily /ˈheɪstɪlɪ/ ad. 匆忙地

了，他惊叫着坐了起来。他一起来，那只傻头傻脑的鸟就立刻飞远了。

"哦，你这只坏鸟！"彼得金一边嚷着，一边冲鸟做着鬼脸。他揉了揉眼睛，然后问现在几点了。

我觉得这个问题很可笑，就回答他说，我们的表丢在海底了，所以我也不知道准确的时间，不过现在太阳刚刚升起一小会儿。

我们的晨泳

彼得金现在开始记起来我们是在什么地方了。他抬头看看晴朗的天，呼吸了一下新鲜空气，高兴得两眼发亮，轻轻地叫了一声："好啊！"然后又揉了揉眼睛。他慢慢地环视四周，当他从灌木丛的缝隙里看到平静的大海时，他就像是被电击了一下，猛地跳起来，甩掉外套，大叫着冲向白色的海滩，跳进水里。

杰克被彼得金的叫声吵醒了。他用胳膊撑起身体，满脸惊诧的表情。看到彼得金在海里游泳，他的脸上开始浮现出笑容。杰克的动作永远是那样的敏捷。他一下子跳起来，脱掉衣服，向后甩了甩头发，就像狮子般地跃过沙滩，冲进海里。他跳进水里时溅起的水花像雨点一样落在彼得金身上。

杰克的游泳和潜水都很出色，他到水里之后，我们将近有一分钟的时间看不到他的影子。当他突然浮出水面的时候，离开岸边已经有好几码了。

看到这些，我的精神也高涨起来，急忙脱掉外

The Coral Island

slipped on a stone while running over the sands, and nearly fell again, much to the joy of Peterkin, who laughed loudly, and called me a "slow-coach". While Jack cried out, "Come along, Ralph, and I'll help you." However, when I got into the water I managed very well, for I was really a good swimmer and diver too. I could not, indeed, **equal**[①] Jack, who was **superior**[②] to any Englishman I ever saw. But I was very much better than Peterkin, who could only swim a little, and could not dive at all.

While Peterkin enjoyed himself near the shore and in running along the beach, Jack and I swam out into the deep water, and **occasionally**[③], dived for stones. I shall never forget my surprise and delight on first seeing the bottom of the sea. As I have before said, the water within the reef was as calm as a pond; and, as there was no wind, it was quite clear from the **surface**[④] to the bottom, so that we could see down easily even when the water was twenty or thirty yards deep.

In the Lagoon[⑤]

When Jack and I dived in places where the water was not so deep, we expected to have found sand and stones, instead of which we found ourselves in what appeared really to be a wonderful garden. The whole of the bottom of the lagoon, as we called the calm water within the reef, was covered with coral of every shape, size, and colour. The most common kind was a sort of branching coral, and some **portions**[⑥] were of a lovely **pale**[⑦] pink colour, others pure white. Among this there grew large quantities of **seaweed**[⑧] of the richest colours imaginable, and of the most graceful forms, while many fishes — blue, red, yellow and green — sported in and out amongst the flower—beds of this under-water-garden, and did not appear to be at all afraid of our **approaching**[⑨] them.

珊瑚岛

套，而且企图像杰克一样跳起来。但是我的脚绊到树枝上，跌倒了。接着，跑过海滩时，我在一块石头上滑了一下，又差点摔倒。这一切都引得彼得金大笑，他还叫我是"慢车"。杰克叫道："快来，拉尔夫，我帮你。"然而到了水里，我就应付自如了，其实我也是个游泳和潜水的好手，但是不能跟杰克相比，在这方面我从来没见过哪个英国人比他更厉害。但是我比彼得金要好得多。彼得金只能游很短的距离，而且根本不会潜水。

彼得金一个人在岸边奔跑、在浅水玩耍的时候，我和杰克游向深水，不时地潜下水底摸石头。我永远也不会忘记第一次看到海底时的惊喜。如我之前所提，因为没有风，珊瑚礁里水平如镜。从海面到海底都很清澈，即便海水有二三十码深，我们仍可以清楚地看到水底。

在环礁湖里

我和杰克潜到不太深的水域，展现在我们面前的是一座美丽的花园，而不是我们想象的那种布满沙子和石头的海底。整个环礁湖的湖底，被形态各异、大小不一和色彩缤纷的珊瑚覆盖着，环礁湖就是我们所说的珊瑚礁里平静的水域。最常见的珊瑚种类是一种呈树枝状的珊瑚，这种珊瑚的某些部分是一种可爱的淡粉色，而其他部分则是纯白色的。这里还有大量的海草，五彩缤纷的颜色超乎我们的想象，许多海草还有着极其优美的外形。红黄蓝绿的鱼儿在这座水下花园里游来游去，对我们这些不

① equal /ˈiːkwəl/ v. 比得上
② superior /suːˈpɪərɪə/ a. 上好的,出众的

③ occasionally /əˈkeɪʒənəlɪ/ ad. 偶尔地

④ surface /ˈsɜːfɪs/ n. 表面,平面

⑤ lagoon /ləˈguːn/ n. 环礁湖

⑥ portion /ˈpɔːʃən/ n. 部分
⑦ pale /peɪl/ a. 苍白的
⑧ seaweed /ˈsiːwiːd/ n. 海草,海藻
⑨ aproach /əˈprəʊtʃ/ v. 靠近,接近

The Coral Island

On coming to the surface for breach, after our first dive, Jack and I rose close to each other.

"Did you ever in your life, Ralph, see anything so lovely?" said Jack, as he threw the water from his hair.

"Never," I replied. "It appears to me like **fairy land**①, I can **scarcely**② believe that we are not dreaming."

"Dreaming!" cried Jack. "Do you know, Ralph, I almost believe that we really are dreaming. But if so, I have made up my mind to make the most of it, and dream another dive. So here goes down again, my boy."

We took the second dive together, and kept beside each other while under water, and I was greatly surprised to find that we could keep down much longer than I ever remember having done in our own seas at home. I believe that this was **owing to**③ the heat of the water, which was so warm that we afterwards found we could remain in it for two and three hours at a time without feeling any unpleasant **effects**④ such as we used to **experience**⑤ in the seas at home.

Jack Supplies Breakfast

When Jack reached the bottom, he took hold of the branches of the coral and moved along on his hands and knees, looking under the seaweed and among the rocks. I observed him also pick up one or two large **shell-fish**⑥ and keep them in his hand, as if he meant to take them up with him, so I also gathered a few. Suddenly he put out his hand to seize a blue and yellow fish, and actually touched its tail, but did not catch it. At this he turned towards me and attempted to smile; but no sooner had he done so than he sprang like an arrow to the surface, where, on following him, I found that he had swallowed a good deal of

① fairy land 仙境
② scarcely /ˈskeəslɪ/ ad. 几乎不,简直没有,勉强

③ owing to /ˈəʊɪŋ tuː/ prep. 由于,因为

④ effect /ɪˈfekt/ n. 影响,效果
⑤ experience /ɪksˈpɪərɪəns/ v. 经历,体验

⑥ shell-fish 水里的贝壳类动物

速之客一点也不害怕。

　　第一次潜水之后我们浮出水面呼吸,杰克和我游得稍微靠近了一点。

　　"拉尔夫,你这辈子见过这么美丽的地方么?"杰克一面甩着头上的水珠一面问我。

　　"从来没有,"我回答说,"这对我来说就像是仙境,我几乎不敢相信这竟然不是在做梦。"

　　"做梦!"杰克叫起来,"你不知道,拉尔夫,我几乎相信这就是在做梦。但就算是做梦,我决定好好地利用它,再做一次潜水梦。来吧,伙计,让我们再潜一次。"

　　我们又一次潜了下去,在水底紧紧挨在一起。我惊奇地发现我们在水底的时间比我在家乡时任何一次潜水的时间都长。我相信这是因为水温的关系,这里的水很暖和。后来我们发觉,我们一次可以在水里待上两三个小时,没有一点不适的感觉,而那种不适是在家乡潜水时经常会遇到的。

杰克弄来的早餐

　　杰克接近湖底的时候,抓住珊瑚枝,用他的膝盖和手移动着,在水草底下和岩石中间寻找什么。我还看见他捡起一两个大海贝抓在手里,好像想要把它们带上岸。我也抓了一些。突然,杰克伸出手去抓一条黄绿相间的鱼,而且竟然碰到了鱼尾巴,但还是没能抓住它。这时他转向我,试图对我笑一下,但他还没有笑出来,就像箭一样射向水面。我也跟着游了上去。原来他呛了很多水。几分钟后他

The Coral Island

water. In a few minutes he recovered, and we both turned to swim to the shore.

"I **declare**①, Ralph," said he, "that I actually tried to laugh under water?"

"So I saw," I replied, "and I saw, too, that you very nearly caught that fish by the tail. It would have done very well for breakfast, if you had."

"Breakfast enough here?" said he, holding up the shell-fish as we landed and ran up the beach. "**Hullo**②, Peterkin! Here you are, boy. Open these while Ralph and I put on our clothes. They'll agree with the coconuts **excellently**③, I have no doubt."

Peterkin, who was already dressed, took the shell-fish, and opened them with the edge of our axe, crying: "Now. that is fine! There's nothing I'm so fond of."

"Ah! that's lucky," said Jack. "I'll be able to keep you in good order now, Master Peterkin. You know you can't dive any better than a cat. So, sir, whenever you are not good, you shall have no shell-fish for breakfast."

"I'm very glad that our breakfast looks so good," said I, "for I feel as if I could eat a lot."

"Here, then, stop our mouth with that!" said Peterkin, holding a large shell-fish to my lips.

I opened my mouth and swallowed it in silence, and really it was very good.

We now **set** ourselves earnestly **about**④ our **preparations**⑤ for **spending**⑥ the day. We had no difficulty with the fire this morning, as the glass in our telescope was an **admirable**⑦ one; and while we roasted a few shell-fish and ate our coconuts, we held a long talk about our plans for the future.

① declare /dɪˈkleə/ v. 宣布,声明

② hullo /ˈhʌˈləʊ/ int. 喂

③ excellently /ˈeksələntlɪ/ ad. 最优地,超群地

④ set about 开始,着手
⑤ preparation /prepəˈreɪʃən/ n. 准备
⑥ spend /spend/ v.（spent, spent）花费,度过
⑦ admirable /ˈædmərəbl/ a. 令人钦佩的，令人赞赏的

恢复过来，我们一起向岸边游去。

"拉尔夫，我告诉你，在水底我几乎笑出来，"杰克说。

"我看出来了，"我回答道，"我也看到你几乎抓住了那条鱼的尾巴。如果你抓到它，那将是一顿很好的早餐。"

"早餐已经足够了！"我们上了岸，向海滩上跑去的时候，他一边举着海贝一边喊，"哎！彼得金，给你，伙计。我和拉尔夫穿衣服的时候你把它们打开。我相信这些海贝和椰子一起吃味道一定很美。"

彼得金已经穿上了衣服。他接过海贝，用斧子的刃撬开它们，大叫道："瞧，这些有多棒！这是我最喜欢的东西了。"

"哦！太好了，"杰克说，"你现在得好好地听我们派遣了。彼得金大人，要知道你就像猫一样不会潜水。所以大人，如果你不听话，就没有海贝吃。"

"我真高兴我们的早餐看起来这么好吃，我觉得我一下子能吃掉好多。"我说。

"给你，闭上你的嘴吃吧！"彼得金说着把一个很大的海贝递到我嘴边。

我不说话了，张开嘴大口吃着海贝，它的味道确实非常好。

现在我们开始认真地为这一天做准备。望远镜上的玻璃非常好用，没费什么力气就点着了火。我们烤着海贝吃着椰子，对于下一步要干什么谈论了很久。

Chapter 5
We Look at the Island

Our first care, after breakfast, was to place the few things we possessed in a hole in a rock at the **farther**[①] end of a small cave, which we discovered near our house. This cave we hoped might be useful to us afterwards as a **store-house**[②]. Then we cut two large sticks off a very hard kind of tree which grew near at hand. One of these was given to Peterkin, the other to me, and Jack armed himself with the axe. We did this because we **purposed**[③] to make a **journey**[④] to the top of the mountains, in order to **obtain**[⑤] a better view of our island. Of course we knew not what dangers we might meet by the way, so we thought it best to be prepared.

Having completed our arrangements and carefully put out our fire, we set out, and walked a short distance along the sea-beach till we came to the entrance of a **valley**[⑥], through which flowed a little stream. Here we turned our back on the sea and struck inland.

The view that **burst**[⑦] upon our sight on entering the valley was truly **splendid**[⑧]. On either side of us there was a gentle rise in the land, which thus formed two hills, about a mile on each side of the valley. These hills — which, as well as the low ground between them, were covered

5
查看海岛

① farther /ˈfɑːðə/ a. 更远的,进一步的

② store-house 堆栈,仓库

③ purpose /ˈpɜːpəs/ v. 打算(做),决意(做)

④ journey /ˈdʒɜːnɪ/ n. 旅程,旅行,行程

⑤ obtain /əbˈteɪn/ v. 获得,得到

⑥ valley /ˈvælɪ/ n. 山谷,溪谷

⑦ burst upon 突然出现

⑧ splendid /ˈsplendɪd/ a. 极好的

　　早饭后,我们首先小心地把少得可怜的财产放在一个小洞穴最深处的石洞里面。那个洞穴是我们在我们的房子旁边发现的。我们希望将来可以用它当仓库。我们想爬上山顶,这样可以将这个岛看得更清楚一点。所以我们就在附近找了一种木质很硬的树,砍了两根大树枝下来。一根给彼得金,另一根给我,杰克则拿着那把斧子。其实我们也不知道在路上会遇到什么危险,但是做些准备总是比较好的。

　　做完准备工作,又小心地熄了火,我们就出发了。沿着海滩走了很短的一段路,我们到了一个山谷的入口,山谷里流淌着一条小溪。在这里我们背朝海洋,来到内陆。

　　进入谷口,我们眼前一亮,视野一下子开阔了许多。我们的两边各有一个慢坡,慢坡在山谷的两边形成两座小山丘,相隔大约一英里。山丘与山丘相连的凹地上长满了树木和灌木丛。山丘向前延伸大约有两英里,和一座小山的山脚连到一起。这座

with trees and bushes — continued inland for about two miles, when they joined the foot of a small mountain. This mountain rose rather **steeply**① from the head of the valley, and was also entirely covered, even to the top, with trees, except on one **particular**② **spot**③ near the left shoulder, where there was a **bare**④ and rocky place of a broken and wild character. Beyond this mountain, we could not see, and we therefore directed out **course**⑤ up the **banks**⑥ of the stream towards the foot of it, **intending**⑦ to climb to the top if that should be possible, as, indeed, we had no doubt it was.

Jack Explains Many Things

Jack, being the wisest and boldest amongst us, took the lead, carrying the axe on his shoulder. Peterkin, with his great stick, came second, as he said he should like to be able to **defend**⑧ me if any danger should **threaten**⑨. I brought up the **rear**⑩, but having been more taken up with the wonderful and strange things I saw before we set out than with thoughts of possible danger, I had very foolishly left my stick behind me. Although, as I have said, the trees and bushes were very thick, they were not so close together as to stop our walking through them. Soon we arrived at the foot of the hill, and prepared to climb it. Here Jack made a **discovery**⑪ which caused us all very great joy. This was a tree of a beautiful appearance, which Jack declared to be the celebrated bread-fruit tree.

"Is it celebrated?" asked Peterkin simply.

"It is," replied Jack.

"That's **odd**⑫, now," answered Peterkin; "I never heard of it before."

① steeply /ˈstiːplɪ/ ad. 险峻地
② particular /pəˈtɪkjʊlə/ a. 特别的
③ spot /spɒt/ n. 地点
④ bare /beə/ a. 赤裸的,极少的
⑤ course /kɔːs/ n. 路线
⑥ bank /bæŋk/ n. 堤,岸
⑦ intend /ɪnˈtend/ v. 计划

⑧ defend /dɪˈfend/ v. 防护,辩护,防卫
⑨ threaten /ˈθretn/ v. 威胁
⑩ rear /rɪə/ n. 后面,背后

⑪ discovery /dɪsˈkʌvərɪ/ n. 发现,发现物

⑫ odd /ɒd/ a. 古怪的

山在山谷的尽头拔地而起,十分陡峭,从山脚一直到山顶都是树。在靠近左山脊的那边有一块特别的地方,那里净是裸露的岩石,地势起伏不定,看起来很荒凉。这座山挡住了我们的视线,因此我们就沿着溪岸向山脚走去。如果可能的话,我们计划爬上山顶,我们打心眼里觉得这是可能的。

杰克解释许多事情

杰克在我们当中最聪明,胆子也最大,他肩上扛着斧子走在前面。彼得金拿着他的大棍子走在第二位,他说一旦发生了危险,他希望能够保护我。我走在后边。一路上看到的奇光异景使我忘记了可能会发生危险,我已经愚蠢地把拐杖丢在后边了。虽然正如我所说的,山谷里的树和灌木长得很茂盛,但是它们没有密到影响我们前进的程度。很快我们就到了山脚下,准备爬山。这时杰克的发现引起我们极大的兴趣。这是一种很美的树,杰克说这就是著名的面包树。

"它真的很有名吗?"彼得金天真地问。

"是的。"杰克答道。

"哦,这就怪了,我以前从没听说过它。"彼得金回答道。

"可能它不像我想象的那样有名,"杰克随手把遮挡住彼得金眼睛的帽子向上推了推说,"但是听

The Coral Island

"Then it's not so celebrated as I thought it was," said Jack, quietly pushing Peterkin's hat over his eyes; "but listen, you little fool, and hear of it now."

Peterkin put on his hat again properly, and was soon listening with as much interest as myself, while Jack told us that this tree is one of the most valuable in the islands of the south; that it **bears**① two, sometimes three, **crops**② of fmit in the year; that the fruit is very like bread, and that it forms the **principal**③ food of many of the islanders.

"So," said Peterkin, "we seem to have every thing ready prepared to our hands in this wonderful island — drink ready bottled in nuts, and bread growing on the trees!"

"Besides," continued Jack, "the **bark**④ of the young branches is made by the natives into cloth; and of the wood, which is hard and of a good colour, they build their houses. So you see, boys, that we have **plenty**⑤ of material to make us comfortable, if we are only clever enough to use it."

"But are you sure that that's it?" asked Peterkin.

"Quite sure," replied Jack, "for I was particularly interested in the **account**⑥ I once read of it, and I remember well what was said of it there. I am sorry, however, that I have forgotten what was said of many other trees which I am sure we have seen today, if we only knew them. So you see, Peterkin, I don't know everything yet."

"Never mind, Jack," said Peterkin, touching his tall companion on the shoulder. "Never mind, Jack; you know a good deal for your age. You're a clever boy, sir — a **promising**⑦ young man, and if you only go on as you have begun, sir, you will —"

The end of this speech was suddenly cut short by Jack pushing Peterkin into a **mass**⑧ of thick bushes, where, finding himself comfortable, he **lay**⑨ still, **sunning**⑩ himself, while Jack and I examined

① bear /beə(r)/ v. 结果实
② crop /krɒp/ n. 农作物,产量
③ principal /ˈprɪnsəp(ə)l,-sɪp-/ a. 主要的

④ bark /bɑːk/ n. 树皮

⑤ plenty /ˈplentɪ/ a. 充足的,相当多的

⑥ account /əˈkaʊnt/ n. 报告,叙述,解释

⑦ promising /ˈprɒmɪsɪŋ/ a. 有希望的,有前途的

⑧ mass /mæs/ n. 块,大多数,质量
⑨ lay /leɪ/ v. 横躺
⑩ sun /sʌn/ v. 晒太阳

着,小傻瓜,你现在听说过它了。"

彼得金又把他的帽子适当地向上放了放,立刻和我一样怀着极大的兴趣听杰克讲。杰克告诉我们这种树在南方海岛上是最有价值的树种之一,它一年结两次果,有时结三次。这种树的果实非常像面包,是许多岛民的主要食物。

"你看,"彼得金说,"在这个奇妙的岛上看来什么东西都给我们预备好了,就在身边,饮料装在坚果里,面包长在树上。"

"除了吃,"杰克接着说,"当地人还拿嫩枝的皮做衣服,还有树干,面包树的木料很硬而且颜色好看,他们用来盖房子。你们看,伙计们,只要我们够聪明,知道怎么用,这儿有许多东西能让我们过得很舒服。"

"但是你能确定它们能用吗?"彼得金问。

"当然能确定。"杰克回答说,"因为有一次在读书的时候,对面包树的描述让我特别感兴趣,而且对于书上讲的东西我记得很清楚。但是很抱歉,今天看到的许多树,我已经忘了书上是怎么说的了,我们要是知道就好了。所以,你看,彼得金,我也并不是每件事都知道的。"

"别介意,杰克,"彼得金拍着他的高个子朋友的肩膀说,"别介意,杰克,对于你这个年龄来说你知道的已经很多了,你是个聪明的年轻人,头儿,一个有希望的年轻人,如果你一直这样发展下去,头儿,你将——"

杰克猛地把彼得金推进了茂密的灌木丛里,从而打断了他的这段演说。当我和杰克查看面包树的

the bread-fruit tree.

The Bread-Fruit Tree

We were much struck with the deep, rich green colour of its broad leaves, which were twelve or eighteen inches long, deeply **toothed**①, and very **smooth**②. The fruit with which it was **loaded**③ was nearly round, and appeared to be about six inches through the middle, with a **rough**④ skin. It was of different colours, from light green to brown and rich yellow. Jack said that the yellow was the ripe fruit. The bark of the tree was rough and light-coloured; the trunk was about two feet thick, and it appeared to be twenty feet high, there being no branches up to that **height**⑤, after which it branched off into a beautiful head. We noticed that the fruits hung in groups of twos and threes on the branches, but as we were anxious to get to the top of the hill we did not try to pluck any at that time.

Our hearts were now very much cheered by our good fortune, and it was with light, quick steps that we climbed up the **steep**⑥ sides of the hill. On reaching the top, a new and, if possible, a **grander**⑦ view met our gaze. We found that this was not the highest part of the island, but that another hill lay beyond, with a wide valley between it and the one on which we stood. This valley, like the first, was also full of rich trees. Among these we saw many bread-fruit trees with their yellow fruits; and also a great many coconut palms. When we had seen all that we could we went down the hill-side, and soon began to climb the second mountain. It was clothed with trees nearly all the way up, but the top was bare, and in some places broken.

时候，彼得金很舒服地躺在灌木丛中晒太阳。

面包树

面包树的叶子给我们留下了深刻的印象，深绿色的叶子宽宽的，十二或十八英寸长，边上有深深的齿，表面非常光滑。面包树的果实几乎呈圆形，直径大约六英寸，外面是粗糙的皮。果实有不同的颜色，从浅绿色、褐色到深黄色。杰克说黄色的是已经成熟的果实。面包树的树皮粗糙，颜色不深。树干大约两英尺粗，看起来有二十英尺高，一直到顶端都没有枝杈。树枝在树顶伸展，形成了一个美丽的树冠。我们注意到面包果两三个一组挂在树枝上，但因为我们急于爬上山顶，所以当时没有打算摘它们。

此时我们被发现的宝物鼓舞着，心情变得轻松了，我们迈着轻快的脚步攀登陡峭的山坡。一到山顶，一个全新的，也可以说是壮观的景象展现在我们面前。我们发现这座山不是海岛的最高点，这座山后面的另一座山才是最高的，两山之间有一条宽阔的山谷。这条山谷也像前边那条一样长满了树。我们看到其中有许多挂着黄色果实的面包树，还有很多椰子树。我们把目力所及之处看遍之后就从另一边下了山，很快就开始爬第二座山。这座山也几乎全被树木覆盖着，但是山顶却是裸露的，而且有些地方起伏不平。

① tooth /tuːθ/ v. 给…装齿
② smooth /smuːð/ a. 平滑的
③ load /ləʊd/ v. 担负
④ rough /rʌf/ a. 粗糙的

⑤ height /haɪt/ n. 高度,高处

⑥ steep /stiːp/ a. 险峻的,陡峭的
⑦ grander /ɡrænd/ a. 宏伟的,壮丽的

From the Mountain-Top

We found this to be the highest point of the island, and from it we saw the country lying, as it were, like a map around us. It **consisted of**① two mountains; the one we guessed at five hundred feet; the other, on which we stood, at one thousand. Between these lay a rich, beautiful valley, as already said. This valley crossed the island from one end to the other, being high in the middle and **sloping**② on each side towards the sea. The large mountain sloped — on the side farthest from where the ship had struck — gently towards the sea; but although, when viewed at a glance, it had thus a regular sloping appearance, a more careful observation showed that it was broken up into many small valleys, mixed with little rocky spots and small but steep **cliffs**③ here and there, with **streams**④ falling over their edges and wandering down the slopes in little white rivers, sometimes shining among the broad leaves of the bread-fruit and coconut trees, or hidden altogether **beneath**⑤ the rich growth of bushes.

At the bottom of the mountain lay a narrow, bright green plain or **meadow**⑥, which ended sharply at the shore. On the other side of the island, **whence**⑦ we had come, stood the smaller hill, from the foot of which started three valleys; one being that which we had come up, with a smaller valley on each side of it, and separated from it by the two low hills before **mentioned**⑧. In these smaller valleys there were no streams, but they were clothed with the same rich growth of trees and bushes.

The island seemed to be about ten miles across, and as it was almost a circle in form, the distance round it must have been thirty miles — perhaps a little more, if we allow for the many bays. The entire island was **surrounded**⑨ by a **beach of**⑩ pure white sand. We now also observed

从山顶看

　　我们发现这是海岛的最高点，从这个角度看，整个海岛就像一幅地图一样展现在眼前。海岛共有两座高山，一座我们估计大约有五百英尺高，我们脚下的这座大约一千英尺高。两山之间是之前提及的富饶美丽的山谷。这条山谷横穿整个海岛，中间稍高，两边向下一直伸向大海。大山的一侧向海边慢慢延伸成一个斜坡，一直伸向我们的船触礁的那片水域。粗看，那斜坡很平滑，但仔细地观察就会发现山坡上有许多小的峡谷，很多地方混杂着小块的岩石和小而陡的悬崖。泉水从崖边上流下来，形成一条条白色的小河，弯弯曲曲地顺坡流下。河水有时在面包树和椰子树阔叶的缝隙中闪闪发光，有时又完全隐没在茂密的灌木丛里。

　　山底有一块狭长的、鲜绿色的平原和草地，与海岸的分界线非常清晰。在岛的另一部分，就是我们来的那个地方，矗立着那座比较小的山，它的山脚有三个峡谷。那座山我们曾经登上过，在它的两边各有一个较小的峡谷，被前面提到的两座小山分开。这些小峡谷没有溪流，但是也被茂密的树林和灌木丛覆盖着。

　　这座岛看上去大约有十英里宽，形状近乎呈圆形，海岸线应该有三十英里，如果算上好几处海湾的话也许比这还长。整个海岛被纯白色的海滩包围着。我们还发现珊瑚礁环绕着海岛，但珊瑚礁离开

---

① consist of 由…组成

② slope /sləʊp/ v. 倾斜

③ cliff /klɪf/ n. 悬崖，峭壁
④ stream /striːm/ n. 流，水流

⑤ beneath /bɪˈniːθ/ prep. 在…之下

⑥ meadow /ˈmedəʊ/ n. 草地
⑦ whence /(h)wens/ pron. 那里(何处)

⑧ mention /ˈmenʃən/ v. 提到，谈到

⑨ surround /səˈraʊnd/ v. 包围，环绕
⑩ beach /biːtʃ/ n. 海滩

that the coral reef completely circled the island, but it was not always the same distance from it; in some places it was a mile from the beach, in others a few hundred yards, but the usual distance was half a mile. The reef lay very low, and the clouds of water from the waves came quite over it in many places. These waves never **ceased**① their war, for however calm the weather might be, there is always a gentle **motion**② in the great Pacific, which, although scarcely noticeable out at sea, reaches the shore at last in a huge wave.

The water within the lagoon, as I have said, was perfectly still. There were three narrow openings in the reef: one opposite each end of the valley, which I have described as crossing the island, the other **opposite**③ our own valley, which we afterwards named the Valley of the Ship. At each of these openings the reef rose into two small green islands, covered with bushes and having one or two coconut palms on each. These islands were very strange, and appeared as if planted for the purpose of marking the way into the lagoon. Our captain was aiming at one of these openings the day the ship struck, and would have reached it, too, I doubt not, had not the ship been **damaged**④. Within the lagoon were several pretty low islands, just opposite our **camp**⑤, and immediately beyond these, out at sea, lay about a dozen other islands at distances from half a mile to ten miles — all of them, as far as we could see, smaller than ours, and **apparently**⑥ with nobody living on them. They seemed to be low coral islands, raised but little above the sea, yet covered with coconut trees.

All this we noted, and a great deal more, while we sat at the top of the mountain. Full of these discoveries, we came back to our house. On the way we came upon the **footmarks**⑦ of some four-footed animal, but whether old or new none of us were able to say. This raised our hopes of

① cease /siːs/ v. 停止，终了
② motion /'məʊʃən/ n. 移动，动作

③ opposite /'ɒpəzɪt/ prep. 对面

④ damage /'dæmɪdʒ/ v. 损害，毁坏
⑤ camp /kæmp/ n. 露营，帐棚

⑥ apparently /ə'pærəntlɪ/ ad. 显然

⑦ footmark /'fʊtˌmɑːk/ n. 足迹

海岛的距离并不是一样长的。有些地方珊瑚礁离开岸边有一英里，而有些地方则只有几百码，平均距离大约是半英里。这些珊瑚礁长得非常低，很多地方几乎被波涛溅起的水雾盖住了。海浪不停地咆哮着，无论天是多么风和日丽，太平洋里却总是微波涌动，虽然在海里几乎感觉不到，但是最后到达岸边时却变成了巨浪。

我前面说过，环礁湖里的水面是相当平静的。珊瑚礁上有三个狭长的开口，我前面讲到的那个横穿海岛的山谷的两端各对着一个开口，另一个正对着后来被我们命名为"船谷"的那个山谷，每一个开口都通向两座绿色的小岛。这些岛上长着灌木，还有一两棵椰子树，小岛非常奇怪，上面那些挺拔的植物仿佛就像是指向环礁湖的路标。船沉的那一天，我们的船长正想沿着这其中的一个开口把船驶向环礁湖。我确信如果船没有触礁的话，是可以到达这里的。环礁湖里还有许多正对着我们营地的可爱的小岛，在离它们不远的海里，还有许多相隔半英里或十英里的小岛。在我们目力所及范围内所有的小岛都比我们这座小，显然没有人居住在那儿，它们是一些长着椰子树的低矮的珊瑚岛，刚刚露出海面。

我们坐在山顶上，把这座海岛仔仔细细地看了个遍，带着这些新发现开始往回走。路上我们发现了一些四蹄动物的足迹，但是这些足迹无论新旧我们都搞不清是什么动物。这激起我们要在岛上抓一些动物吃的欲望。因此回到家的时候，我们的精神很好，很快地准备好晚餐，对今天的这次旅行很满意。

obtaining some animal food on the island, so we reached home in good spirits, quite prepared for supper, and highly satisfied with our journey.

After much talk, in which Peterkin took the lead, we decided that there were no **natives**[1] on the island, and went to bed.

讨论了很长时间之后，当然大部分时间都是彼得金在说话，我们确定这座岛上没有土著人，然后就睡觉了。

① native /ˈneɪtɪv/ n. 本地人

Chapter 6
A Shark

For several days after the journey which I have described above, we did not **wander**① far from our house, but gave our time to forming plans for the future and making our present home comfortable.

There were various causes that led us to do so little. In the first place, although everything around us was so delightful, and we could without difficulty obtain all that we required for our comfort, we did not quite like the idea of **settling down**② here for the rest of our lives, far away from our friends and our native land. Then there was a little uncertainty still as to there being natives on the island, and we had a kind of faint hope that a ship might come and take us off. But as day after day passed, and neither natives nor ship appeared, we gave up all hope of an early **deliverance**③, and began to work hard at our home.

During this time, however, we had not been quite **idle**④. We had several times reed, in different ways, to cook the coconut, but none of these improved it. Then we removed our goods, and made our home in the cave, but found the change so bad that we gladly returned to the house. Besides this, we swam very **frequently**⑤, and talked a great deal; at least Jack and Peterkin did — I listened.

6
鲨　鱼

① wander /ˈwɒndə/ v. 游荡

② settle down 安下心来, 定居

③ deliverance /dɪˈlɪvərəns/ n. 救出,救助,释放
④ idle /ˈaɪdl/ a. 懒惰的,闲散的

⑤ frequently /ˈfriːkwəntlɪ/ ad. 经常地,频繁地

　　我说的这次旅行过后好几天，我们没有再到远处去，而是把大部分时间用来筹划未来和把我们现在的家建得舒适一点。

　　这么做的原因有几个。首先，尽管我们周围的一切都是那么的令人愉快，不费什么力气就可以获得我们所需的一切，但是我们却不愿意一辈子都待在这里，远离祖国和朋友。其次，这个岛上到底有没有土著人还是不能确定，我们还存着一线希望，盼望着一天有一条船把我们带走。但是时间一天天地过去，既没有看到土著人，也没有见到船，我们就放弃了尽早离开的念头，开始努力地营造我们的家。

　　这段时间里，我们也并没有闲着。我们尝试用不同的方法烧熟椰子，但都失败了。在这之后，我们把所有的东西都搬到一个大石洞里，在那里建了一个家，但是发现这次搬家的决定是错误的，我们还是愿意搬回原来的房子。除了这些之外，我们还常常游泳、聊大天，至少杰克和彼得金说得很多，我则听着。

The Coral Island

Among other useful things, Jack, who was always working at something, turned about three inches of the iron from the oar into an excellent knife. First he **beat**① it quite **flat**② with the axe. Then he made a rude handle and tied the iron to it with our piece of rope, and ground it to an edge on a piece of stone. When it was finished he used it to shape a better handle, to which he fixed it with a **strip**③ of his cotton **handkerchief**④. The rope thus set free was used by Peterkin as a fishing line. He **merely**⑤ tied a piece of shell-fish to the end of it. This the fish were allowed to swallow, and then they were pulled quickly **ashore**⑥. But as the line was very short and we had no boat, the fish we caught were extremely small.

Our Log Boat

One day Peterkin came up from the beach, where he had been fishing, and said in a very **cross**⑦ tone: "I'll tell you what, Jack, I want you to swim out with me on your back, and let me fish in deep water!"

"Dear me, Peterkin," replied Jack, "I had no idea you were taking the thing so much to heart, else I would have got you out of that difficulty long ago. Let me see" — and Jack looked down at a piece of wood on which he had been working with a far-away look, which he always put on when trying to find a way out of a difficulty.

"What do you say to building a boat?" he asked, looking up quickly.

"Take far too long," was the reply; "can't wait. I want to begin at once!"

Again Jack considered. "I have it!" he cried. "We'll cut down a large tree, and put the trunk of it in the water, so that when you want to fish you've nothing to do but to swim out to it."

① beat /biːt/ v. 打
② flat /flæt/ a. 平坦的,扁平的

③ strip /strɪp/ n. 长条,条状
④ handkerchief /ˈhæŋkətʃiːf/ n. 手帕

⑤ merely /ˈmɪəli/ ad. 仅仅,只不过
⑥ ashore /əˈʃɔː/ ad. 在岸上,上岸

⑦ cross /krɒs/ a. 生气的

除了现有的东西,喜欢动手的杰克用那块从船桨上取下来的大约三英寸长的铁做了一把很棒的小刀。他先用斧子把它敲得平平的,然后做了一个简陋的木柄,把铁片用那段绳子绑在木柄上。最后在一块石头上磨出刀刃。做好后,他用这把刀子削了一个更好看的木柄,然后从他的手绢上撕下一块布条把刀子绑好。解下来的没用的绳子被彼得金用来当渔线了。他在线的一端系上一块贝肉,等鱼吞下它,就飞快地把鱼拉上来。但因为渔线太短,我们又没有船,抓上来的鱼都非常小。

我们的独木舟

一天,彼得金从海滩上钓鱼回来,怒气冲冲地说:"告诉你,杰克,我想让你背着我游泳。我坐在你背上,好在深水里钓鱼!"

"天啊!彼得金,"杰克回答说,"我根本不知道你对这事这么上心,否则的话我早就帮你想出办法了,让我想想看。"杰克低下头沉思地望着他正在摆弄的一块木头,那种表情在他试图解决什么棘手的问题时常常能看到。

"咱们造条船,你说怎么样?"他快速抬起头问。

"时间太长了,等不了,我需要马上开始!"彼得金回答说。

杰克又考虑了一下。"有办法了!"他叫道,"我们砍下一棵大树,把树干放到水里,这样一来,你想钓鱼了,只需游到树干那儿就可以了。"

The Coral Island

This was agreed on, so we **started off**① to a spot, not far distant, where we knew of a tree that would **suit**② us, which grew near the water's edge. As soon as we reached it, Jack threw off his coat, and, with strong blows of the axe, cut at it for a quarter of an hour without ceasing. Then, while he sat down to rest, I continued the work. Then Peterkin made an **attack**③ on it, so that when Jack once more began to give it powerful blows, a few minutes' cutting brought it down with a **terrible**④ sound.

"Hurrah!" cried Jack. "Let us cut off its head."

So saying he began to cut through the trunk again, at about six yards from the thick end. This done, he cut three strong, short poles from the thicker branches, with which to roll the **log**⑤ down the beach into the sea; for, as it was nearly two feet thick at the large end, we could not move it without such helps. With the poles, however, we rolled it slowly into the sea.

Having thus been successful in getting our boat into the water, we next shaped the **poles**⑥ into rude oars, and then tried to get on. This was easy enough to do; but after seating ourselves on the log with one leg on either side, it was with the greatest difficulty that we kept it from rolling round and throwing us into the water. Not that we **minded**⑦ that much; but we **preferred**⑧, if possible, to fish in dry clothes. To be sure, our trousers were necessarily wet, as our legs were in the water on each side of the log; but as they could be easily dried, we did not care. After half an hour's **practice**⑨, we were able to keep on the log **fairly**⑩ easily. Then Peterkin laid down his oar, and having put a whole shell-fish on his line, dropped it into deep water.

① start off 出发（动身，开始）
② suit /suːt/ v. 适合，满足

③ attack /əˈtæk/ n. 攻击，抨击
④ terrible /ˈterəbl/ a. 可怕的，糟糕的

⑤ log /lɒɡ/ n. 圆木

⑥ pole /pəʊl/ n. 极（点）

⑦ mind /maɪnd/ v. 介意，留心
⑧ prefer /prɪˈfɜː/ v. 较喜欢，宁可

⑨ practice /ˈpræktɪs/ n. 练习
⑩ fairly /ˈfeəlɪ/ ad. 相当地

　　大家都同意这个主意，说干就干，我们知道在不远的地方，有一棵长在水边的大树，正合适。到了那儿，杰克马上脱掉外衣，用斧子用力地砍起来，他连续地砍了大约一刻钟。然后是我接着干，他坐下来休息。后来轮到彼得金向大树发起进攻，结果当再次轮到杰克挥斧猛砍时，只消几分钟，大树就轰然一声倒下了。

　　"啊哈！"杰克叫道，"我们来把树冠砍掉。"
　　说着，他就开始在离较粗的一端大约六码的地方把树干再截断。截断以后，他又从粗树枝上砍下三根结实的短棍。用这三根棍子，我们把树干滚过沙滩推进海里。没有棍子，我们根本就推不动它，因为树干粗的一端直径大约有两英尺。现在有了木棍的帮助，我们慢慢地把它滚进海里了。

　　把船成功地弄到海里之后，我们又把那三根木棍削成简陋的船桨，然后试着爬上船。爬上船是件很容易的事，难的是两腿跨坐在树干上，又不能让树干翻过来，把我们掀到海里。虽然我们并不是特别在乎落到水里，但是如果可能，我们还是希望能穿着干衣服钓鱼。事实上，裤子是非湿不可的，因为我们是跨坐在树干上，腿是伸进水里的，但因为裤子很快就能干，我们也并不在意。经过半个小时的练习，我们已经很容易在树干上保持平衡了。然后彼得金放下他的桨，把整个一块贝肉都系到绳子上抛进深水里。

Peterkin Catches a Fish

"Now then, Jack," said he, "be careful; keep away from that seaweed. There! that's it; gently now, gently. I see a fellow at least a foot long down there, coming to — Ha! that's it. Oh, blow! he's off."

"Did he **bite**①?" said Jack, sending the log on a little with his oar.

"Bite? Yes! He took it into his mouth, but the moment I began to pull he opened his mouth and let it out again."

"Let him swallow it next time," said Jack, laughing.

"There he is again!" cried Peterkin, his eyes shining. "Look out! Now then! No! Yes! No! Why, the fish won't swallow it!"

"Try to pull it up by the mouth, then! "cried Jack. "Do it gently."

A heavy **sigh**② and a sad look showed that poor Peterkin had tried but that the fish had got away again.

"Never mind, my boy," said Jack; "we'll move on and **offer**③ it to some other fish."

So saying, Jack began to use his oar; but **hardly**④ had he moved from the spot, when a fish with a **huge**⑤ head and a little body **rushed**⑥ from under a rock and swallowed the shell-fish at once.

"Got him this time — that's a fact! "cried Peterkin, pulling in the line. "He's swallowed it right down to his tail, I declare. Oh, what a big one!"

As the fish came to the surface, we bent forward to see it, and the log **turned round**⑦. Peterkin threw his arms round the fish's neck, and in another **instant**⑧ we were all in the water!

A shout of laughter burst from us as we rose to the surface like three

彼得金抓到一条鱼

"注意,杰克,"他说,"当心,避开那块海草。这儿,对,轻一点,轻轻地。我看到一个家伙起码在一英尺深的地方,向着——哈!好的。噢,该死!它逃了。"

"咬钩了吗?"杰克问,用桨又向前划了一点。

"咬钩了吗?当然!它吃进嘴里,但是我要拉绳子的时候,它又张开嘴把食饵吐出来了。"

"下次等它吞下去再说,"杰克笑着说。

"它又来了!"彼得金大声叫道,眼睛发着光,"小心!注意!不!对!不!真奇怪,那鱼就是不咬钩!"

"那就试试勾住鱼嘴把它弄上来!轻轻地拉。"杰克叫道。

沉重的叹息和痛苦的表情都告诉我们可怜的彼得金又没有成功,那条鱼又逃掉了。

"别在意,伙计,"杰克说,"我们接着来引其他的鱼上钩。"

杰克边说边拿起桨,但还没等我们离开原地,就有一条头大身子小的鱼从岩石中窜出来,一口吞下了贝肉。

"这回可抓住了,没说的!"彼得金边叫边拉起渔线。"我敢说它把肉吞到肚子里了。噢,这条可真够个儿的!"

鱼被拉出水面,我们都探下身子去看,树干翻了,彼得金只来得及用胳膊抱住鱼头,我们就都落到水里了!

---

① bite /baɪt/ v. 咬

② sigh /saɪ/ n. 叹息

③ offer /ˈɒfə/ v. 提供,企图

④ hardly /ˈhɑːdlɪ/ ad. 几乎不

⑤ huge /hjuːdʒ/ a. 巨大的,极大的

⑥ rush /rʌʃ/ v. 冲,闯

⑦ turn round 旋转(转变,逆转)

⑧ instant /ˈɪnstənt/ n. 瞬间

drowned **rats**① and seized hold of the log. We soon recovered our position, and sat more carefully, while Peterkin **secured**② the fish, which had almost **escaped**③ during our **struggles**④. It was hardly worth having, however; but, as Peterkin said, it was better than the little ones he had been catching for the last two or three days; so we laid it on the log before us, and having put another shell-fish on the line, dropped it in again for another.

Attacked by a Shark

Now, while we were thus busy with our sport, our attention was drawn to a movement on the surface of the sea, just a few yards away from us. Peterkin shouted to us to row in that direction, as he thought it was a big fish and we might have a chance of catching it. But Jack, instead of doing so, said, in a deep, earnest tone of voice, which I never before heard him use:

"Pull up your line, Peterkin; seize your oar; quick — it's a shark!"

The fear with which we heard this may well be imagined, for it must be remembered that our legs were hanging down in the water, and we could not pull them up without the log **turning over**⑤. Peterkin **instantly**⑥ **pulled up**⑦ the line, and seizing his oar, **rowed**⑧ his hardest, while we also did our best to **make for**⑨ the shore. But we were a good way off, and the log being, as I have before said, very heavy, moved but slowly through the water. We now saw the **shark**⑩ quite clearly, swimming round and round us. From its quick and unsteady movements, Jack knew it was making up its mind to attack us, so he urged us to row for our lives, while he himself set us the example. Suddenly he shouted,

① rat /ræt/ n. 鼠
② secure /sɪˈkjʊə/ v. 固定，使…安全
③ escape /ɪsˈkeɪp/ v. 逃脱，避开，溜走
④ struggle /ˈstrʌɡl/ v. 挣扎

我们抓住树干，从水里钻出来，看到三个人湿得像落汤鸡，不禁大笑起来。很快我们又重新爬上树干，这次必须更小心地坐好，彼得金也把那条鱼放好以防它逃掉，刚才我们在水中挣扎时差点儿让它溜了。尽管这条鱼并不算太好，但彼得金说得对，无论如何这总比他两三天前抓的那些小鱼要好多了；我们把它放在树干前面，渔线上又绑好一块贝肉，放进水里准备再钓一条。

受到鲨鱼的攻击

虽然我们正忙着玩这个新把戏，但是我们的注意力还是被几码远的海面上一个奇怪的动静吸引过去了。彼得金认为那是条大鱼就嚷着要我们划过去，好有机会抓住它。但杰克非但没有按他的要求去做，反而用一种从没听到过的低沉而严肃的语气对我们说：

"把你的渔线收上来，彼得金，抓紧桨，快，那是鲨鱼！"

⑤ turn over 滚动，翻过来
⑥ instantly /ˈɪnstəntlɪ/ ad. 立即地，即刻地
⑦ pull up 拉起
⑧ row /rəʊ/ v. 划，划船
⑨ make for 有助于（相有利，促进）
⑩ shark /ʃɑːk/ n. 鲨鱼

听到这话，可以想象出我们有多害怕，因为你一定还记得我们的腿都伸到水里，而且不可能把腿抬出水面而不弄翻树干。彼得金立即把渔线拉上来，抓住他的桨，用尽力气划起来。我们大家都拼命地向岸上划去，但是我们离岸太远了。更糟的是，就像我前面说过的，这根树干很重，在水面上移动得十分缓慢。现在我们可以清楚地看到鲨鱼，它在一圈一圈地绕着我们游。杰克催促我们使劲划好逃命，因为他知道鲨鱼那快速而又躁动不安的动作预示着它正在下决心准备进攻，他自己竭尽全力

The Coral Island

"Look out! There he comes!" and in a second we saw the great fish dive close under us, and turn half over on his side. But we all beat the water with our oars, which **frightened**① it away for that time, but we saw it immediately after circling round us as before.

"Throw the fish to him!" cried Jack, in a quick, low voice. "We'll reach the shore in time yet, if we can keep him off for a few minutes."

Peterkin stopped one instant to obey the **command**②, and then rowed again with all his might. No sooner had the fish fallen into the water than we observed the shark to disappear. In another moment his nose rose above the water; his wide mouth, armed with a **fearful**③ **double**④ row of teeth, appeared. The dead fish was swallowed and the shark disappeared again. But Jack was wrong in thinking that it would be satisfied. In a very few minutes it returned to us, and its quick movements led us to fear that it would attack us at once.

"Stop rowing!" cried Jack suddenly. "I see it coming up behind us. Now obey my orders quickly. Our lives may **depend**⑤ on it. Ralph, Peterkin, do your best to keep the log from turning over. Don't look out for the shark. Don't look behind you. Do nothing but keep the log from moving."

Peterkin and I instantly did as we were ordered, being only too glad to do anything that gave us a chance or a hope of escape, for we had great **faith**⑥ in Jack's courage and **wisdom**⑦. For a few seconds, that seemed long minutes to my mind, we sat thus silently; but I could not help looking back, although I had been told not to. On doing so, I saw Jack sitting perfectly still, with his oar raised, his mouth **shut**⑧ closely, and his **eyebrows**⑨ bent over his eyes, which looked out fiercely beneath them down into the water. I also saw the shark, quite close under the log, in the act of rushing towards Jack's foot. I could hardly keep back a

① frighten /ˈfraɪtn/ v. 使惊吓,惊恐

② command /kəˈmɑːnd/ n. 命令,指挥,控制

③ fearful /ˈfɪəfʊl/ a. 担心的,可怕的
④ double /ˈdʌbl/ n. 两倍

⑤ depend /dɪˈpend/ v. 依靠,相信,信赖

⑥ faith /feiθ/ n. 信任,信仰
⑦ wisdom /ˈwɪzdəm/ n. 智慧

⑧ shut /ʃʌt/ v. 关上,闭起

⑨ eyebrow /ˈaɪbraʊ/ n. 眉毛

地划,为我们做榜样。突然他大叫道:"小心!它来了!"刹那间我们见到那条大鲨鱼潜到我们底下,身体半翻转过来。我们全都用桨狠命地拍打着水面,暂时把它吓跑了,但我们马上又见到它像刚才那样围着我们打转。

"把鱼扔给它!如果我们能把它赶走几分钟,就能及时上岸,"杰克叫道,声音急促而低沉。

彼得金立刻就照着要求做了,然后马上又操起桨用力划起来。鱼刚落到水里,鲨鱼就消失了。但它的鼻子立刻又冒出了水面,接着露出了那张大嘴,张大的嘴巴里是两排令人心惊胆战的牙齿。死鱼被吞下去之后大鲨鱼消失了。但是杰克的判断是错误的,鲨鱼根本不会满足。只几分钟,它又回来了,那迅猛的动作使我们担心它会立即向我们进攻。

"别划了!"杰克突然叫道,"我见到它朝我们后面来了。现在,马上听我的命令,我们能不能活命就靠它了。拉尔夫、彼得金,你们俩必须尽最大的努力不要让树干翻过来。不要留心寻找鲨鱼,也不要回头看,什么都不要做,只要保持树干不动。"

一心只想找到机会和生存希望的我和彼得金立刻照命令做了,因为我们深深信服杰克的勇气和智慧。我们默默地坐在那儿,虽然只几秒钟,对我来说却是漫长的。尽管杰克告诉我们不要向后看,我还是禁不住回过头去,只见杰克一动不动地坐在那儿举着桨,嘴唇紧闭,双眉紧锁,一双眼睛紧紧地盯着水里。我也看到了那条鲨鱼,它就在离我们的树干不远的地方,朝着杰克的脚冲过来。看到这些,我差一点叫出声来。接着鲨鱼跃出水面,杰克

The Coral Island

cry on seeing this. In another moment the shark rose. Jack drew his leg suddenly from the water and threw it over the log. The great head rubbed against the log as it passed, and we saw its huge mouth, into which Jack instantly pushed the oar, and drove it down its throat. So forceful was this act that Jack rose to his feet in doing it; the log was thus rolled completely over, and we were once more thrown into the water. We all rose in a moment.

"Now then, swim out for the shore!" cried Jack. "Here, Peterkin, catch hold of my **collar**①, and swim as hard as you can."

Peterkin did as he was told, and Jack swam out with such force that he **cut through**② the water like a boat; while I, having only myself to carry, **succeeded**③ in keeping up with him. As we had by this time drawn quite near to the shore, in a few minutes more we were in water not deep enough for the shark to swim in; and, finally, we landed in safety, though very tired and not a little frightened by this terrible **affair**④.

① collar /ˈkɒlə/ n. 衣领

② cut through 刺穿,穿透
③ succeed /səkˈsiːd/ v. 成功

④ affair /əˈfeə/ n. 事件,事情,事务

立即把腿从水里抽上来,移到另一面,鲨鱼冲过来时那巨大的脑袋擦着树干而过,我们清楚地看到了那张大嘴。说时迟,那时快,杰克猛地把手里的桨插进鲨鱼的喉咙。杰克跳起来插桨时动作是那么勇猛,树干一下子翻了个底朝天,我们再一次落入水里,马上又都浮了上来。

"喂,快向岸边游!"杰克叫道,"彼得金,抓住我的衣领,尽力向前游。"

彼得金照着吩咐做了,杰克就像条船似的破浪前进,我在没有什么负担的情况下,终于跟上了他。这时我们离岸已经很近了,只用了几分钟我们就游入浅海,这里的海水太浅,鲨鱼已经不可能游进来了。我们终于安全地上了岸,然而这次可怕的经历弄得我们筋疲力尽,胆战心惊。

Chapter 7
A Garden, Some Nuts and Other Things

Our fight with the shark was the first great danger that we had met since landing on this island, and we were very much moved by it, especially when we considered that we had so often, without knowing it, **run into**① the same danger before while swimming. We were now forced to take to fishing again in the water near the shore, until we should succeed in building a boat.

What troubled us most, however, was that we could no longer go for our morning swims. We did, indeed, continue to wash ourselves by the side of the sea, but Jack and I found that one of our greatest joys was gone when we could no longer dive down among the beautiful coral **groves**② at the bottom of the lagoon. We had come to be so **fond of**③ this, and to take such an interest in watching the shapes of coral and the play of the many beautiful fish **amongst**④ the forests of red and green seaweeds, that we knew the **appearance**⑤ of the fish and the places where they were to be found.

We had also become very good divers. At times, when Jack **happened to**⑥ feel full of fun, he would seat himself at the bottom of the sea on one of the big pieces of coral, and then make faces at me, in

7
花园、坚果及其他

　　和鲨鱼搏斗是我们上岛后遇到的第一件让人心惊胆战的事情。特别是想到在不知情的情况下，经常在同样危险的环境下游泳，我们都十分后怕。现在我们被迫在靠近岸边的水里捕鱼，除非我们能成功地造好一条小船。

　　然而，最让我们苦恼的是我们不能再晨泳了，实际上只能在海滩边洗洗澡。但是我和杰克发现，如果我们再也不能潜到环礁湖底去欣赏美丽的珊瑚树丛，就失去了生活中最大的乐趣。我们曾经怀着极大的兴趣到海底去欣赏珊瑚的各种形状，观看各种美丽的鱼在红的、蓝的水草森林中游来游去，这样我们认识了各种各样的鱼，知道在什么地方可以找到它们，我们太喜欢这件事了。

　　渐渐地，我们还成了十分优秀的潜水员。那时，只要杰克觉得好玩，他就可以坐在海底珊瑚的大树枝上，冲我做鬼脸，想尽办法让我在水底笑出来。开始的时候我没有心理准备，他几乎得逞，我蹿上水面大笑。但是后来当我识破他的诡计之后，我那

① run into 陷入

② grove /grəʊv/ n. 小树林
③ fond of 喜欢
④ amongst /ə'mʌŋst/ prep. 在…之中,在…之间(= among)
⑤ appearance /ə'pɪərəns/ n. 外观,外表

⑥ happened to 发生（碰巧,正巧,偶然）

The Coral Island

order, if possible, to make me laugh under water. At first, when I was not expecting it, he nearly succeeded, and I shot to the **surface**① in order to laugh; but afterwards I knew what he was trying to do, and being naturally of a grave nature, I had no difficulty in stopping myself.

I often used to wonder how poor Peterkin would have liked to be with us; and at times he expressed much **sorrow**② at not being able to join us. I used to do my best to comfort him, poor fellow, by telling him of all the **wonders**③ that we saw; but this, instead of satisfying, seemed only to make him more **anxious**④ to come with us, so one day he agreed to try to go down with us. But although a brave boy in every other way, Peterkin was very afraid of the water, and it was with difficulty we got him to **consent**⑤ to be taken down, for he could never have managed to push himself down to the bottom without help. But we had only pulled him down a yard or so into the deep clear water when he began to struggle and **kick**⑥, so we were forced to let him go, when he rose out of the water, gave a frightful roar, and struck out for the shore with the greatest possible **haste**⑦.

Now all this pleasure we were to do without, and when we thought about it, Jack and I felt very sad. I could see, also, that Peterkin felt sorry for us, for when we talked about this matter he did not make fun about it.

The Water Garden

As, however, a man's difficulties usually **set** him **upon**⑧ trying to find a way to get out of them, so this, our difficulty, made us think of searching for a place among the rocks where the water should be deep enough for diving, yet so circled by rocks as to prevent sharks from

① surface /'sɜːfɪs/ n. 表面，平面

② sorrow /'sɒrəʊ/ n. 悲伤，哀惜

③ wonder /'wʌndə/ n. 奇迹，惊奇

④ anxious /'æŋkʃəs/ a. 焦急的,忧虑的

⑤ consent /kən'sent/ v. 同意,承诺

⑥ kick /kɪk/ v. 踢

⑦ haste /heɪst/ n. 急速,急忙

⑧ set upon 决心要拿到，着手

不苟言笑的天性使我没费多大力气就控制住了自己。

我老是想弄清楚彼得金为什么那么想和我们在一起，他常常抱怨我们潜水时他特伤心。我曾经尽我最大的努力去安慰他，可怜的孩子，我告诉他我们在海底所有的惊奇发现，但令人失望的是，这只能使他更加渴望和我们在一起，因此有一天他同意试着跟我们潜一下水。其实在其他方面彼得金都是一个勇敢的孩子，但是他十分怕水，我们费了不少口舌，他才同意让我们带着他下去，如果没人帮他，他就根本不能自己潜入水底。可我们刚刚把他带到一码左右深的水里，他就开始又蹬又踢地挣扎，我们只好放了他。他一露出水面就尖声怪叫，急不可耐地用力游到岸边。

现在，所有这些好玩的事情都不能做了。每当想起这事时，我和杰克都非常沮丧。而且我能看出来，彼得金也觉得我们怪倒霉的，因为当我们谈起这事时，他没有拿它开玩笑。

水中花园

其实，困难常会促使人们努力去想办法解决它。因此现在的困难促使我们在岩礁里找到一片够深的、能让我们潜水的水域，但这片水域应该是被岩礁环绕着的，这样可以阻止鲨鱼向我们进攻。后来

getting at us. And such a place we afterwards found. It was not more than ten minutes' walk from our house, and was in the form of a small deep **bay**①, the entrance to which, besides being narrow, was not deep enough for a fish so large as a shark to get in; at least, not unless he should be a very thin one.

Inside of this bay, which we called our Water Garden, the coral was much more wonderful, and the seaweed plants far more lovely and brightly coloured than in the lagoon itself. And the water was so clear and still that, although very deep, you could see the smallest object at the bottom. Besides this, there was a **rock**② which overhung the water at its deepest part, from which we could dive pleasantly, and on which Peterkin could sit and see not only all the wonders I had described to him, but also see Jack and me **creeping**③ among the seaweeds at the bottom, like — as he expressed it — "two great white sea animals."

During these dives of ours to the bottom of the sea, we began to find out something of the manners and customs of the animals, and to make discoveries of wonderful things, the like of which we never before thought of. Among other things, we were deeply interested in the work of the little coral animal which, I was **informed**④ by Jack, is supposed to have entirely made many of the islands in the Pacific Ocean. And certainly, when we considered the great reef which these animals had formed round the island on which we were cast, and observed the **ceaseless**⑤ way in which they built their coral houses, it did seem as if this might be true.

I also became much interested in the **manners**⑥ and appearance of other water creatures, and was not content with watching those I saw during my dives in the Water Garden. I made a hole in the coral rock close to it; this I **filled**⑦ with salt water, and put into it different shellfish and other animals, in order to watch more closely how they passed

① bay /beɪ/ n. 海湾

② rock /rɒk/ n. 岩石,巨石

③ creep /kriːp/ v. 爬

④ inform /ɪnˈfɔːm/ v. 通知，告诉

⑤ ceaseless /ˈsiːslɪs/ a. 不停的，不绝的

⑥ manner /ˈmænə/ n. 样子，方式

⑦ fill /fɪl/ v. 装满,填充

我们找到了一块这样的地方。这块水域离我们住的地方只有不超过十分钟的路。它是一个小而深的海湾，开口特别的窄，而且也不太深，像鲨鱼那样的庞然大物是进不来的，除非它是条特别瘦的鲨鱼。

我们把这个海湾命名为"水中花园"，和其他水域相比，这里的珊瑚长得更美，水草类植物比环礁湖里的更好看，颜色也更亮丽。那里的水清澈见底，尽管很深，你也能看见海床上一个很小的东西。除此以外，还有一块巨石在海湾的最深处悬空而出，从那里我们可以轻松地跳进水里潜下去，而且彼得金也可以坐在那儿，他不但能看到我向他描述的全部美景，还能看见我和杰克在长满水草的水底爬行，正如彼得金所描述的那样，我俩"像两只又白又大的海洋动物"。

在海底潜水的时候，我们开始发现了一些海底动物的行为方式和生活习性，还发现了许多我们从前想都没有想到过的美妙东西。在这些东西里，小小的珊瑚虫勤奋的工作引起了我们极大的兴趣。杰克告诉我，太平洋上的许多岛屿可能完全是由珊瑚构成的。的确，我们落脚的小岛就被由珊瑚虫构成的巨大岩礁环绕着，当我们凝望珊瑚礁，看到珊瑚虫以永不停息的方式构筑它们的家园时，这种说法也就显得更令人信服了。

我对其他的水生动物的外貌和行为方式也产生了极大的兴趣，已经不满足于观察那些在潜到"水中花园"时看到的东西了。在靠近"水中花园"的珊瑚石上，我挖了一个洞，在里面灌满了海水，抓了一些不同种类的贝类和其他海洋动物放在里面，为的是更仔细地观察它们的生活方式。望远镜上的

their time. The big glass from our telescope also now became a great **treasure**① to me, as by looking at the animals through it, they appeared larger, and so I could see more clearly the forms and actions of these strange creatures of the sea.

We Plan to Walk Round the Island

Having now got ourselves into a very comfortable **position**②, we began to talk of the plan which we had long thought of carrying out — namely, to travel **entirely**③ round the island; in order, first, to find out whether it contained any other things which might be useful to us; and, second, to see whether there might be any better place for us to live than that on which our house now stood. Not that there was anything about it which we did not like — in fact, we looked upon our house as a home — but if a better place did **exist**④, there was no reason why we should not make use of it. At any rate, it would be well to know of it.

We had much earnest talk over this matter. But Jack said that, before starting on such a **journey**⑤, we should supply ourselves with good arms, for as we intended not only to go round all the shore, but to go up most of the valleys. Before we came home, we should be likely to meet with, he should not say dangers, but at least with everything there was on the island — whatever that might be.

"Besides," said Jack, "it won't be a good thing for us to live on coconuts and shell-fish always. No doubt they are very **excellent**⑥ in their way, but I think a little animal food now and then would be pleasant as well as good for us; and as there are many small birds among the trees, some of which are **probably**⑦ very good meat. I think it would be a fine plan to make **bows**⑧ and arrows, with which we could easily knock them over."

大镜片现在也成了我的一件大宝贝,透过它这些奇特的海洋生物变得更大,我可以更清楚地观察它们的外形和动作。

我们计划周游海岛

① treasure /ˈtreʒə/ n. 宝物,财富

② position /pəˈzɪʃən/ n. 位置,状态

③ entirely /ɪnˈtaɪəlɪ/ n. 完全地

④ exist /ɪɡˈzɪst/ v. 存在

⑤ journey /ˈdʒɜːnɪ/ n. 旅行,行程

⑥ excellent /ˈeksələnt/ a. 极好的,优秀的

⑦ probably /ˈprɒbəb(ə)lɪ/ ad. 大概,或许

⑧ bow /bəʊ/ n. 弓,弓形物

我们现在过得很舒服,因此开始谈论很早以前就想做的一件事,即彻底地周游一遍海岛。目的是,第一,找一找岛上是否还有其他可能对我们有用的东西;第二,去看看岛上是否有其他地方比现在这儿更适合居住。这并非表示我们对现在的住所不满意,实际上,我们把现在住的地方当成我们的家,但是如果有一个更好的地方,我们没有理由不去利用它。不管怎么说,找一找总是比较好。

对这件事我们做了认真的讨论。杰克说在我们开始出发之前应该用合适的武器来武装自己,因为我们不但打算环游海岛,而且还要去绝大多数的山谷。在我们回家之前,可能会遇到什么事,杰克不把它们叫作危险,但是至少是在岛上存在的事,不管它们可能是些什么。

"还有,"杰克说,"我们现在依靠贝类和椰子为生,这不一定是一个好办法。虽然它们在这一类食物里是很好的了,但是我想时常吃一些肉类食物对我们是很有好处的。树上有许多小鸟,其中有一些有可能是很好的肉食。我想最好做一套弓箭,有了它我们就能轻而易举地把鸟射下来。"

· 079 ·

The Coral Island

"First **rate**①!" cried Peterkin. "You will make the bows, Jack, and I will make the arrows. The fact is, I am quite tired of throwing stones at the birds. I began the very day we **landed**②, I think, and have kept on up to the present time, but I've never hit anything yet."

"You forget," said I, "you hit me one day on the leg."

"Ah, true," replied Peterkin, "and a great row you made about it. But you were at least four yards away from the parrot I was trying to hit; so you see what a bad **shot**③ I am."

"But, Jack." said I, "you cannot make three bows and arrows before tomorrow, and would it not be a **pity**④ to waste time, now that we have made up our minds to go on this journey? Suppose that you make one bow and arrow for yourself, and we can take our sticks?"

"That's true, Ralph. It is quite late, and I doubt if I can make even one bow before **dark**⑤. To be sure, I might work by firelight, after the sun goes down."

We had, up to this time, been used to going to bed with the sun, as we had no real reason to work at nights, and, indeed, our work during the day was usually hard enough — what with fishing and **improving**⑥ our house, and diving in the Water Garden and wandering in the woods — so that, when night came, we were usually very glad to **retire to**⑦ our beds. But now that we wanted to work at night, we felt a wish for a light.

"Won't a good fire give you light enough?" asked Peterkin.

"Yes," replied Jack, "quite enough; but then it will give us a great deal more than enough heat."

"True," said Peterkin; "I forgot that. It will cook us."

"Well," said Jack, "I've been thinking over this **subject**⑧ before.

珊瑚岛

① rate /reɪt/ n. 比率,等级

② land /lænd/ v. 登陆,登岸

③ shot /ʃɒt/ n. 射手

④ pity /ˈpɪtɪ/ n. 遗憾,同情,可惜

⑤ dark /dɑːk/ n. 黑暗

⑥ improve /ɪmˈpruːv/ v. 改良,改善

⑦ retire to /rɪˈtaɪə/ 就寝

⑧ subject /ˈsʌbʒɪkt/ n. 题目,主题

"太好了!"彼得金叫起来,"杰克你做弓,我做箭。实际上我已经对扔石头打鸟感到厌烦了。我想起来我们一上岛,我就开始用石头打鸟,一直坚持到现在,可还是什么也没有打到。"

"你忘了,有一天你打中了我的腿。"我说。

"哦,那倒是真的,为这事你还使劲嚷嚷呢。你当时离我要打的那只鹦鹉至少有四码远,你们看我有多没准。"彼得金回答。

"但是,杰克,"我说,"你们不可能在明天之前造好三套弓箭。我们现在应该把主要精力放在海岛上,这样浪费时间不是很可惜吗?我和彼得金可以用我们的大棍子,你给自己造一套弓箭,怎么样?"

"这也对,拉尔夫,现在太晚了,我不敢肯定是不是能在天黑之前做完一只弓。如果完不了,太阳落山之后,我可以在火光底下做完它。"

以前的这个时候,虽然太阳还在天上,我们也已经上床了,因为晚上我们没有必要干活儿,再说,白天的事常常把我们累得够呛,捕鱼、修缮房子、在"水中花园"潜水、在树林里转悠,因此到了晚上我们通常非常乐意去睡觉。但是现在我们要在晚上工作,就很希望有一盏灯。

"火生得大一点是不是能照得更亮?"彼得金问。

"是的,"杰克回答,"够亮的,而且它能给我们比充足的热量多得多的东西。"

"对呀!"彼得金说,"我都忘了,它能烧熟饭。"

"喔,"杰克说,"我以前也一直在想这个问题:在岛上应该生长着一种坚果,土著人用

· 081 ·

There is a certain nut growing in these islands which the natives use to give them a light, and I know all about it and how to **prepare**① it for burning."

"Then why don't you do it?" said Peterkin. "Why have you kept us in the dark so long, you wicked fellow?"

Preparations②

"Because," said Jack, "I have not seen the tree yet, and I'm not sure that I should know either the tree or the nuts if I did see them. You see, I forget what they were said to look like. I believe the **nut**③ is quite small; and I think that the leaves are white, but I am not sure."

"Eh! Ha! Hum!" cried Peterkin. "I saw a tree like that every day!"

"Did you?" cried Jack. "Is it far from here?"

"No, not half a mile."

"Then lead me to it," said Jack, **seizing**④ his axe.

In a few minutes we were all three pushing through the bushes of the forest, led by Peterkin.

We quickly came to the tree Peterkin had told us about, which, after Jack had closely examined it, we **concluded**⑤ must be the right one. Its leaves were of a beautiful **silvery**⑥ white, very different from the dark green leaves of the trees round it. We **immediately**⑦ filled our pockets with the nuts, after which Jack said:

"Now, Peterkin, climb that coconut tree and cut me one of the long branches."

This was soon done, but it cost some trouble for the trunk was very high, and as Peterkin usually pulled nuts from the younger trees, he did

① prepare /prɪ'peə/ v. 准备，筹备

② preparation /ˌprepə'reɪʃn/ n. 准备，预备

③ nut /nʌt/ n. 坚果

④ seize /siːz/ v. 突然抓住

⑤ conclude /kən'kluːd/ v. 推断
⑥ silvery /'sɪlvərɪ/ a. 像银的，银色的
⑦ immediately /ɪ'miːdjətlɪ/ ad. 立即 conj. 一…(就)

它当灯，我对它非常了解，还知道怎么把它点着。"

"那么你为什么不动手去做呢？"彼得金埋怨道，"你为什么让我们在黑暗里待了那么长时间，你这坏蛋。"

准备工作

"因为，"杰克说道，"我还没有看到这种树，而且如果我确实看到了它们，我也不敢确定这就是我想要的东西。你看，我忘了书上是怎么描述它们的样子了。我记得这种坚果很小，而且树叶子是白色的，但是我不敢肯定。"

"啊哈！"彼得金大叫着，"我每天都看到这种树！"

"真的吗？离这儿远吗？"杰克也叫起来。

"不远，还不到半英里。"

"那就带我去吧。"杰克说着抓起了他的斧子。

几分钟之后我们在彼得金的带领下穿过茂密的灌木林。

我们很快来到了彼得金所讲的那棵树下。杰克靠近它查看一番后，确定这一定是我们要的那种。它的叶子是一种美丽的银白色，在周围其他树的深绿色树叶衬托下显得非常特殊。我们很快在口袋里装满了这树的坚果，然后杰克说：

"喂，彼得金，你爬上那棵椰子树，帮我砍一个长树枝下来。"

这事很快就办到了。但是彼得金爬树的时候还是遇到了一些麻烦，因为他平时都是爬一些小一点

The Coral Island

not often climb the high ones.

Jack now took one of the little leaves, and, cutting out the hard, stick-like middle, hurried back with it to our camp. Having made a small fire, he cooked the nuts slightly, and then took off the outsides. After this he wished to make a hole in them, which, not having anything better at the time, he did with the point of our pencil case. Then he put the middle part of the coconut leaf through the hole in each one, and on putting a light to the nut at the top, we found to our joy that it burned with a clear, beautiful flame. When he saw it, Peterkin jumped up and danced round the fire for at least five minutes.

"Now, boys," said Jack, putting out the light, "the sun will set in an hour, so we have no time to lose. I shall go and cut a young tree to make my bow out of, and you had better each of you go and **select**① good strong sticks, and we'll set to work at them after dark."

So saying, he put his axe on his shoulder and went off, followed by Peterkin, while I took up a piece of coconut cloth and began to **examine**② it. I was still **occupied**③ with this, and was sitting in the same position, when my companions came back.

"I told you so!" cried Peterkin, with a loud laugh. "Oh, Ralph, you're **hopeless**④. See, there's a stick for you. I was sure, when we left you looking at that bit of stuff, that we would find you still looking at it when we came back, so I just cut a stick for you as well as for myself."

"Thank you, Peterkin," said I. "It was kind of you to do that, instead of being cross with me for being a **lazy**⑤ fellow, as I **deserve**⑥."

"Oh, as to that," answered Peterkin, "I'll be cross with you yet, if you wish it; only it would be of no use if I did, for you'd still go your own way."

As it was now getting dark we lighted our light, and placing it in a **holder**⑦, made of two crossing branches, inside our hut, we seated

的树摘椰子，很少爬这么高的树。

这时杰克拿了片椰子树上的嫩叶子，把其中坚硬的木质部分切下来，拿着它急急忙忙地回到了住地。他点了一小堆火，把坚果稍微烤了一下，剥掉外面的皮。然后他想在上面戳一个洞，因为手边没有更好的工具，他就用了铅笔套的尖。接着他用椰子树叶中间部分穿过每个坚果的洞，把最上面的一个点燃。当明亮美丽的火焰点燃的时候，我们欣喜若狂。看到火苗燃起来，彼得金绕着火又蹦又跳足足有五分钟。

"嗨，伙计们，"杰克边熄火边说，"离太阳下山还有一个小时，我们不能再耽误时间了。我去砍一棵小树做弓。你们俩最好也去找些好的大树枝，天黑之后我们就开始工作。"

说着，他就扛起斧子走了出去，彼得金跟在他后面。我则拿起一块椰子皮，开始仔细研究。当我的伙伴们回来的时候，我还坐在同一地方，拿着它看。

"叫我说着了！"彼得金笑着叫道，"哦，拉尔夫，你真是无可救药。看，这是你的树枝。我们走的时候，你就在看这些东西，我敢肯定等我们回来的时候，你一定还在看它们，所以就给你砍了一个树枝，我还给自己砍了一枝。"

"谢谢你，彼得金，"我说，"你真是个好心人，我这么懒，你该骂我才是。"

"噢，这个嘛，"彼得金回答，"你要愿意，我会冲你发脾气的。但是这对你来说毫无作用，你还是我行我素。"

天黑下来了，我们点亮了灯，把灯放在用两个树枝十字交叉做成的架子上。之后，我们就待在屋

① select /sɪˈlekt/ v. 选择，挑选

② examine /ɪɡˈzæmɪn/ v. 检查

③ occupy /ˈɒkjʊpaɪ/ v. 占领，占

④ hopeless /ˈhəʊplɪs/ a. 没有希望的，绝望的

⑤ lazy /ˈleɪzɪ/ a. 懒惰的
⑥ deserve /dɪˈzɜːv/ v. 应受

⑦ holder /ˈhəʊldə/ n. 支持物

ourselves on our beds and began to work.

"I intend to keep the bow for my own use," said Jack, cutting with his axe at the piece of wood he had brought. "I used to be quite a good shot once. But what's that you're doing?" he added, looking at Peterkin, who had **drawn**① the end of a long pole into the **hut**②, and was trying to fit a small piece of iron to the end of it.

"You see, Jack," answered Peterkin, "I think I should like to have a **spear**③."

"Well, if length is power," said Jack, "no one will be able to beat you."

The pole which Peterkin cut was fully twelve feet long, being a very strong but light young tree, which **merely**④ required thinning at one end to be a very good spear.

"That's a very good idea," said I.

"Which — this?" asked Peterkin, pointing to the spear.

"Yes," I replied.

"Hum!" said he. "You'd find it a very strong and real idea if you had it pushed through your body, old boy!"

"I mean the idea of making it is a good one," said I, laughing. "And, now I think of it, I'll change my plan too. I don't think much of the stick, so I'll make a **sling**⑤ out of this piece of cloth. I used to be very fond of slinging — ever since I read of David killing Goliath, the **Philistine**⑥—and I was once thought to be very good at it."

A Very Strange Noise

So I set to work to make a sling. For a long time we all worked very busily without speaking. While we were thus **engaged**⑦ we were surprised

① draw /drɔː/ v. 拉,拖
② hut /hʌt/ n. 小屋

③ spear /spɪə/ n. 矛

④ merely /ˈmɪəlɪ/ ad. 仅仅

⑤ sling /slɪŋ/ n. 投石器

⑥ Philistine /ˈfɪlɪstaɪn/ n. 非利士人

⑦ engage /ɪnˈgeɪdʒ/ v. 使忙碌

里坐在各自的床上开始工作。

"我想把这一张弓留给自己用,"杰克一边用斧子在他拿来的一块木头上砍着,一边说道,"我曾经是个好射手。你在做什么呢?"他看着彼得金加了一句。彼得金正把一根长杆子拖进我们的小茅屋,想要把一小块铁安在它末尾。

"你看,杰克,我想做一个渔叉。"彼得金回答说。

"不错,如果长度代表威力的话,没人能击败你。"杰克说。

彼得金砍的杆子足足有十二英尺长,是棵分量轻但非常结实的小树,只要把它的一端弄细就能是一个很好的渔叉。

"这是个好主意,"我说。

"哪个,是这个吗?"彼得金指着他的渔叉问。

"是的。"我回答。

"哼!"他说,"老伙计,如果我用它刺穿你,你就会知道它有多厉害。"

"我是说做个渔叉是个好主意,"我笑着说,"我正想这件事,我也准备改变一下计划。我对用树枝做棍子已经不感兴趣了,我要用这个椰子皮做个投石器。我过去很喜欢投石,那是在我读了大卫杀了哥利亚,那个非利士人的故事以后。而且人们都认为我很擅长这个。"

非常奇怪的声音

于是我就开始做投石器。我们都忙着各自手中的活,很长时间没有人说话。正忙的时候,从远处

The Coral Island

to hear a **distant**① but most strange and **frightful**② cry. It seemed to come from the sea, but was so far away that we could not clearly tell its true direction. Rushing out of our house, we hurried down to the beach and stayed to listen. Again it came, quite loud on the night air. The moon had risen, and we could see the islands in and beyond the lagoon quite **plainly**③, but there was no object that we could see to account for such a cry. A strong wind was blowing from the point whence the sound came, but this **died away**④ while we were gazing out to sea.

"What can it be?" said Peterkin, in a low voice, while we all crept close to each other.

"Do you know," said Jack, "I have heard that sound twice before, but never so loud as to-night. Indeed, it was so faint that I thought I must have merely fancied it, so, as I did not wish to **alarm**⑤ you, I said nothing about it."

We listened for a long time for the sound again, but as it did not come, we went back to the house and **continued**⑥ our work.

"Very strange," said Peterkin, quite gravely. "Do you believe in **ghosts**⑦, Ralph?"

"No," I answered, "I do not. But I must say that strange sounds for which I cannot account, such as we have just heard, make me feel a little **uneasy**⑧."

"What do you say to it, Jack?"

"I neither believe in ghosts nor feel uneasy," he replied. "I never saw a ghost myself, and I never met with anyone who had; and I have generally found that strange things have almost always been **accounted for**⑨, and found to be quite simple on close examination. I certainly can't imagine what that sound is; but I am quite sure I shall find out before long, and if it is a ghost I'll — I'll —"

① distant /ˈdɪstənt/ a. 遥远的,远的
② frightful /ˈfraɪtfʊl/ a. 可怕的
③ plainly /ˈpleɪnlɪ/ ad. 平坦地,明白地
④ die away 渐熄(减弱,消失)
⑤ alarm /əˈlɑːm/ v. 使…惊慌
⑥ continue /kənˈtɪnjuː/ v. 继续,连续
⑦ ghost /gəʊst/ n. 鬼,幽灵
⑧ uneasy /ʌnˈiːzɪ/ a. 不自在的,心神不安的
⑨ account for 说明（原因等）

　　传来了一种既非常奇怪又很恐怖的声音，这声音吓了我们一跳。听起来，声音来自海里，但是因为很远，我们不能说出它的确切位置。我们冲出屋子，急急忙忙地跑到海边，仔细地听。声音又传来了，在夜空中听起来很响亮。月亮已经升起来了，我们可以清楚地看到环礁湖内外的小岛。但是我们没有看见是什么东西发出的这种声音。从发出声音的地方吹来一阵很强的风，当我们紧盯着海面的时候风势减弱了。

　　"那能是什么？"彼得金小声问道，我们都渐渐地贴近了对方。

　　"知道吗？"杰克说，"以前我听到过两次这种声音，但是都没有今晚这么大。实际上，前两次声音太小了，我想也许是我的幻觉。我也不想吓着你们，所以就什么也没说。"

　　我们等了很长时间，但是再没有听到那声音，我们就回到家里，继续干我们的活。

　　"真是奇怪，"彼得金非常严肃地说，"拉尔夫，你相信有鬼吗？"

　　"不，"我回答，"我不相信。但是我必须承认我也不知道刚才听见的奇怪的声音是怎么回事，这让我有点担忧。"

　　"杰克，你怎么看？"

　　"我既不相信鬼神也不觉得担心，"他回答，"我自己从来没有见过鬼也没遇到谁见过。我发现许多奇怪的事最后总能被说清楚，通过仔细研究就会发现事情很简单。当然我现在想象不出这声音是什么。但我确信不久能够找出答案，如果它是鬼的话，我就——我就——"

"Eat it!" cried Peterkin.

"Yes, I'll eat it! Now, then, my bow and two arrows are finished, so if you're ready we'd better go to bed."

By this time Peterkin had **thinned down**① his spear, and tied an iron point very cleverly to the end of it; I had formed a sling, the lines of which were made of thin strips of coconut cloth; and Jack had made a bow, nearly five feet long, with two arrows, feathered with two or three large **feathers**② which some bird had dropped. Jack said that if arrows were well feathered they did not require iron points, but would fly quite well if merely **sharpened**③ at the point, which I did not know before.

We Practise with Our Weapons

Although thus prepared for a start on the next day, we thought it **wise**④ to have some practice in the use of our arms before starting, and on this we spent the whole of the next day. And it was well we did so, for we found that our arms were not at all perfect, and that we were far from perfect in the use of them. First, Jack found that the bow was much too strong, and he had to thin it. Also the spear was much too heavy, and so had to be made thinner, although Peterkin would on no account shorten it. My sling worked very well, but I was so much out of practice that my first stone **knocked off**⑤ Peterkin's hat, and narrowly **missed**⑥ making a second Goliath of him. However, after having spent the whole day in practice, we began to find some of our former cleverness returning — at least Jack and I did. As for Peterkin, being **naturally**⑦ good with his hands, he soon used his spear well, and was able to run as hard as he could at a coconut, and hit it in the middle once out of every five times.

① thin down 弄细,变细

② feather /ˈfeðə/ n. 羽毛 v. 用羽毛装饰

③ sharpen /ˈʃɑːpən/ v. 使尖锐,使敏捷

④ wise /waɪz/ a. 明智的

⑤ knock off 敲落
⑥ miss /mɪs/ v. 漏掉,错过

⑦ naturally /ˈnætʃərlɪ/ ad. 天生地

"吃了它!"彼得金叫道。

"对!我就吃了它!现在,我的弓和两只箭已经做好了,如果你们也做完了,我们就睡觉吧。"

这会儿彼得金把他的渔叉弄细了,又在一端巧妙地绑了一个铁头。我的投石器也做好了,带子是用薄薄的椰子皮条做的。杰克做了一张弓,差不多五英尺长,还做了两只箭。箭上装饰着两三根从鸟身上掉下来的大羽毛。杰克说如果箭装上羽毛,就不用装铁头,只要把它的头削尖就能平稳地飞行,我以前不知道这一点。

试用我们的武器

虽然本来打算第二天我们就出发上路,但是我们觉得在出发之前试用一下我们的武器是明智的做法,于是就用了整整一天的时间练习。我们这么做是对的,因为我们发现我们的武器远不是完美无缺的,而且在使用上我们还十分生疏。首先杰克发现他的弓太硬了,不得不把它弄细一点。彼得金的渔叉也太重了,虽然他决不肯截断它,但也必须得弄细一点。我的投石器十分好用,但是我的技术都已生疏了,我的第一块石头竟打掉了彼得金的帽子,差点把他变成我的弹下冤鬼哥利亚二世。然而在整整一天的练习之后,我们开始发现以前的机灵劲儿又回来了,至少我和杰克是这样。至于彼得金,因为他天生手臂强壮,他很快就能很灵活地用他的渔叉了。他用吃奶的劲儿向一个椰子冲过去,每五次里能有一次把渔叉叉进椭子中间。

But I think that we owed much of our **rapid**① success to Jack, who said that, since we had made him captain, we should obey him, and he kept us at work from morning till night on the same thing. Peterkin wished very much to run about and stick his spear into everything he passed; but Jack **put up**② a coconut, and would not let him leave off running at that for a moment, except when he wanted to rest. We laughed at Jack for this, but we both felt that it did us much good.

That night we examined and **repaired**③ our arms before we lay down to rest, although we were very tired, in order that we might be ready to start out on our journey at **daylight**④ on the following morning.

① rapid /'ræpɪd/ *a.* 迅速的，飞快的

② put up 举起

③ repair /rɪ'peə/ *v.* 修理，补救，补偿

④ daylight /'deɪlaɪt/ *n.* 日光

　　我想我们取得这么神速的进步应该归功于杰克，自从我们选他当头儿之后，他说我们必须服从他。他让我们从早到晚都做同样的练习。彼得金渴望拿着他的渔叉到处乱跑，把它叉在他见到的任何东西上，但是杰克挂起一个椰子给他叉，一会儿也不让他乱跑，除非他想休息的时候。我们都因为这而嘲笑杰克，但是我们俩都认为这对我们十分有好处。

　　晚上，在上床睡觉之前，我们检查了一遍我们的武器，又做了些改进。虽然我们已经很累了，但是为了明天一大早的旅行，我们应该做好准备。

Chapter 8
Strange Clouds

Hardly had the sun shot its first ray across the **bosom**① of the broad Pacific, when Jack jumped to his feet, and, shouting in Peterkin's ear to wake him, ran down the beach to take his usual swim in the sea. We did not, as we usually did, go that morning to our Water Garden, but, in order to **save**② time, washed ourselves in the lagoon just opposite the house. Our breakfast was eaten without loss of time, and in less than an hour afterwards all our **preparations**③ for the journey were completed.

In addition to his usual dress, Jack tied a **belt**④ of coconut cloth round his **waist**⑤; into this he put the axe. I was also advised to put on a belt and carry a short stick in it; for, as I truly said, the sling would be of little use if we should chance to come very close to any wild animal. As for Peterkin, although he carried such a long, and I must add, frightful-looking spear over his shoulder, we could not make him leave his stick behind. "For," said he, "a spear, when close to an enemy, is not worth a **button**⑥." I must say that it seemed to me that the stick was, to use his own language, not worth a button either; for the head was very rough, something like the stick which I remember to have seen in picture books of Jack the Giant-Killer, besides being so heavy that he

8
奇怪的水雾

① bosom /ˈbʊzəm/ n. 胸部

② save /seɪv/ v. 节省

③ preparation /prepəˈreɪʃən/ n. 准备
④ belt /belt/ n. 带,腰带
⑤ waist /weɪst/ n. 腰部

⑥ button /ˈbʌtn/ n. 纽扣

　　当太阳的第一道光线刚照耀到太平洋的宽阔胸膛上，杰克就跳起来了，他冲着彼得金的耳朵大声地把他叫醒，然后就跑向海边开始他日常的晨泳。为了赶时间，今天我们不像往常那样在"水中花园"里游泳，而是在就在房子对面的环礁湖里洗了个澡。早餐也只用了很少的时间。不到一个小时，出发的全套准备工作就完成了。

　　除了平常的穿着，杰克在腰上系了一根椰子皮做的带子，把斧子插在上面。他也让我在腰上系根带子，在上面插根短木棍。因为，说实话，如果我们近距离遭遇野兽，我的投石器一点用处也没有。至于彼得金，虽然他在肩上扛着那根长长的，我必须加上一句，样子很吓人的渔叉，但我们还是不能让他丢掉他的棍子。虽然他说："如果我们遇到敌人，这玩意儿还不如一只纽扣有用。"我必须说，在我看来这根大棍子，确实像彼得金自己说的，比不上一只纽扣。棍子的前端非常粗糙，有些像我在杰克的连环画《凶猛杀手》中见到的棍子。只是这根棍子很重，彼得金不得不用两只手握住，才能用

required to hold it with both hands in order to use it at all. However, he took it with him, and **in this manner**① we **set out**② upon our travels.

We did not consider it necessary to carry any food with us, as we knew that wherever we went we should be certain to fall in with coconut trees; having these, we were well supplied, as Peterkin said, with meat and drink and cloth! I was careful, however, to put the glass from the telescope into my pocket, **in case**③ we should want a fire.

Half a mile's walk took us round a bend in the land which **shut out**④ our house from view, and for some time we advanced at a quick pace without speaking, though our eyes were not idle, but noted everything in the woods, on the shore, or in the sea that was interesting. After passing the hill that formed one side of our valley — the Valley of the Ship — we saw another small valley lying before us in all the loveliness of tropical plant life. We had, indeed, seen it before from the mountain-top, but we had no idea that it would turn out to be so much more lovely when we were close to it. We were about to begin to examine this valley, when Peterkin stopped us and directed our attention to a very strange appearance in front of us along the shore.

A **Puzzling**⑤ Sight

"What's that, think you?" said he, **levelling**⑥ his spear as if he expected an **immediate**⑦ attack from the object in question, though it was quite half a mile distant.

As he spoke, there appeared a white cloud above the rocks as if of **steam**⑧. It rose upwards to a height of several feet, and then disappeared. If this had been near the sea, we should not have been so greatly surprised, as it might in that case have been the waves, for at this part

① in this manner 用这种方式,这样
② set out 出发,开始

③ in case 如果,万一
④ shut out 关在外面（隔开）

它。但是他仍然带着它。我们就这样开始了我们的行程。

我们认为携带食物是没必要的，因为我们知道无论走到哪里，都肯定会在周围发现许多的椰子树。有了这些，我们需要的任何东西就都有了，正如彼得金说的，肉、饮料、衣服都有！然而我还是加了些小心，把望远镜的玻璃片放在口袋里，说不定我们会需要火呢。

走了半英里之后，我们拐了一个弯，我们的房子被挡在视线之外。有时我们不说话加快脚步赶路，但是眼睛却不闲着，在树林里、岸上和海里寻找我们感兴趣的东西。在穿过"船谷"边的一座山丘之后，我们看到另一座小山谷横在我们面前，里面长满了美丽的热带植物，其实我们以前在山顶上已经看到过这座山谷，但是我们没有料到的是，在近处它变得更可爱。我们想进到山谷里看看，但彼得金阻止住了我们，他指着前面海滩上的一个非常奇怪的东西让我们看。

⑤ puzzling /'pʌzlɪŋ/ a. 令人迷惑的
⑥ levelling /'levəlɪŋ/ n. 调整
⑦ immediate /ɪ'miːdjət/ a. 立即的,直接的
⑧ steam /stiːm/ n. 蒸气

令人困惑的景象

"你们看那会是什么？"彼得金说，虽然那东西离我们大约有半英里远，但是他举起渔叉，好像认为那个来路不明的东西会马上发起进攻。

他说话的时候，在岩石的上方出现了一团就像是水蒸气似的白色水雾。它向上升起了大约有几英尺高，然后就消失了。如果它靠近大海，我们对它们也不会感觉惊奇，因为那很可能是海浪造

The Coral Island

of the **coast**① the coral reef approached so near to the island that in some parts it almost **joined**② it. There was therefore no lagoon between, and the heavy waves of the ocean beat almost up to the rocks. But this white cloud appeared about fifty yards inland. The rocks at this place were rough, and they stretched across the **sandy**③ beach into the sea. Hardly had we ceased expressing our surprise at this sight, when another cloud flew upwards for a few seconds, not far from the spot where the first had been seen, and disappeared; and so, from time to time, these strange sights continued.

We were now quite sure that the clouds were **watery**④, but what caused them we could not **guess**⑤, so we determined to go and see. In a few minutes we gained the spot, which was very rough, and quite wet with the falling of the water. We had much difficulty in **passing over**⑥ with dry feet. The ground also was full of holes here and there. Now, while we stood anxiously waiting for the appearance of these clouds, we heard a low sound near us, which quickly increased to a loud noise, and a moment afterwards a thick cloud of water burst upwards from a hole in the rock and shot into the air with much force, and so close to where Jack and I were standing, that it nearly touched us. We sprang to one side, but not before the water came down and wetted us both to the skin.

Peterkin, who was standing farther off, escaped with a few drops, and burst into a fit of laughter on seeing our state.

"Mind your eye!" he shouted **eagerly**⑦. "There goes another!"

The words were hardly out his mouth when there came up a cloud from another hole, which served us exactly in the same manner as before.

Peterkin shouted with laughter; but his joy was quickly ended by the

① coast /kəʊst/ n. 海岸，海滨
② join /dʒɔɪn/ v. 参加，结合，加入
③ sandy /ˈsændɪ/ a. 沙的，多沙的

④ watery /ˈwɔːtərɪ/ a. 水的，潮湿的
⑤ guess /ges/ v. 猜测，推测
⑥ pass over 越过

⑦ eagerly /ˈiːgəlɪ/ ad. 渴望地

成的现象。在这边的海岸上，珊瑚礁和海岛靠得很近，在有些地方几乎连在二起了。因此在那里没有环礁湖，海里的海浪几乎都要拍打到岩石上面了。但是这团白色的水雾延伸至内陆大约有五十码。这地方的礁石都很粗糙，它们从海边的沙地一直延伸到海里。正当我们对这一景象不再感到奇怪的时候，几秒钟后，另一团水雾在离我们第一次看见它不远的地方又升了起来，一会儿又消失了，就这样，一次又一次，这种奇怪的景象持续着。

我们现在十分肯定这是一片水雾，但是我们猜不出来它是怎么形成的，所以决定上前去看看。几分钟后，我们到了那儿。那地方高低不平，而且很潮湿，到处都是水，走在上面难免弄湿我们的脚。地上到处是小洞。我们正站在那里焦急地等待着这些水雾的出现，突然听见身旁有一种很低沉的声音，很快声音变大了，不一会儿厚厚的一团水雾以很大的冲力从礁石的一个小洞里冲出来，它离我和杰克站的地方很近，几乎碰到我们。我们急忙向旁边一跳，但是水点已经落下来，把我们全身都弄湿了。

彼得金站得比较远一些，只溅到一两滴，看到我们的窘境他爆发出一阵大笑。

"当心！"他急叫着，"它们又来了！"

他的话音还没落，水雾又从另一个石洞里冲出，像刚才一样弄得我们全身透湿。

彼得金笑着叫着，但是很快在靠近他站的那个地方传来了一阵声音，他的快乐被打断了。

noise occurring close to where he stood.

"Where will it come up this time, I wonder?" he said, looking anxiously about, and preparing to run.

Suddenly there came a loud noise; a fierce cloud of water burst between Peterkin's legs, blew him off his feet, surrounded him with water, and threw him to the ground. He fell with so much force that we feared he must have broken some of his bones, and ran anxiously to help him; but by good **fortune**① he had fallen into a bush, in which he now lay.

It was now our turn to laugh; but we were not yet quite sure that he was unhurt, and as we knew not when or where the next cloud might arise, we helped him quickly to jump up and **hurry**② from the spot.

"What's to be done now?" said Peterkin sadly.

"Make a fire, my boy, and dry ourselves," replied Jack.

"And here is material ready to our hand," said I, picking up a dry branch of a tree as we hurried up to the woods.

In about an hour after this, our clothes were again dry.

While they were **hanging up**③ before the fire, we walked down to the beach, and soon observed that these strange clouds formed immediately after the fall of a huge wave, never before it; and that they did not form except when the wave was an extremely large one. From this we concluded that there must be an underground **channel**④ in the rock into which the water was driven by the larger waves, and finding no way of escape except through these small holes, was thus **forced up**⑤ through them. **At any rate**⑥, we could not think of any other reason for these strange clouds, and this seemed a very simple and **probable**⑦ one.

① fortune /ˈfɔːtʃən/ n. 运气

② hurry /ˈhʌrɪ/ v. 忽忙，催促

③ hang up 悬挂，挂断

④ channel /ˈtʃænl/ n. 通道，频道，海峡
⑤ force up 迫使上升
⑥ at any rate 无论如何，至少
⑦ probable /ˈprɒbəbl/ a. 很可能的

"我不知道，这次它从什么地方冲出来？"他说，看起来很担心，而且随时准备跑。

突然传来一声巨响，一股猛烈的水雾从彼得金的两腿之间冲出，冲得他两腿悬空，全身湿透，摔倒在地。他摔得很重，我们都担心他会跌断骨头，急忙跑过去帮他。但是幸运的是他跌到了灌木丛里，现在还躺在那儿。

现在轮到我们笑起来，但是我们还不敢肯定他安然无恙，而且也不知道下一次水雾会在什么时候什么地方冲出来，所以我们扶着彼得金急急忙忙跳开，逃离了这个地方。

"我们现在该干什么？"彼得金沮丧地说。

"点把火，伙计，把我们弄干。"杰克回答说。

"点火的材料到手了。"我们急速穿过树林时，我边说边抓了一把干树枝。

大约一个小时之后，我们的衣服干了。我们趁衣服在火边挂着的时候，向海边走去，我们很快发现大浪刚一落下，水雾就形成了，大浪打来之前决不会出现这种情况，而且只有浪头非常大，水雾才能形成。基于这些现象，我们想在岩石底下一定有一条暗沟，大浪把海水压进沟里，水找不到出路，被迫从岩石的小洞里喷出来。无论如何，我们都想不出其他的原因来解释这些奇怪的水雾，这看来是最简单最有可能的解释。

The Coral Island

A Strange Fish

"I say, Ralph, what's that in the water? Is it a shark?" said Jack, just as we were about to leave the place.

I immediately ran to the **overhanging**① rock, from which he was looking down into the sea, and bent over it. There I saw a very faint pale object of a **greenish**② colour, which seemed to move slightly while I looked at it.

"It's like a fish of some sort," said I.

"Hullo! Peterkin!" cried Jack. "**Fetch**③ your spear, here's work for it."

But when we tried to reach the object, the spear was too short.

"There now," said Peterkin, "you were always telling me it was too long".

Jack now drove the spear hard towards the object, and let go his hold; but although it seemed to be well aimed, he must have missed, for the handle soon rose again; and when the spear was drawn up, there was the **pale green**④ object in exactly the same spot, slowly moving its tail.

"Very odd," said Jack.

But although it was certainly very odd and though Jack and all of us drove the spear at it **repeatedly**⑤, we could neither hit nor drive it away, so we were **forced**⑥ to continue our journey without discovering what it was. I wondered very much at this strange appearance in the water, and could not get it out of my mind for a long time afterwards. However, I **quieted**⑦ myself by making up my mind that I would pay a visit to it again at some other time.

一条奇怪的鱼

"我说,拉尔夫,在水里的那是什么?是鲨鱼么?"我们正要离开的时候杰克问我。

我急忙跑到一块突出的岩石上,杰克正在那里弯着腰往海里看。从岩石上往下看,我看见水里有一个呈绿色的模糊不清的物体,似乎正在缓慢地摆动着。

"看起来像一种鱼。"我说。

"喂!彼得金!"杰克叫道,"把你的渔叉拿来,这儿有活儿可干了。"

但是当我们想用渔叉够那个东西时,发现渔叉太短了。

"怎么样,"彼得金说,"你们还老说这个太长了。"

杰克抓住渔叉对准那东西使劲扎下去。虽然看起来他瞄得很准,但是一定是扎偏了,因为渔叉的柄又很快浮上来,而且当渔叉拽上来之后,那个淡绿色的东西还在那个地方,慢慢地摆动着它的尾巴。

"真奇怪。"杰克说。

这东西真是太奇怪了,虽然杰克和我们都用渔叉试了好几次,但是我们既没有叉到它也没能把它赶走,我们不得不带着这个疑问继续我们的旅程。但是我对水里的那个奇怪的东西很好奇,在以后很长一段时间里,我都无法把它忘记,我安慰自己说以后一定要再来一次。

---

① overhang /ˌəʊvəˈhæŋ/ v. 悬于…之上,逼近

② greenish /ˈgriːnɪʃ/ a. 带绿色的

③ fetch /fetʃ/ v. 拿来,取来

④ pale green 浅绿

⑤ repeatedly /rɪˈpiːtɪdlɪ/ ad. 重复地,再三地

⑥ force /fɔːs/ v. 强迫,强夺,加压力

⑦ quiet /ˈkwaɪət/ v. 使…减少,使…安心

Chapter 9
The Second Day of Our Journey

Our **examination**① of the little valley proved to be most helpful. We found in it not only the same trees as we had already seen in our own valley, but also one or two others of a different kind. We had also the pleasure of discovering a strange vegetable, which Jack thought must certainly be that of which we had read as being among the South Sea Islands, and which was named **taro**②. Also we found a large supply of **yams**③, and another root like a **potato**④ in appearance. These were all quite new to us. We each put one of these roots in our pocket, intending to use them for our supper; of which more later. We also saw many beautiful birds here, and **traces**⑤ of some four-footed animals again.

In the **meantime**⑥ the sun began to **descend**⑦, so we returned to the shore, and pushed on round the cloud-producing rocks into the next valley. This was that valley of which I have spoken as running across the entire island. It was by far the largest and most beautiful that we had yet looked upon. Here were trees of every shape and size and colour which it is possible to think of, many of which we had not seen in the other valleys; for, the stream in this valley being larger, and the earth much richer than in the Valley of the Ship, it was clothed with a thicker

9
我们旅行的第二天

① examination /ɪɡˌzæmɪˈneɪʃn/ n. 考查，检查

② taro /ˈtɑːrəʊ/ n. 芋头
③ yam /jæm/ n. 番薯，甜薯
④ potato /pəˈteɪtəʊ/ n. 马铃薯，土豆

⑤ trace /treɪs/ n. 痕迹，踪迹
⑥ meantime /ˈmiːnˈtaɪm/ ad. 与此同时
⑦ descend /dɪˈsend/ v. 降

　　我们在小山谷里查看一番结果是很有用的，我们不但发现了一些和我们的山谷里一样的树，而且还发现了一两个不同的树种。我们还高兴地发现了一种奇怪的蔬菜，杰克想这一定是我们读到过的生长在南海群岛的那种蔬菜，书上把它们叫作芋头。我们还找到了许多的山药和一种外观像土豆的块根。这些都是我们以前从来没有见过的。我们每人都抓了一些放进口袋里，打算把它们当作晚餐，虽然现在离晚餐还有很长的一段时间。我们在这里还见到了许多美丽的鸟，并发现了一些四蹄动物的足迹。

　　在太阳快要下山的时候，我们回到岸边，费了很大劲，绕过了那块能喷雾的大石头，进入了下一个山谷。这个山谷就是我前面讲到的横穿整个海岛的那个山谷。这是我们迄今所见过的最大最漂亮的山谷。这里的树大大小小，奇形怪状，还有许多想都想不到的漂亮颜色，其中有很多是我们在其他的山谷里没见过的。因为在这儿溪水的流量更大，土壤也比"船谷"更肥沃，上面覆盖着茂密的树木和

· 105 ·

growth of trees and plants.

Some trees were dark shining green, others of a rich and warm colour, pleasantly different from those of a pale light green, which were everywhere common. Among these we saw the broad dark heads of the bread-fruit, with its **golden**① fruit; the **pure**②, silvery leaves of the tree bearing the nuts from which we obtained our light, and several kinds which were very like the **pine**③; while here and there, in groups and in single trees, rose the tall forms of the coconut palms, waving their **graceful**④ leaves high above all the rest.

New Trees

Now, while we were gazing round us in silent admiration, Jack uttered a cry of surprise, and pointing to an object a little to one side of us, said:

"That's a **banyan**⑤ tree."

"And what's a banyan tree?" asked Peterkin, as we walked towards it.

"A very strange one, as you shall see presently," replied Jack. "There is a wonderful thing about it. What a big one it is, to be sure!"

"*It*!" repeated Peterkin. "Why there are dozens of banyans here! What do you mean by talking bad English? Is your sense **deserting**⑥ you, Jack?"

"There is but one tree here of this kind," replied Jack, "as you will see if you examine it."

And, sure enough, we did find that what we had supposed was a forest of trees was really only one. Its bark was of a light colour, and had a shining appearance, the leaves being spear-shaped, small, and of

各种植物。

与那些随处可见的浅绿色树木不同，有些树是明亮的深绿色，还有一些是绚丽的暖色，令人赏心悦目。在这些树中我们见到了长着宽大的深色树冠的面包树，果实金灿灿的；还有果实被我们刚用来点灯的那种树，叶子是纯银白色；还有其他几种很像松树；高大的椰子树不管是几棵连成一片还是独立生长的都随处可见，它们那美丽的枝叶在其他树木之上优雅地摆动着。

新树种

正当我们环顾四周暗暗赞叹的时候，杰克惊讶地叫了起来，他指着离我们较近的一棵树说：

"那是棵榕树。"

"什么是榕树？"我们朝着它走过去的时候彼得金问。

"一棵奇妙的树，马上你就会看到了。"杰克答道，"这种树有种奇妙的特征。哎呀，多大的一棵树啊！"

"一棵！"彼得金说，"嗨，这儿有好多棵榕树！你说的是英文吗？难道你神志不清了吗，杰克？"

"这儿的确就只有一棵榕树，仔细看你就会明白了。"杰克回答说。

这是真的，我们发现我们想象中的一整片的树林实际上只是一棵树。榕树的树皮是浅颜色的，有些发亮。叶子是尖的，不大，呈漂亮的绿色。

---

① golden /ˈɡəʊldən/ a. 金(黄)色的
② pure /pjʊə/ a. 纯的，纯洁的
③ pine /paɪn/ n. 松树

④ graceful /ˈɡreɪsfʊl/ a. 优雅的

⑤ banyan /ˈbænjən/ n. 榕树

⑥ deserting /dɪˈzɜːt/ v. 放弃，遗弃

The Coral Island

a beautiful green. But the wonderful thing about it was, that the branches, which grew out from the trunk like the arms of a cross, sent down long **shoots**① to the ground, which, taking root, had themselves become trees, and were covered with bark like the tree itself. Many of these shootse had descended from the branches at **various**② distances, and some of them were so large and strong that it was not easy at first to tell the child from the parent trunk. The shoots were of all sizes and in all conditions of growth, from the trunks we have just **mentioned**③ to small ropes which hung down and were about to take root, and thin brown **threads**④ still far from the ground, which waved about with every motion of the wind.

In short, it seemed to us that, if there were only space enough for it, this single tree would **at length**⑤ cover the whole island.

Shortly after this we came upon another strange tree, which, as its interesting shape afterwards proved extremely useful to us, must be described. Its **proper**⑥ name Jack did not know. However, there were quantifies of fine nuts upon it, some of which we put in our pockets. But its trunk was the wonderful part of it. It rose to about twelve feet without a branch, and was not of great thickness — far from it, it was very thin for the size of the tree — but, to make up for this, there were four or five wonderful **outgrowths**⑦ in this trunk. These I cannot better describe than by asking the reader to suppose that five boards of two inches thick and three feet broad had been placed round the trunk of the tree, with their, *edges* closely fixed to it, from the ground up to the branches, and that these boards had been covered over with the bark of the tree, and had become one with it. Without them the trunk could not have supported its heavy and leafy top. We found very many of these nut trees. They grew **chiefly**⑧ on the banks of the stream, and were of all sizes.

① shoot /ʃuːt/ n. 芽

② various /ˈveərɪəs/ a. 各种各样的

③ mention /ˈmenʃən/ v. 说起,提到
④ thread /θred/ n. 线

⑤ at length 终于(最后,详细地)

⑥ proper /ˈprɒpə/ a. 适当的,正确的

⑦ outgrowth /ˈaʊtɡrəʊθ/ n. 自然结果,发展

⑧ chiefly /ˈtʃiːflɪ/ ad. 主要地

但是最奇妙的是树干上长出的枝杈像手臂一样向四面伸展，长长的嫩枝扎到地里，在那里生根，于是这些枝杈又长成了树，树外面也包着和母树相同的树皮。许许多多的嫩枝从树枝的不同位置长出来，有些又粗又大，第一眼看上去很难分辨出哪棵是从母树上分出的小树。这些嫩枝大小不同，生长的状况也各异，有刚才提到长成树干的；也有绳索状悬挂下来，即将入地生根的；还有些枝条像棕色的细线，它们离地面很远，在风中摇曳着。

总之，在我们看来，只要有足够的空间，这棵树最后就有可能长满整个海岛。

这之后不久我们又发现了另一种奇怪的树，因为这种形状的树后来对我们极其有用，我要仔细地把它那奇妙的外观描述一番。杰克也不知道它确切的名字。树上面长满了许多成色好的坚果，我们摘了一些放在口袋里，但是树干是整棵树里最棒的部分，它一直长到十二英尺高都没分枝，而且并不很粗。就它的个头来说算是很细的了。为了补偿这一点，主树干上长着四五个令人惊奇的派生树干。那派生干的样子我没法更好地描述，只能请读者想象一下五块两英寸厚三英尺宽的木板，环绕在从地面到分枝这一截树干上，其边缘与主干紧紧相连，派生干的外面也裹着树皮，和主干连为一体。没有这些，这种树根本不可能撑起枝叶茂密的树冠。我们发现了许多这样的坚果树。它们有大有小，主要长在溪流两边的岸上。

The Coral Island

While we were examining a small tree of this kind, Jack cut off a piece of a board with his axe, and found the wood to be firm and easily cut. Then he struck his axe into it with all his force, and very soon cut it off, close to the tree, first, however, having cut it across above and below. By this means he satisfied himself that we could now obtain short boards, as it were already cut, of any size and **thickness**① that we desired; which was a very great discovery indeed — perhaps the most important we had yet made.

We now made our way back to the coast, intending to camp near the beach, as we found that the **mosquitoes**② were a trouble in the forest. On our way we could not help admiring the birds which flew and called all round us. The colours of many of these birds were **extremely**③ bright — bright green, blue, and red being the common colours. We tried several times **throughout**④ the day to bring down one of these, both with the bow and the sling — not for mere sport, but to find out whether they were good for food. But we always missed, although once or twice we were very near hitting. As evening drew on, however, a **flock**⑤ of birds flew over. I sent a stone into the middle of them, and had the good fortune to kill one of them.

We were surprised, soon after, by a loud **whistling**⑥ noise above our heads; and on looking up, saw **a flock of**⑦ wild ducks flying towards the coast. We watched these, and observing where they came down, followed them up until we came upon a most lovely blue lake, not more than two hundred yards long, circled by green trees. Its smooth surface, in which we could see every leaf and branch quite clearly, was covered with various kinds of wild ducks, feeding among the rushes and broad-leaved water-plants which **floated**⑧ on it; while many other water-birds ran up and down most busily on its edge. These all flew quickly away

① thickness /'θɪknɪs/ n. 厚度,浓度

② mosquito /mə'skiːtəʊ/ ad. 非常,极其

③ extremely /ɪk'striːmli/ ad. 非常,极其

④ throughout /θruː'aʊt/ ad. 自始至终

⑤ flock /flɒk/ n. 群

⑥ whistling /'(h)wɪslɪŋ/ n. 啸声

⑦ a flock of 一群,一组,许多

⑧ float /fləʊt/ v. 浮动,飘,散播

我们找了棵小树观察,杰克用斧子砍下了一块木板,发现这种树的木质很硬但又很容易砍伐。接着,他走到树旁,先上下横着砍了几斧,然后就挥斧猛砍,很快就把树放倒了。他很满意,这样一来,我们现在就能有短木板了,和已经砍下来的一样,想要多大多厚都行。这是一个非常重大的发现——可能是迄今为止最重大的一项。

我们现在返回海滨,准备在靠近沙滩的地方露营,因为我们发现树林里的蚊子令人烦恼。在路上我们对在四周飞翔啼叫的鸟儿赞叹不已。这些鸟儿的颜色特别明快——亮绿、蓝色,还有红色,都是很常见的颜色。白天我们用弓和投石器试了好几次想打下一只来——不仅仅是为了好玩,而是还想看看鸟肉能不能吃。虽然有一两次我们几乎要打中了,但是最终一只都没打到。然而当夜色降临的时候,一群鸟儿飞了过来,我朝鸟群中间扔了块石头,居然幸运地打死了一只。

紧接着,一阵很响的鸣叫声从头顶上传来让我们大吃一惊,抬头一看,一群野鸭子正向海滩飞去。我们望着它们,想看看它们到底飞到什么地方。后来,野鸭子把我们带到了一个十分美丽的蓝色湖泊。这湖不到二百码长,四周长满了绿树。湖水很平静,我们能清楚地看见每片树叶和每根树枝在水里的倒影。那里有各种各样的野鸭子,在草丛和漂浮在水面上的阔叶水生植物中间觅食,还有许多其他种类的水鸟在湖边跑来跑去。我们一露面它们就一下子都飞走了。沿着湖边我们还发现湖里有鱼,但叫不出名字。

The Coral Island

the instant we made our appearance. While walking along the edge we observed fish in the water, but of what sort we could not tell.

Now, as we neared the shore, Jack and I said we would go a little out of our way to see if we could not get one of those ducks; so, directing Peterkin to go straight to the shore and made a fire, we separated, **promising**① to join him again soon. But we did not find the ducks, although we made a careful search for half an hour. We were about to make our way back, when we came across one of the strangest sights that we had yet **beheld**②.

The Pigs

Just in front of us, at a **distance**③ of about ten yards, grew a fine tree, which certainly was the largest we had yet seen on the island. Its trunk was at least five feet round, with a smooth grey bark; above this the spreading branches were clothed with light green leaves, among which were groups of bright yellow fruit — so many as to **bend down**④ the branches with their great weight. This fruit was about the size of an orange. The ground at the foot of this tree was thickly covered with the fallen fruits; in the middle of which lay sleeping at least twenty pigs, of all ages and sizes, having quite filled themselves up with the fruit.

Jack and I could **scarce**⑤ hold in our laughter as we gazed at these fat, **ugly**⑥ animals, while they lay breathing heavily among the **remains**⑦ of their supper.

"Now, Ralph," said Jack, in a low **whisper**⑧, "put a stone in your sling — a good big one — and shoot at that fat fellow with his back towards you. I'll try to put an arrow into that little pig over there."

"Don't you think we had better wake them up first?" I whispered.

① promising /ˈprɒmɪsɪŋ/ a. 有希望的,有前途的

② behold /bɪˈhəʊld/ v. 看到

③ distance /ˈdɪstəns/ n. 距离,间距

④ bend down 俯身(弯腰)

⑤ scarce /skeəs/ a. 缺乏的,不足的
⑥ ugly /ˈʌɡlɪ/ a. 丑陋的,难看的
⑦ remain /rɪˈmeɪn/ n. 剩余物,残骸
⑧ whisper /ˈ(h)wɪspə/ n. 耳语

等接近海滩的时候，我和杰克说我们应当再多费些力气，看能不能抓到一只野鸭子。我们叫彼得金先去海边生火。分手的时候，我们答应彼得金会很快回去找他。虽然我们仔仔细细地找了半个小时，却没有抓到鸭子。正当我们准备回去的时候，突然发现了一种景象，一种我们所见过的最为奇特的景象。

猪

就在我们正前方，大约十码远的地方长着一棵茂盛的树，这肯定是我们在岛上见过的最大一棵树。树干大约有五英尺粗，长着光滑的灰色树皮，向四周伸展的树枝上长满了浅绿色的树叶，在树叶之间挂着一簇簇明黄色的果实——果子那么多，把树枝都压弯了。这种果子的大小和橘子差不多。树脚下堆了厚厚一层落果，至少有二十只不同年龄和大小的猪正躺在落果中间睡觉，它们个个都吃得饱饱的。

当我和杰克看到这些又丑又胖的家伙时，几乎禁不住要大笑起来，这些家伙正喘着粗气躺在它们吃剩的晚饭上。

"喂，拉尔夫，"，杰克小声说，"在你的投石器上装一块石头，装一块大的啊，打那头背冲着你的胖家伙，我用箭射那边那头小猪。"

"我们是不是最好先把它们弄醒？趁它们睡觉的

The Coral Island

"It seems **cruel**① to kill them while asleep."

"If I wanted sport, Ralph, I would certainly wake them up; but as we only want meat, we'll let them lie. Besides, we are not sure of killing them, so shoot away."

At these words, I slung my stone with so good an aim that it hit against the pig's side as if against the head of a **drum**②; but it had no other effect than to make the animal start to its feet with a frightful cry of surprise, and rush away. At the same instant Jack shot, and the arrow **pinned**③ the little pig to the ground by the ear.

"I've missed, **after all**④!" cried Jack, running forward with raised axe, while the little pig uttered a loud cry, tore the arrow from the ground, and ran away with it, along with the whole **herd**⑤, into the bushes and disappeared, though we heard the noise they made long afterwards in the distance.

"That's a pity, now," said Jack, **rubbing**⑥ the point of his nose.

"Very," I replied, stroking mine.

"Well, we must **make haste**⑦ and get back to Peterkin," said Jack. "It's getting late." And without further words we threaded our way quickly through the woods to the shore.

When we reached it, we found wood laid out, the fire lighted and beginning to burn up, with other signs of preparation for our camp, but Peterkin was not to be found. We wondered very much at this, but Jack said that he might have gone to fetch water, so he gave a shout to let him know that we had arrived, and sat down upon a rock. while I threw off my coat and seized the axe, intending to **split**⑧ up one or two pieces of wood. But I had scarcely moved from the spot when, in the distance, we heard a most frightening shout which was followed up by **a burst of**⑨ cries from the pigs, and a loud hurrah.

① cruel /ˈkruəl/ a. 残酷的，残忍的

② drum /drʌm/ n. 鼓

③ pin /pɪn/ v. 钉住
④ after all 毕竟，到底

⑤ herd /hɜːd/ n. 兽群，人群，牧人

⑥ rub /rʌb/ v. 擦，搓，摩擦

⑦ make haste 赶快

⑧ split /splɪt/ v. 劈开

⑨ a burst of 突然一阵

时候把它们弄死似乎是有点太残忍了。"我也小声说。

"拉尔夫，如果我想闹着玩，当然得把它们弄醒，但是咱们只想吃肉，还是让它们躺着罢。再说，咱们也不敢肯定一定能杀死它们，所以还是快干吧。"

杰克说完，我就用力把石头投出去，真准呀，石头打中了猪的肋部，那声音就像敲在一面鼓上。但这除了让这头动物蹦起来惊叫着跑掉之外，没有任何的效果。同时杰克也射出了他的箭，箭刺穿了小猪的耳朵，把它钉在了地上。

"还是射偏了！"杰克叫着举着斧子冲过去，那头小猪惨叫着，把箭从地上拔起来，带着它和同伴一起跑入灌木丛不见了，尽管很长时间以后我们还能听见远处猪群发出的叫声。

"唉，真可惜。"杰克揉着鼻尖说。

"太可惜了。"我也揉着鼻尖说。

"唉，我们得赶紧回去找彼得金，"杰克说，"现在天已经晚了。"我们不再多说什么，赶忙穿过树林向海边走去。

我们到海滩上的时候，发现柴火都摆好了，火也点了，开始旺起来，我们还能看到宿营的其他准备工作，但却没见着彼得金的影子。我们很奇怪，杰克说彼得金可能是去取水了。他大叫了一声好让彼得金知道我们已经回来了，然后就坐在一块大岩石上，我则脱掉外衣，拿起斧子，准备劈一两块柴火。我还没挪窝，就听见远处传来了十分吓人的叫声，接着是猪的狂叫和大声地欢呼。

The Coral Island

"I do believe," said I, "that Peterkin has met with the pigs."

"Hurrah!" shouted Peterkin in the distance.

We turned **hastily**① towards the direction from which the sound came, and soon saw Peterkin walking along the beach towards us with a little pig stuck on the end of his long spear.

"Well done, my boy!" cried Jack, hitting him on the shoulder when he came up. "You're the best shot among us."

"Look here, Jack!" said Peterkin, as he took the animal from his spear. "Have you seen that hole," said he, **pointing to**② the pig's ear; "and are you **familiar**③ with this arrow, eh?"

"Well, I declare!" said Jack.

"Of course you do," said Peterkin; "but **pray**④ stop declaring this time, for I'm very hungry, I can tell you; and it's a **serious**⑤ thing to charge a whole herd of pigs with their huge mother leading them."

Supper

We now began to prepare supper; and, truly, a good show of food we made, when all was laid out on a flat rock in the light of the **blazing**⑥ fire. There was, first of all, the little pig; then there was the taro root, and the yam, and the potato, and lastly, the bird.

We found great difficulty in making up our minds how we were to cook the pig. None of us had ever **cut up**⑦ one before, and we did not know exactly how to begin; besides, we had nothing but the axe to do it with, our knife having been forgotten. At last Jack jumped up and said:

"Don't let us waste more time talking about it, boys. Hold it up, Peterkin. There, lay the back leg on this piece of wood — so"; and he cut it off with a large **portion**⑧ of the body at a single blow of the axe.

① hastily /ˈheɪstɪlɪ/ ad. 匆忙地,急速地,慌张地

② point to 指向
③ familiar /fəˈmɪljə/ a. 熟悉

④ pray /preɪ/ v. 祈祷,恳求
⑤ serious /ˈsɪərɪəs/ a. 严肃的,认真的

⑥ blazing /ˈbleɪzɪŋ/ a. 强烈的,燃烧的,炫目的

⑦ cut up 切碎

⑧ portion /ˈpɔːʃən/ n. 一部分,一份

"我敢肯定彼得金也遇到了那群猪。"我说。

"噢!"彼得金在远处大叫着。

我们急忙向着声音传来的地方跑去,很快就看到彼得金沿着沙滩向我们走来,一只小猪叉在他那根长长的渔叉上。

"好样的,小伙子!"当我们赶到时,杰克拍着彼得金的肩膀叫道,"你是我们当中最好的射手。"

"看这儿,杰克,"彼得金说着,把猪从渔叉上拿下来,指着猪耳朵说,"你看见这个洞了么?你一定也认识这支箭,对么?"

"噢,可真怪呀!"杰克说。

"你当然觉得奇怪,"彼得金说,"但是我恳求你现在别大惊小怪了,我已经很饿了,真的,去袭击一群由一个身材庞大的妈妈带领的猪群可不是闹着玩的。"

晚　饭

我们现在开始准备晚饭,事实上,当我们在火光的照耀下把所有的东西放在一块平整的岩石上时,发现我们的食物很丰盛。首先是一头小猪,其次有芋头,山药和土豆,最后还有鸟。

怎样动手做这头猪呢?这个主意可真难拿。在这之前我们谁都没有杀过猪,根本不知该如何下手。而且除了斧子我们没有其他的工具,我们谁都没有想起那把刀子。最后杰克跳起来说:

"伙计们,我们别再浪费时间讨论了。把它拿起来,彼得金。好的,把它的后腿放在这块木头

The Coral Island

"Now the other — that's it." And having thus cut off the two back legs, he made several cuts in them, pushed a sharp pointed stick through each, and put them up before the blaze to roast. The bird was then cut open, washed clean in **salt**① water, and **treated**② in the same way. While these were cooking, we made a hole in the sand under the fire, into which we put our vegetables and covered them up.

The taro root was egg-shaped about ten inches long and four or five **thick**③, it was of a **grey**④ colour, and had a thick skin. We found it **somewhat**⑤ like an **Irish**⑥ potato, and very good. The yam was **roundish**⑦, and had a rough brown skin. It was very sweet and tasted nice. The potato, we were surprised to find, was quite sweet and very good, as also were the pig and the bird too, when we came to taste them.

In fact this was **decidedly**⑧ the best supper we had enjoyed for many a day; and Jack said it was very much better than we ever got on board ship; and Peterkin said he feared that if we should remain long on the island he would think of nothing but eating; at which Jack replied that he need not fear that, for he did so already! And so, having eaten our fill, we laid ourselves comfortably down to sleep, upon a bed of branches under a coral rock.

① salt /sɔːlt/ *a.* 含盐的
② treat /triːt/ *v.* 处理

③ thick /θɪk/ *a.* 厚的
④ grey /ɡreɪ/ *a.* 灰色的
⑤ somewhat /ˈsʌm(h)wɒt/ *ad.* 多少，几分
⑥ Irish /ˈaɪərɪʃ/ *a.* 爱尔兰的
⑦ roundish /ˈraʊndɪʃ/ *a.* 圆的
⑧ decidedly /dɪˈsaɪdɪdlɪ/ *ad.* 毫无疑问

上——行了！"他一斧子就把后腿连同好大一块肉砍下来了，"现在，另外一条后腿——就是它。"就这样他砍下了猪的两条后腿，又在上面砍了几下，然后把它们分别穿到一根根尖尖的棍子上，放在火上烤。鸟也切开了，在海水里洗干净后也如法炮制。烤肉的时候，我们在火堆底下的沙地上挖了一个洞，把那些菜放进去盖好。

芋头是蛋形的，大约十英寸长，四或五英寸粗，呈灰色，皮厚厚的。我们发现它有些像爱尔兰土豆，很不错。山药圆乎乎的，棕色的皮很粗糙。它的味道很甜，口感也好。还有土豆，我们惊奇地发现它也甜丝丝的，味道很棒。品尝猪肉和鸟肉的时候，我们也觉得相当不错。

实际这是许多天以来我们最棒的一顿晚饭。杰克说这要比我们在船上吃过的饭菜好多了；彼得金说如果我们得在岛上再多待些时候，他恐怕除了吃，其他什么也不想了；杰克说他不必担心这点，因为他现在已经这样了！过后我们把自己填得饱饱的，舒舒服服地躺在珊瑚礁底下树枝铺成的床上睡着了。

Chapter 10
Back to Our House

When we awakened on the following morning, we found that the sun was already quite high in the sky, so I became sure that a heavy supper does not help one to rise early. However, we felt very strong and well, and very ready to have our breakfast. First, however, as was our **custom**①, we had our morning swim.

We had not **advanced**② on our journey much above a mile or so, when, on turning a point that showed us a new and beautiful group of islands, we were suddenly stopped by the **frightful**③ cry which had so **alarmed**④ us a few nights before. But this time we were **by no means**⑤ so much alarmed as on the occasion before, because at that time it was night, and now it was day; and I have always found, though I am unable to account for it, that daylight **sends away**⑥ many of the fears that attack us in the dark.

On heating the sound, Peterkin hastily levelled his spear.

"Now, what can it be?" said he, looking round at Jack. "I'll tell you what it is; if we are going to be kept in a **constant**⑦ condition of fear and surprise, as we have been for the last week, the sooner we're

10
回　家

　　第二天早晨当我们醒来时，发现太阳已经升得很高了。我由此认定一顿丰盛的晚餐不会让人早起。但我们个个觉得身强力壮，非常乐意吃早饭，可头一件事，就是去晨泳，这是我们的老习惯了。

　　我们上路后还没走多远，大约只有一英里多吧，就来到一个转弯处，一个新奇而美丽的群岛展现在我们面前。这时，我们突然停住了脚步，因为耳边传来前几天夜里弄得我们惊慌失措的可怕叫声。但这次我们无论如何也不会像上次那么惊慌，因为那时是夜晚，而现在是白天。尽管我不能明确说出为什么会是这样，但是我总觉得，白天明亮的光线能把许多在夜晚折磨我们的恐惧赶跑。

　　听到这声音，彼得金急忙端起他的渔叉。

　　"喂，这是什么声音？"他转过头看着杰克，"我告诉你，如果我们永远处在恐惧和惊慌里，就像上星期一样，那我们越早离开这个岛越好，尽管这里有山药、椰子、猪还有土豆！"

---

① custom /'kʌstəm/ *n.* 习惯，风俗
② advance /əd'vɑːns/ *v.* 前进，增加
③ frightful /'fraɪtfəl/ *a.* 可怕的，不愉快的
④ alarmed /ə'lɑːmd/ *a.* 惊恐的，忧虑的
⑤ by no means 决不，并没有
⑥ send away 赶出，解雇
⑦ constant /'kɒnstənt/ *a.* 始终如一，不断的

The Coral Island

out of this island the better, **in spite of**[①] the yams and coconuts and pigs and potatoes!"

As Peterkin said this, we heard the cry again, louder than before.

"It comes from one of these islands," said Jack.

"It must be a ghost, then," said Peterkin, "for I never heard any living thing make a noise like that."

We all turned our eyes towards the group of islands, where, on the largest, we observed strange objects moving on the shore.

"Soldiers they are — that's a fact!" cried Peterkin, **gazing at**[②] them in the greatest surprise.

And, **in truth**[③], what Peterkin said seemed to me to be correct, for, at the distance from which we saw them, they appeared to be an army. There they stood, in **ranks**[④], in lines and in **squares**[⑤], with blue coats and white trousers. While we were looking at them, the **dreadful**[⑥] cry came again over the water, and Peterkin said that he thought it must be an army sent out to kill the natives. At this Jack laughed, and said:

"Why, Peterkin, they are **penguins**[⑦]!"

"Penguins?" repeated Peterkin.

"Yes, penguins, Peterkin, penguins — nothing more or less than big sea-birds, as you shall see one of these days, when we pay them a visit in our boat, which I mean to set about building the moment we get back to our house."

"So, then, our dreadful shouting ghosts, and our blood-thirsty soldiers," said 'Peterkin, "have changed to penguins — big sea-birds! Very good. Then I say that we should continue our journey as fast as possible, or our island will be turned into a dream before we get completely round it."

Now, as we continued on our way, I thought much over this new

① in spite of 尽管

② gaze at 凝视（注视）

③ in truth 事实上（的确）

④ rank /ræŋk/ n. 等级，阶级

⑤ square /skweə/ n. 正方形

⑥ dreadful /'dredfʊl/ a. 可怕的

⑦ penguin /'peŋgwɪn/ n. 企鹅

彼得金正说着，那叫声又传来了，而且比前一次更响。

"声音是从那边的一个岛上传来的。"杰克说。

"那一定是鬼了，"彼得金说，"我从没听过哪种活物发出这种声音。"

我们都转过去望着那边的群岛，发现在最大的那个岛上有一群奇怪的东西在岸边移动。

"他们是士兵，事实明摆着！"彼得金边叫边睁圆了眼睛盯着他们。

说真的，我也认为彼得金说得没错，因为从我们这儿望过去，他们真像一支军队，他们穿着蓝色的外衣和白色的裤子，一排排、一行行、一个个方阵地站着。就在我们看他们的时候，又一阵令人毛骨悚然的叫声越过水面传来。彼得金说他认为这一定是派来杀害土著人的军队。听到这话，杰克大笑着说：

"什么呀，彼得金，它们是企鹅啊！"

"企鹅？"彼得金重复着。

"是的，企鹅。彼得金，是企鹅，那只不过是一种大的水鸟。我打算回去后就着手造一条船，到时候我们划船过去看看，你很快就会明白了。"

"这么说，那叫声吓人的魔鬼和嗜血如命的士兵，"彼得金说，"都变成了企鹅，一种大水鸟啦！太好了。要是这样，我说，我们应该尽快继续旅行，要不然我们还没来得及绕岛一圈，这儿就变成仙岛了。"

我们接着朝前走，我还在想着这个新发现和那些怪模怪样的鸟。杰克对它们也了解得很少。我开

The Coral Island

discovery and the strange appearance of these birds, of which Jack could only give us a very slight account; and I began to long to begin our boat, in order that we might go and look at them more narrowly. But **by degrees**① these thoughts left me, and I began to be much **taken up**② again With the interesting character of the country which we were passing through.

Nearing Home

The second night we passed in much the same manner as the first, at about two-thirds of the way round the island, as we thought, and we hoped to sleep on the night following at our house. I will not here note so **particularly**③ all that we said and saw during the course of this second day, as we did not make any further important discoveries. The shore along which we travelled, and the various pans of the woods through which we passed, were very like those which have already been treated of. There were one or two **observations**④ that we made; however, and these were as follows:

We saw that, while many of the large **fruit-bearing**⑤ trees grew only in the valleys, and some of them only near the banks of the streams, where the soil was especially rich, the coconut palm grew everywhere; not only on the hill-sides, but also on the **seashore**⑥, and even, as has been already said, on the coral reef itself, where the soil, if we may use the name, was nothing better than **loose**⑦ sand mixed with broken shells and coral rock. So near the sea, too, did this useful tree grow, that in many cases its roots were washed by the water from the waves. Yet we found the trees growing thus on the sands to be quite as fine as those growing in the valleys, and the fruit as good, also.

We found several more herds of pigs in the woods, but we did not

① by degrees 渐渐地，逐渐地
② take up 开始，从事

③ particularly /pəˈtɪkjʊlərɪ/ ad. 特别，尤其

④ observation /ˌɒbzəˈveɪʃən/ n. 观察

⑤ fruit-bearing 结果的

⑥ seashore /ˈsiːʃɔː/ n. 海岸，海滨

⑦ loose /luːs/ a. 宽松的，不牢固的

始盼望快点造好船，这样就能在近处见到它们了。我渐渐丢开这些想法，又开始被路上的奇光异景迷住了。

快到家了

第二个夜晚差不多和头一个一样被打发掉了，我们觉得我们的环岛旅行大约已经走了三分之二的路程，大伙儿都盼着下一个夜晚可以睡在我们自己的房子里。这里我就不再详细讲第二天的所见所闻，因为在旅途中并没有什么新的重大发现。沿途的海滩和树林与前面见过的没有什么区别，只有一两样新发现，它们是：

我们见到许多高大的果树只长在山谷里，其中一些甚至只长在靠近河岸的地方，因为那里的土壤最肥沃。但是椰子树无处不在，它不仅长在山崖边，也长在海滩上，甚至像我前面说的，它们还长在珊瑚礁上，那里的土壤，如果也可以这么叫的话，不过是一些散沙混上些破碎的贝壳和珊瑚石。这种有价值的树在紧靠大海的地方也照样生长，在很多地方树根被海水冲刷着。但我们发现沙地上的椰子树与山谷里面的长得一样好，果实也一样甜美。

kill any of them, having more than enough for our present needs. We saw, also, many of their footmarks in this **district**①.

During the rest of the day we **pursued**② our journey, and examined the other end of the large valley, which we found to be so much like the parts already **described**③, that I shall not say anything about what we saw in this place. We arrived at our house in the evening, and found everything just in the same condition as we had left it three days before.

When we lay down that night under the shelter of the house, we fell immediately into very deep sleep. I am quite sure about this, for Jack afterwards **admitted**④ the fact, and Peterkin, although he **denied**⑤ it, I heard breathing loudly in his sleep two minutes after lying down. In this condition we remained all night and the whole of the following day without awakening once, or so much as moving our places. When we did awake it was near **sunset**⑥ and we **merely**⑦ rose to swallow some food. As Peterkin said, we took breakfast at **teatime**⑧, and then went to bed again, where we lay till the following morning.

After this we rose feeling very wide awake, but much alarmed for fear that we had lost **count**⑨ of a day. However, on considering the subject, we were all three of the same opinion as to how long we had slept, and so our minds were put at ease.

My Hole in the Rock

For many days after this, while Peterkin and Jack were busily employed in building a little boat out of the natural boards of the nut tree, I spent much of my time in examining with the glass from the telescope the strange things that were **constantly**⑩ happening in my hole in the rock. Here I saw those strange animals which stick, like little red, yellow, and green **masses**⑪, to the rocks, put forth, as it were, many

① district /'dɪstrɪkt/ n. 区，地区，行政区
② pursue /pə'sjuː/ v. 继续从事
③ describe /dɪ'skraɪb/ v. 描述

④ admit /əd'mɪt/ v. 承认
⑤ deny /dɪ'naɪ/ v. 否认

⑥ sunset /'sʌnset/ n. 日落
⑦ merely /'mɪəlɪ/ ad. 仅仅，只不过
⑧ teatime 下午茶时间

⑨ count /kaʊnt/ n. 计数

⑩ constantly /'kɒnstəntlɪ/ ad. 不断地，经常地
⑪ mass /mæs/ n. 块，大多数

在树林里，又发现了几群野猪，但是一只也没有杀，我们目前的食物已经足够了。在这里我们还见到许多野猪的脚印。

在这一天剩下的时间里，我们继续前行，抵达到这条大山谷的另一端。我们发现这里和前面已经描述过的景象极其相似，所以我无须赘述这里的见闻。傍晚时分，我们回到了我们的房子，发现这里的一切同我们三天前离开时一模一样。

那天晚上我们在房子里刚躺下就沉沉入睡了。我敢肯定是这样，因为杰克过后承认了这一点，至于彼得金，我听到他刚躺下两分钟就鼾声大作，尽管他极力否认。就这样我们睡了一整夜和第二天一整天，中间没有醒过一次，更没有挪动一下地方。当我们醒来时，太阳已经快下山了，我们起来草草地吃了几口饭。正像彼得金所说的那样，我们在下午茶的时间吃早饭，然后又睡，一直睡到第二天早晨。

起来后，我们都觉得神清气爽，但很害怕我们记录的日期会少了一天。但是因为我们三个人对于睡了多长时间这个问题的意见是一致的，心才放了下来。

石头上的小洞

这以后的许多天，杰克和彼得金都在忙着用坚果树上的天然木板造小船，而我则把大部分时间都花在了岩石的小洞上，我用望远镜的镜片观察那里面不断发生着的奇特的事情。我看到那些粘在岩石上的一堆堆浅红、黄色和绿色的奇怪动物，伸展开

arms and wait till little fish or other small animals touched them. Then they instantly seize them, fold arm after arm around them, and so take them inside.

Here I saw the ceaseless working of those little coral animals whose efforts have built up vast rocks and huge reefs round the islands of the Pacific. And I observed that many of these animals, though extremely small, were very beautiful, coming out of their holes in a circle of **fine threads**①. Here I saw strange little shell-fish opening a hole in their backs and putting out a thin, **feathery**② hand, with which, I doubt not, they **dragged**③ their food in to their mouths. Here, also, I saw those **crabs**④ which have shells only in the front of their bodies, but no shell whatever on their very **tender**⑤ tails, so that, in order to protect them, they **thrust**⑥ them into the empty shells of some other shell-fish, and when they grow too big for one, change into another. But, most strange of all, I saw an animal which had the wonderful power, when it became ill, of casting its inside and its teeth away from it, and getting an entirely new set in the course of a few months! All this I saw, and a great deal more, by means of my hole in the rock and my glass; but I will not set down more particulars here, as I have still much to tell of what happened to us while we remained on this island.

① fine thread 细纹,细线
② feathery /ˈfeðərɪ/ a. 柔软如羽毛的
③ drag /dræg/ v. 拖,拉
④ crab /kræb/ n. 蟹
⑤ tender /ˈtendə/ a. 温和的,亲切的,未成熟的
⑥ thrust /θrʌst/ v. 插入,推挤,刺

许许多多的触手,等待着小鱼或其他小动物,一旦它们碰到它,就立即被抓住,触手一只只地收回来,小动物就被吞吃掉了。

这里我也看到那些小小的珊瑚虫,它们不停地工作着,凭着自己的努力在太平洋群岛周围建起了巨大的岩石和珊瑚礁群。我发现这些动物虽然体积极小,但美丽无比,它们像一圈细丝一样,从洞里出来。我还见到一种奇怪的小海贝,它们在背部开了一个小口,伸出一只细长的、像羽毛似的触须。我敢肯定,它们一定是用触须抓住食物送入口中。我在这里还见过那种只有一半硬壳的螃蟹,它的硬壳只长在身体的前半部,软软的尾部却没有壳。因此,为了保护自己,它们必须钻进其他贝类的空壳里。当它们长大时,空壳容不下了,就另换一个。但最令人不可思议的是我见过的一种动物,它有一种神奇的力量,它生病的时候,竟然能把整个内脏和牙齿一同排出来抛掉,而在几个月的时间里又长出一套全新的来!上述这一切,都是我用望远镜,在岩石上的小洞里看到的,我还看到了更多的东西,但不能在这里一一述说了,我们滞留海岛期间发生了许多事,要讲的还多着呢。

Chapter 11
Diamond① Cave

"Come, Jack." cried Peterkin, one morning about three weeks after we had come back from our long journey, "let's be **cheerful**② today, and do something at which we can run about. I'm quite tired of **hammering**③ and bamming, cutting and **butting**④ at that little boat of ours, that seems as hard to build as Noah's. Let us go to the mountaintop, or have a hunt after the wild ducks, or make a dash at the pigs. I'm quite **flat**⑤ — flat as a board; in fact, I want something to **toss**⑥ me up, as it were. Eh, what do you say to it?"

"Well," answered Jack, throwing down the axe with which he was just about to proceed towards the boat, "if that's what you want, I would **advise**⑦ you to make a journey to the cloud-making rocks. The last one we had to do with tossed you up a fine height; perhaps the next will send you higher, who knows, if you're at all **reasonable**⑧ in what you expect!"

"Jack, my dear boy," said Peterkin gravely, "you are really becoming too fond of fun. It's a thing I don't at all approve of, and if you don't give it up, I fear that, for the good of both of us, we shall have to part."

11
钻石洞

① diamond /'daɪəmənd/ n. 钻石

② cheerful /'tʃɪəfʊl/ a. 高兴的,快乐的
③ hammer /'hæmə/ v. 锤击,敲打
④ butting /'bʌtɪŋ/ n. 撞
⑤ flat /flæt/ a. 单调的
⑥ toss /tɔːs/ v. 抛,扔,掷

⑦ advise /əd'vaɪz/ v. 劝告

⑧ reasonable /'riːznəbl/ a. 合理的,有道理的,适度,通情达理的

"嗨,杰克,"在我们长途旅行回来后大约三个星期的一个早上,彼得金喊着,"我们今天要高高兴兴的,做一些能游游逛逛的事。围着我们那条小船砰砰地敲呀打呀,砍呀削呀,拼呀接呀,真让我烦死了,这看起来就像建诺亚方舟一样难。我们去山顶吧,或者去打野鸭子,或者去打那群猪。我觉得生活平淡无味,无聊透了;说实话,在某种程度上,我需要一些能让我兴奋的事。噢,你们说怎么样?"

"好吧,"杰克扔下斧子说,刚才他拿着斧子正要去造船,"如果你想找刺激的话,我就建议你到那块能喷雾的岩石去。我们没躲掉的最后那次喷发把你扔得够高的,也许下一次能把你抛得更高,谁知道呢,如果你的期望合情合理的话。"

"杰克,我的老兄,"彼得金严肃地说,"你现在变得太爱开玩笑了。我一点也不喜欢你这样,如果你不改的话,恐怕彼此分手对我们大家都有好处。"

· 131 ·

"Well, then, Peterkin," replied Jack with a smile, "what would you have?"

"Have?" said Peterkin. "I would have nothing, I didn't say I wanted to have; I said that I wanted to do."

"By the way," said I, "I remember now that we have not yet discovered the nature of the appearance that we saw near the cloud-making rocks, on our journey round the island. Perhaps It would be well to go for that purpose."

"**Humph**①!" cried Peterkin, "I know the nature of it well enough."

"What was it?" said I.

"It was of a strange nature, to be sure!" said he, with a wave of his hand, while he rose from the log on which he had been sitting and put on his belt, into which he pushed his huge stick.

"Well, then, let us away to the cloud-making rocks," cried Jack, going up to the house for his bow and arrows; "and bring your spear, Peterkin. It may be useful."

We now, having made up our minds to examine into this matter, set out **eagerly**② in the direction of the cloud-making rocks, which, as I have before mentioned, were not far from the place where we were now living. On arriving there we **hastened**③ down to the edge of the rocks and **gazed**④ over into the sea, where we observed the pale-green object still easily to be seen, moving its tail slowly backwards and forwards in the water.

"Most strange!" said Jack.

"Very **unusual**⑤!" said I.

"Takes the prize!" said Peterkin.

珊瑚岛

"好了，彼得金，"杰克笑着说，"那么你想要什么？"

"要什么？"彼得金说，"我不会要任何东西，也没说我想要。我是说我想干点什么。"

"顺便说一句，"我说，"我现在想起上次环游海岛时在喷雾的岩石旁边看到的怪东西了，我们还没有发现这是怎么回事呢。出于这个目的去那儿看看也许是件好事。"

"哼！"彼得金叫起来，"我很清楚这是怎么回事。"

"怎么回事？"我问。

"那是一种怪物，没错！"他挥舞着胳膊从一根圆木上站起，他刚才一直坐在那儿，他扎上腰带，把他那根大棍子别在腰带里面。

"好吧，那我们就到那块能喷雾的岩石去吧。"杰克叫着，到屋里去取他的弓箭；"带上你的渔叉，彼得金，也许会有用的。"

我们决心对这件事进行调查后，就满怀渴望地向那块能喷雾的岩石走去。我前面已经说过，那地方离我们现在住的地方不远。到了那儿，我们就急忙来到岩石边上向海里看去。发现那个淡绿色的东西仍然清晰可见，它在水里慢慢地来回晃动着尾巴。

"真是奇怪！"杰克说。

"太不寻常了！"我说。

"抓住它！"彼得金说。

---

① humph /hʌmf/ v. 发哼声

② eagerly /ˈiːɡəlɪ/ ad. 渴望地

③ hasten /ˈheɪsn/ v. 催促,赶快,急忙

④ gaze /ɡeɪz/ v. 注视,凝视

⑤ unusual /ʌnˈjuːʒʊəl/ ad. 异常的,罕见的

The Strange Fish Again

"Now, Jack," he added, "you made such a poor **figure**[①] when you last tried to stick that object, that I would advise you to let me try it. If it has got a heart at all, I'll promise to send my spear right through the middle of it; if it hasn't got a heart, I'll send it through the spot where its heart ought to be."

"Go on then, my boy," replied Jack with a laugh.

Peterkin immediately took the spear, held it for a second or two above his head, then sent it like an arrow into the sea. Down it **went straight**[②] into the centre of the green object, passed quite through it, and came up immediately afterwards, **pure**[③] and **unmarked**[④], while the strange tail moved quietly as before!

"Now," said Peterkin gravely, "that animal is **heartless**[⑤]; I'll have nothing more to do with it."

"I'm pretty sure now," said Jack, "that it is merely some form of light; but I must say I do not understand why it remains always in that **exact**[⑥] spot."

I did not understand it either, and thought with Jack that it must be natural light, of which appearance we had seen much while on our way to these seas.

"But," said I, "there is nothing to stop us from diving down to it, now that we are sure it is not a shark."

"True," answered Jack, **stripping off**[⑦] his clothes; "I'll go down, Ralph, as I'm better at diving than you are. Now then, Peterkin, out of the road!"

Jack stepped forward, joined his hands above his head, bent over

奇怪的鱼又出现了

"我说,杰克,"彼得金接着说,"你上次叉它的时候,差得太多了。现在我建议你让我试试。如果它还真有心脏的话,我保证让我的渔叉直接穿过心脏;如果没有心脏,我就把渔叉叉进它的要害。"

"来吧,伙计。"杰克笑着答道。

彼得金立即拿起渔叉,把它举过头顶,握了一两秒钟之久,然后把它像箭一样射向海里。渔叉径直地叉向那绿色物体的中部,一下子穿过去,又很快地浮上来,没有任何痕迹,那条奇怪的尾巴还像从前一样平静地摆动着。

"哎呀,"彼得金一脸严肃地说,"这东西根本就没有心脏,我现在是没有招儿了。"

"我现在差不多全明白了,"杰克说,"这仅仅是某种光。但是我得说我还弄不明白它为什么总是在这个地方出现。"

我也不知道这是为什么,但同意杰克这一定是一种自然光的看法,我想起来在去海边的路上我们曾多次看到这种光线出现。

"不过,"我说,"既然肯定那东西不是鲨鱼了,就没有什么能阻止我们潜下去看看了。"

"对,"杰克边说边甩掉他的外衣,"拉尔夫,我下去,我比你潜得好。喂,彼得金,让一下!"

杰克迈步向前,两手交叉在头上,身子贴近岩石,一下子跳进大海。有那么一瞬间,他潜水时激

① figure /ˈfɪɡə/ n. 数字

② go straight 直走,改过自新
③ pure /pjʊə/ a. 纯的,纯粹的
④ unmarked /ˌʌnˈmɑːkt/ a. 无记号的,未被注意的
⑤ heartless /ˈhɑːtlɪs/ a. 狠心的,无情的

⑥ exact /ɪɡˈzækt/ a. 精确的

⑦ strip off 剥去

the rocks, and dived into the sea. For a second or two the water thrown up by his dive **hid**[1] him from view; then the water became **calm**[2], and we saw him swimming far down in the middle of the green object. Suddenly he went below it, and disappeared completely from our sight! We gazed anxiously down at the spot where he had disappeared for nearly a minute, expecting every moment to see him rise again for breath; but fully a minute passed, and still he did not appear again. Two minutes passed! and then **a flood of**[3] alarm rushed in upon my **soul**[4], when I considered that, during all the time I had known him, Jack had never remained under water more than a minute at a time; indeed, not often so long.

Jack Disappears

"Oh, Peterkin!" I said, in a voice that **trembled**[5] with **increasing**[6] fear, "something has happened. It is more than three minutes now."

But Peterkin did not answer, and I observed that he was gazing down into the water with a look of great fear, while his face was overspread with a **deadly**[7] paleness. Suddenly he jumped to his feet, and rushed about in a dreadful state, crying, "Oh, Jack, Jack! He is gone! It must have been a shark, and he is gone for ever!"

For the next five minutes I know not what I did; the **depth**[8] of my feelings almost took away my senses. But I was **recalled**[9] to myself by Peterkin seizing me by the shoulder and gazing wildly into my face, while he **exclaimed**[10]:

"Ralph! Ralph! perhaps he has only fainted. Dive for him, Ralph!"

It seemed strange that this did not occur to me before. In a moment I

① hid /hɪd/ v. 藏,隐藏,遮蔽
② calm /kɑːm/ a. 平静的,冷静的

③ a flood of 一大片,大量
④ soul /səʊl/ n. 灵魂,精神

⑤ tremble /'trembl/ v. 战栗,微动
⑥ increase /ɪn'kriːs/ v. 增加,提高

⑦ deadly /'dedlɪ/ ad. 非常地,如死一般地

⑧ depth /depθ/ n. 深度
⑨ recall /rɪ'kɔːl/ v. 回想起,召回,恢复

⑩ exclaim /ɪk'skleɪm/ v. 大叫,呼喊,大声叫

起的波浪挡住了他的身影；然后水面平静下来了，我们看到他已经深深地潜到了那个绿色物体中间。突然，他向下一沉，从我们的视线里完全消失了！我们焦急地注视着他消失的那个地方，将近有一分钟，不停地盼望着能看到他上来换气。但是整整一分钟过去了，他还是没出现。两分钟过去了！无边的恐惧向我袭来，我想到我和杰克认识这么长时间，他每次潜入水底从来没有超过一分钟。真的，从来没这么长。

杰克不见了

"噢,彼得金！"我说,由于越来越害怕声音都发抖了,"一定是发生了什么事,现在已经超过三分钟了。"

但彼得金没有回答,我发现他正惊恐万分地盯着水底,脸色像死人一样苍白。突然他跳起来,吓人地又跑又叫,"噢！杰克,杰克！他死了,一定是有鲨鱼。他再也回不来了！"

在后来的五分钟里我不知道我做了些什么,深深的痛苦几乎使我丧失理智。当彼得金抓住我的肩膀,疯狂地看着我的脸的时候,我才清醒过来,彼得金狂叫着：

"拉尔夫！拉尔夫！也许他只是昏倒了,下去救他。拉尔夫！"

怪事,我刚才怎么就没想到这个办法呢。我没

rushed to the edge of the rocks, and, without waiting to **throw off**① my garments, was on the point to spring into the waves, when I observed something black rising up through the green object. In another moment Jack's head rose to the surface, and he gave a wild shout, throwing back the water from his hair, as he always did after a dive. Now we were almost as much surprised at seeing him appear, well and strong, as we had been at first at his non-appearance. To the best of our **judgment**②, he had been nearly ten minutes under water, perhaps longer, and it required no effort of our **reason**③ to make known to us that this was utterly impossible for **mortal**④ man to do and keep his strength and senses. It was therefore with a strange feeling that I held down my hand and **assisted**⑤ him to climb up the steep rocks. But no such feeling came over Peterkin. When Jack gained the rocks and sat himself on one, breathing deeply, he threw his arms round his neck and burst into a flood of tears.

"Oh, Jack, Jack! "said he. "Where were you? What kept you so long? "

After a few moments Peterkin became calm enough to sit still and listen to Jack's explanation.

The Mystery⑥ Explained

"Now, **lads**⑦," said Jack, "that green object is not a shark; it is a stream of light **issuing**⑧ from a cave in the rocks. Just after I made my dive, I observed that this light came from the side of the rock above which we are now sitting; so I swam towards it, and saw an opening into some place or other that appeared to be light within. For one instant I stopped to think whether I ought to go in. Then I made up my mind,

① throw off 抛弃,摆托

② judgment /'dʒʌdʒmənt/ n. 裁判,宣告

③ reason /'riːzn/ n. 理由,原因,理智,理性
④ mortal /'mɔːtl/ a. 人世间的

⑤ assist /ə'sɪst/ v. 协助

⑥ mystery /'mɪstərɪ/ n. 神秘,神秘的事物

⑦ lad /læd/ n. 少年,小伙子
⑧ issue /'ɪʃjuː/ v. 发行,流出

来得及脱掉外衣就立即冲到岩石边上,就在要跳进波涛中的一刹那,我看见一个黑色的东西从那团绿色物体里升上来。紧接着杰克的脑袋从水中冒出来。他大叫一声,甩甩头上的水,就像以前他每次潜完水那样。看到他毫发未损地出来了,我们差不多和起初看他老不出来一样感到吃惊。就我们所能判断的来说,杰克在水底呆了将近十分钟,也许更长,不用费劲,理性就能告诉我们,人要是潜这么长时间的水而仍能具备体力和意识是根本不可能的。因此,带着这样一种奇怪的感觉,我伸手把杰克拉上陡峭的岩石。但彼得金却没有同感。当杰克爬上岩石坐在我身边大口喘气的时候,他用胳膊搂住杰克的脖子,突然大哭起来。

"哦,杰克,杰克!"他说,"你到哪儿去了?你怎么待了这么长时间啊?"

不久彼得金就平静了下来,静静地坐在那儿听杰克的解释。

奇妙的解释

"听我说,小伙子们,"杰克说,"那个绿色的东西不是鲨鱼,而是从一个岩洞里发出的光束。我一潜下去,就发现这束光是从我们坐的这块石头下面的那块石头边上发出来的。于是我就朝它游过去,看到了一个通向某个地方的口子,里面显得很亮。我停了一下,想是不是应该进去,接着我下了决心,冲了进去。你看,彼得金,虽然

and dashed into it. For you see, Peterkin, although I take some time to tell this, it happened in the space of a few seconds, so that I knew I had **wind**① enough in me to serve to bring me out of the hole and up to the surface again.

"Well, I was just **on the point of**② turning — for I began to feel a little uncomfortable in such a place — when it seemed to me as if there was a faint light right above me. I swam upwards, and found my head out of water. This pleased me greatly, for I now felt that I could take in air enough to allow me to return the way I came. Then it all at once **occurred to**③ me that I might not be able to find the way out again; but, on glancing downwards, my mind was put quite at rest by seeing the green light below me streaming into the cave, just like the light that we had seen streaming out of it, only what I now saw was much brighter.

Exploring④ **the Cave**

"At first I could **scarcely**⑤ see anything as I gazed round me, it was so dark; but after a time my eyes became used to it, and I found that I was in a huge cave, part of the walls of which I observed on each side of me. The **roof**⑥ just above me was also to be seen, and I fancied that I could see beautiful shining objects there; but the farther end of the cave was in **darkness**⑦. While I was looking round me in great wonder, it came into my head that you two would think I was **drowned**⑧; so I dived down again in a great hurry, rose to the surface, and — here I am!"

When Jack ended his story of what he had seen in this cave, I could not rest satisfied till I had dived down to see it; which I did, but found it so dark, as Jack had said, that I could scarcely see anything. When I came back, we had a long talk about it, during which I observed that

① wind /wɪnd/ n. 风,气味,气息

② on the point of 即将(正要,接近)

③ occur to 想起

④ explore /ɪks'plɔː/ v. 探测,探索

⑤ scarcely /'skɛəslɪ/ ad. 几乎不,简直不

⑥ roof /ruːf/ n. 屋顶,顶部

⑦ darkness /'dɑːknɪs/ n. 黑暗

⑧ drown /draʊn/ v. 淹没,溺死

我得花些时间讲这事,但是在当时只有几秒钟,我知道肺里的空气足够让我从洞里出来,然后再升到水面。

哦,当我正要转身的时候,因为我开始觉得在这种地方有些不舒服,我发现好像有一束微弱的光线就在我头上。我向上游去,发现自己的头露出水面。这让我高兴得不得了,因为我觉得我可以吸入足够的空气让我能沿原路回去。接着我突然想到我也许找不到回去的路。但是,当我向下一瞥,就不像刚才那么紧张了,我看见那束绿色的光线涌入我下面的石洞里,就像我们见到的光线从那里射出来一样,只是我当时看见的更亮一些。"

在石洞里的探险

"那里面太黑了,我向四周看去,开始的时候几乎什么也看不见。但是过了一会儿我的眼睛就适应了,我发现自己在一个大石洞里,我的两边是墙,上面还可以看见洞顶。我想我能在里面看到一些美丽的、闪闪发光的东西。但是在石洞深处是一片黑暗。正当我非常惊奇地往四处张望时,突然想起来你们两个会认为我被淹死了。所以我就匆匆忙忙又潜下去,升到水面,然后就到这儿了!"

听杰克讲完他在石洞里看到的景象后,我一直到潜下去亲眼目睹的时候才算心满意足。下去之后,我发现正如杰克所说的那样,里面太黑了,几乎看不见任何东西。我回到水面,和杰克谈论了好长时间,这时我发现彼得金脸上的表情极为

The Coral Island

Peterkin had a most sad expression on his face.

"What's the matter, Peterkin?" said I.

"The matter?" he replied. "It's all very well for you two to be talking away like fishes about the wonders of this cave, but you know I must be content to hear about it, while you are enjoying yourselves down there like mad sharks. It's really too bad."

"I'm very sorry for you, Peterkin, indeed I am," said Jack, "but we cannot help you. If you would only learn to dive —"

"Learn to fly, you might as well say!" answered Peterkin, in a very cross tone.

We both laughed and shook our heads, for it was clear that nothing was to be made of Peterkin in the water. But we could not rest satisfied till we had seen more of this cave; so, after further talk, Jack and I determined to try if we could take down a stick with us, and set **fire**① to it in the cave.

This we found to be very difficult, but we did it at last by the following **means**②. First, we took the bark of a certain tree, which we cut into strips, and **fastened**③ together with a kind of **gum**④, which we also obtained from another tree; neither of which trees, however, was known by name to Jack. This, when prepared, we **wrapped up**⑤ in a great number of pieces of coconut cloth, so that we were sure it could not get wet during the short time it should be under water. Then we **rolled up**⑥ some dry grass and a few small pieces of wood, which, with a little bow and **drill**⑦ like those described before, we wrapped up in coconut cloth. When all was ready we laid aside our garments, with the **exception**⑧ of our trousers, which, as we did not know what rough climbing on rocks we might be **subjected to**⑨, we kept on.

Then we advanced to the edge of the rocks, Jack carrying one

① set fire 纵火,放火烧

② means /miːnz/ n. 方法,手段

③ fasten /ˈfɑːsn/ v. 拴紧,使固定,系

④ gum /ɡʌm/ n. 树胶

⑤ wrap up 掩饰,伪装,使全神贯注,围好围巾,包起来

⑥ roll up 袅袅上升(卷起,到达)

⑦ drill /drɪl/ n. 钻孔机,钻子,播种机

⑧ exception /ɪkˈsepʃən/ n. 例外

⑨ subject to 易受…的

沮丧。

"怎么了,彼得金?"我说。

"怎么了?"他回答,"你们俩倒好,自由自在地谈论着洞里的奇观,可你们知道我只能满足于坐在这儿听着,而你们像疯狂的鲨鱼在底下痛痛快快地玩。这实在太糟糕了。"

"很抱歉,彼得金,我真的很抱歉,"杰克说,"但是我们没办法帮你,如果你能学会潜水——"

"那你还不如说学会飞好。"彼得金怒气冲冲地说。

我们都笑起来,摇着头,因为很明显,彼得金整个是只旱鸭子。但是我们都迫不及待地想再去看看那个岩洞,因此我们又谈论了一会儿,我和杰克决定如果可能我们就带一根火把下去,点着了在石洞里照亮。

我们发现这是相当困难的,但是我们最终还是想出了这么一个办法:首先我们剥下一种树的树皮,把它们撕成条,然后用从另一棵树上找到的树胶牢牢把它们粘在一起,但这两种树杰克都叫不上名字。这些都做好之后,我们就在外面缠上大量的椰子皮,这样我们能保证它在水里短时间内不会被弄湿。然后我们又卷了些干草和几块小木头,还拿了前面提过的小弓钻,把它们裹在椰子皮里。一切就绪后,我们就脱下外衣,放到一边,但还穿着裤子,因为不知道会遇到什么样的粗糙不平的岩石,所以我们没脱裤子。

我们到了岩石边上,杰克拿着那包火把,我拿着另外一包点火的东西。

The Coral Island

bundle①, with the stick, I the other, with the things for **producing**② fire.

"Now don't worry for us, Peterkin, should we be gone some time," said Jack; "we'll be sure to come back in half an hour at the very latest, however interesting the cave should be, that we may ease your mind.""

"**Farewell**③! " said Peterkin, coming up to us with a look of deep but **unreal**④ sadness, while he shook hands and kissed each of us on the **cheek**⑤. "Farewell! And while you are gone I shall rest my weary **limbs**⑥ under the shelter of this bush, and think of the **changefulness**⑦ of all things earthly, and especially of the condition of a poor sailor boy!"

So saying, Peterkin waved his hand, turned from us, and cast himself upon the ground with a look of great sadness, which was so well done that I almost thought it real. We both laughed, and, springing from the rocks together, dived head first into the sea.

The Cave

We gained the inside of the underwater cave without difficulty, and, on coming out from the waves, supported ourselves for some time by **treading**⑧-water, while we held the two bundles above our heads. This we did in order to let our eyes become used to the darkness. Then, when we could see enough, we swam to a rock, and landed in safety. Having got the water out of our trousers, and dried ourselves as well as we could, we **proceeded to**⑨ light the stick. This we did without difficulty in a few minutes; and no sooner did it **burn up**⑩ than we were stuck **speechless**⑪ with the wonderful objects that were shown to our gaze.

The roof of the cave just above us seemed to be about ten feet high, but grew higher as it went back into the distance, until it was lost in darkness. It seemed to be made of coral, and was supported by great

① bundle /'bʌndl/ n. 捆,束
② produce /prə'djuːs/ v. 产生,生产,提出

③ farewell /'feə'wel/ n. 告别
④ unreal /ʌn'rɪ(ː)əl/ a. 不真实的
⑤ cheek /tʃiːk/ n. 面颊
⑥ limb /lɪm/ n. 肢,臂,腿
⑦ changefulness /'tʃeɪndʒfʊlnɪs/ n. 不确定性

⑧ tread /tred/ v. 踏,行走

⑨ proceed to 往下进行(另一件事)
⑩ burn up 烧尽
⑪ speechless /'spiːtʃlɪs/ a. 非言语能表达的

杰克说:"即使我们走的时间长了点儿,彼得金,也别惦着我们。我们保证至多半个小时就回来,不管那个石洞会多么有趣,我们不会让你担心的。"

"再见!"彼得金说,他走过来和我们握手,分别吻了我们的脸颊,他看起来很沮丧,但是又不像真的,"再见,你们走了以后,我就四仰八叉地躺在这片灌木的阴影里,好好歇着,想想世事的变化无常,特别是一个可怜水手的处境。"

彼得金边说边向我们挥挥手,然后转过身,一下子躺在地上,看起来痛苦万分。他装得实在太好了,差点让我相信这是真的。我们俩都笑了,一起从岩石上跳起,一头潜入海里。

岩　洞

我们没遇到什么麻烦就到了水底的岩洞里,我们从海浪里露出头来,把两包东西举过头顶,靠踩水浮了一会儿。我们这样做是为了让眼睛适应黑暗。我们在能看清楚之后,就游向一块岩石,平安地爬了上去。我们把裤子里的水倒出去,尽可能地把自己弄干,然后开始点那根火把。我们没费什么劲儿很快就点着了它。火把一点燃,映入眼帘的美景顿时使我们目瞪口呆。

我们头上的洞顶看上去大约有十英尺高,但是它向远处延伸时变得高了些,然后就消失在黑暗里了。洞顶看起来是珊瑚构成的,被同样也是由珊瑚构成的大柱子支撑着。洞顶很多地方悬垂着巨大的

columns① of the same material. Huge spear-shaped masses (as they appeared to us) hung from it in various places. These, however, were formed of a kind of coral, which seemed to flow in a watery form towards the point of each, where it became rock. A good many drops fell, however, to the rock below, and these formed little points, which rose to meet the points above. Some of them had already met, and thus we saw how the columns were formed, which at first seemed to us as if they had been placed there by some human builder to support the roof.

As we advanced farther in, we saw that the floor was made of the same material as the columns; and it presented the strange appearance of little waves, such as are formed on water when **gently**② blown upon by the wind. There were several openings on either hand in the walls, that seemed to lead into other caves; but these we did not go into at this time. We also observed that the roof was strangely marked in many places, as if it were a **noble**③ church; and the walls, as well as the roof, shone in the light and threw back **flashes**④, as if they were covered with **precious**⑤ stones.

Although we proceeded far into this cave, we did not come to the end of it, and we were **obliged to**⑥ return more speedily than we would have liked to have done, as our stick was nearly **burnt down**⑦. We did not observe any openings in the roof, or any signs of places **whereby**⑧ light might enter; but near the entrance to the cave stood a huge mass of pure white coral rock, which caught and threw back the little light that found an entrance through the cave's mouth, and thus produced, we thought, the pale-green object which had first drawn our attention to the place. We thought, also, that the light-turning power of this rock was that which gave forth the light that faintly lit up the first part of the cave.

Before diving through the entrance again we put out the small piece

① column /ˈkɒləm/ n. 圆柱

② gently /ˈdʒentlɪ/ ad. 轻轻地,温柔地

③ noble /ˈnəʊbl/ a. 高尚的,高贵的
④ flash /flæʃ/ n. 闪光
⑤ precious /ˈpreʃəs/ a. 宝贵的,珍贵的
⑥ be obliged to 被迫做
⑦ burn down 烧成平地(烧毁,烧光)
⑧ whereby /(h)weəˈbaɪ/ ad. 借此(在…旁,凭什么)

石笋（在我们看来是这样），石笋是由某种珊瑚构成的，它们像水一样朝笋尖流，在那儿变成了岩石。但是有很多滴落到了下面的岩石上，形成了一个个小石笋，这些石笋挺起身来迎接上面的石笋。其中有些石笋已经连在一起了，由此我们知道了这些柱子是怎么形成的。当我们第一眼看到它们时，还以为它们是被人类建筑师放在这里来支撑洞顶的呢！

我们继续向前走，发觉地面是用和柱子一样的材料构成的，地面上有些奇异的波纹，就像微风过后水面上泛起的涟漪。在两边的墙上都有些开口，可能是通向另一些岩洞的。但是这次我们没有进去。我们还发现洞顶的许多地方有些奇怪的标志，就像是一座高雅的教堂。墙壁和洞顶一样，发着光，反射着光线，仿佛表面覆盖着宝石。

虽然我们在岩洞里继续向前走了很远，但是没有走到尽头。尽管我们不大愿意但还是不得不尽快往回走，因为火把已经快燃尽了。我们没有在洞顶发现任何的开口，或者任何一块能让光线射进来的地方，但是在靠近入口的地方，有一块巨大的纯白色珊瑚石，它接收和反射着进出洞口的微弱的光线。我们想这大概就是第一次把我们的注意力吸引到这儿来的那个淡绿色东西的成因。我们还认为，由于这块白石头具有折光能力，它才发出微弱的光芒，照亮了岩洞的入口处。

在再次潜过入口之前我们把烧剩的那根火把弄灭，把它放在一个干燥的地方。我们想如果将来有一天我们潜进洞时不巧把照明的火把弄湿了，

The Coral Island

of our stick that remained, and left it in a dry spot; thinking that we might possibly need it, if at any future time we should chance to wet our stick for lighting us while diving into the cave. As we stood for a few minutes after it was out, waiting till our eyes became **accustomed to**[①] the darkness, we could not help **remarking**[②] the deep quiet and the **unearthly**[③] darkness of all around us.

"Now, Ralph, are you ready?" said Jack, in a low voice that seemed to **echo**[④] up into the roof above.

"Quite ready."

"Come along, then," said he; and diving off the rock into the water, we swam through the narrow entrance. In a few seconds we were on the rocks above, and receiving the welcome of our friend Peterkin.

可能需要用这根剩的。火把灭了之后，我们在那里站了几分钟，等着我们的眼睛逐渐适应黑暗。我们不禁感觉到极度的安静和死一般的黑暗包围着我们。

"喂，拉尔夫，你准备好了吗？"杰克说，他那低沉的声音在洞顶回荡着。

"完全好了。"

"那么来吧，"他说着离开了岩石潜入水里。我们游过窄窄的入口。几秒钟之后我们回到了水面的岩石上，受到了我们的朋友彼得金的欢迎。

① accustom to 习惯于（养成…的习惯）
② remark /rɪˈmɑːk/ v. 评论，注意，述及
③ unearthly /ʌnˈɜːθlɪ/ a. 怪异的，异常的
④ echo /ˈekəʊ/ v. 发回声，随声附和，摹仿

Chapter 12
Pig Sticking

It was pleasant to us to breathe the pure air, and to enjoy the glad sunshine after our long walk in the Diamond Cave, as we named it; for although we did not stop more than half an hour away, it seemed to us much longer. While we were dressing, and during our walk home, we did our best to satisfy poor Peterkin, who seemed very sorry that he could not dive. There was no help for it, however.

After having told all we could to Peterkin about the Diamond Cave, we were making our way **rapidly**[①] **homewards**[②] when a well-known sound came to our ears.

"That's the ticket!" was Peterkin's strange cry, as he started up and **lifted**[③] his spear.

"Listen!" cried Jack. "These are your friends, Peterkin. They must have come over **on purpose**[④] to pay you a **friendly**[⑤] visit, for it is the first time we have seen them on this side the island."

"**Come along**[⑥]!" cried Peterkin, hurrying towards the wood, while Jack and I followed, smiling.

More noises, much louder than before, came down the valley. At this time we were just **opposite**[⑦] the small valley which lay between the

12
杀 猪

在我们命名的"钻石洞"里走了很长时间后,又呼吸到新鲜的空气,沐浴着明媚的阳光,真是件令人高兴的事,虽然我们在洞里逗留的时间没有超过半小时,但是我们感觉要比这长得多。我们在穿衣服的时候以及在回家的路上,都尽力宽慰可怜的彼得金,但于事无补,他看上去对不会潜水感到特别难过。

我们把在"钻石洞"里见到的一切都告诉了彼得金,然后就径直向家走去,这时一种熟悉的声音又在耳边响起。

"就是它!"彼得金惊跳起来,举起渔叉怪叫道。

"听!"杰克叫道,"是你的朋友,彼得金。它们一定是远道而来对你进行友好访问的,我们这可是头一次在岛的这一边见到它们啊。"

"跟我来!"彼得金叫着急忙向树林跑去,我和杰克微笑着跟在后面。

① rapidly /'ræpɪdlɪ/ ad. 迅速地
② homewards /'həʊmwədz/ ad. 回家

③ lift /lɪft/ v. 升高,举起
④ on purpose 故意,有意
⑤ friendly /'frendlɪ/ a. 友好的,友善的

⑥ come along 一道走,一起来

⑦ opposite /'ɒpəzɪt/ a. 相反的,对面的

The Coral Island

Valley of the Ship and Diamond Cave.

"I say, Peterkin," cried Jack, in a whisper.

"Well, what is't?"

"Stop a bit, man. These pigs are just up there on the hill-side. If you go and stand with Ralph under that rock, I'll run round behind and drive them through the valley, so that you'll have a better chance of **picking out**① a good one. Now, mind you get a fat young pig, Peterkin," added Jack, as he jumped into the bushes.

"Won't I just!" said Peterkin, **licking**② his lips, as we took our station beside the rock. "I feel quite a tender liking for young pigs in my heart. Perhaps it would be more correct to say in my —"

"There they come!" cried I, as a loud shout from Jack sent the whole herd down the hill. Now Peterkin, being unable to keep still, crept a short way up a very steep **grassy**③ hill, in order to get a better view of the pigs before they came up; and just as he raised his head above its top, two little pigs, which had run faster than their companions, rushed over the top with the **utmost**④ haste. One of these **brushed**⑤ close past Peterkin's ear, the other, unable to stop its **flight**⑥, went, as Peterkin himself afterwards expressed it, "**bash**⑦" into his arms with a sudden cry, which was caused more by the force of the blow than the will of the animal, and both of them **rolled down**⑧ to the foot of the hill. No sooner was this reached than the little pig recovered its feet, threw up its tail, and ran crying from the spot. But I sent a large stone after it, which, being fortunately well aimed, hit it behind the ear, and brought it to the earth.

"Fine, Ralph! That's your sort!" cried Peterkin, who, to my surprise and great joy, had risen to his feet unhurt, though covered with earth.

珊瑚岛

① pick out 挑出

② lick /lɪk/ v. 舔

③ grassy /ˈɡrɑːsɪ/ a. 绿色的,像草的

④ utmost /ˈʌtməʊst/ a. 极度的,最远的
⑤ brush /brʌʃ/ v. 刷,掠过
⑥ flight /flaɪt/ n. 飞行
⑦ bash /bæʃ/ v. 猛击,猛撞
⑧ roll down 滚下

　　进到山谷之后,声音更嘈杂也更大了。这时我们正好在"船谷"和"钻石洞"之间的小山谷对面。

　　"喂,彼得金。"杰克小声叫道。

　　"哎,什么事?"

　　"等一等,伙计,这群猪正好在山腰上,如果你和拉尔夫站在那块岩石底下,我跑步绕到后面,把它们赶进山谷,你就更有机会挑一只好的啦。喂,你不是想要一只小肥猪吗?"杰克跳入灌木丛时又加了一句。

　　"我当然想啦!"我们在岩石旁边站好后,彼得金舔着他的嘴唇说,"其实我心里并不是很想要小猪,也许更确切地说,我——"

　　"它们来了!"当杰克大叫一声把这群猪赶下山时,我喊道。这会儿彼得金可闲不住了。他向一座很陡的长满青草的小山上爬了一小段路,想在猪群冲过来之前看得更清楚些。他刚刚在山顶露出头来,两只跑在前面的小猪崽,飞快地冲过山顶。其中一只紧贴着彼得金的耳朵冲过去,另一只已经收不住脚了——就像彼得金自己后来讲的那样——突然尖叫一声一头撞进彼得金的怀里。由此产生的冲击力远比猪期盼的大,彼得金和猪一起滚到了山脚下。刚滚到山脚,小猪崽就立即站起来,甩起尾巴,嚎叫着跑开了。我向它扔了一块大石头,恰好打中了它的耳朵后面,把它打倒在地上。

　　"好样的!拉尔夫,干得好!"彼得金叫着,让我又惊又喜的是,他虽然满身都是土,但没有受伤,已经站起来了。

The Coral Island

He rushed madly towards the valley, which the cries of the pigs told us they were now approaching. I had made up my mind that I would not kill another, as, if Peterkin should be successful, two were more than enough for our wants at the present time. Suddenly they all **burst forth**① two or three little ones **in advance**② and a huge old pig with a herd of little ones at her **heels**③.

"Now, Peterkin," said I, "there's a nice little fat one; just spear it."

Peterkin Makes Shoes

But Peterkin did not move, he allowed it to pass **unharmed**④. I looked at him in surprise, and saw that his lips were closed and his eyebrows bent, as if he were about to fight with some **awful**⑤ enemy.

"What is it?" I asked, with some fear.

Suddenly he lifted his spear, ran forward, and, with a shout that nearly **froze**⑥ my blood, speared the old pig to the heart. Indeed, the spear went in at one side and came out at the other!

"Oh, Peterkin!" said I, going up to him. "What have you done?"

"Done? I've killed their mother, that's all," said he, looking with a **somewhat**⑦ fearful expression at the dead animal.

"Hallo! What's this?" said Jack, as he came up. "Why, Peterkin, you must be fond of hard meat. If you mean to eat this old pig, she'll try your teeth, I fancy. What made you stick her, Peterkin?"

"Why, the fact is I want a pair of shoes."

"What have your shoes to do with the old pig?" said I, smiling.

"My present shoes have certainly nothing to do with her," replied Peterkin; but she will have a good deal to do with my future shoes. The fact is, when I saw you hit that pig so well, Ralph, it struck me that

他发疯似的向山谷冲去，猪叫声表明它们正朝这边跑来，我打定主意不再杀猪了，因为如果彼得金得手的话，眼下两头猪对我们来讲已经太多了。突然间猪群出现了——两三头小猪崽跑在前边，接着是一群小猪紧跟着一头巨大的老母猪。

　　"嘿，彼得金！"我叫道，"那儿有一头很棒的小肥猪，叉它！"

彼得金做鞋

　　但彼得金没有动，他让那头小猪平平安安地跑过去了。我奇怪地看着他。他的嘴唇紧闭，眉头紧锁，好像要同什么可怕的敌人搏斗一样。

　　"怎么啦？"我有点担心地问。

　　突然彼得金举起渔叉向前跑去，大叫一声，几乎让我全身的血液都要凝固了，他把渔叉叉向了老母猪的心脏。真的，那渔叉从猪身的一侧叉进去又从另一侧穿出来。

　　"哦，彼得金！你在干什么？"我边说边向他跑过去。

　　"干什么？我杀了猪妈妈，就是这样子。"说着，彼得金用一种有些害怕的表情看着那头死猪。

　　"哎！这是什么呀？"杰克跑过来的时候问道，"哟，彼得金，你一定喜欢吃老猪肉。如果你想吃这头老猪的话，我想这对你的牙齿一定是个考验。彼得金，你为什么想杀它呢？"

　　"噢，事实上我想要双鞋子。"

　　"你的鞋和这头老猪有什么关系？"我笑着问。

　　"我现在穿的鞋当然和它没关系，"彼得金回答

① burst forth 忽然发生，突然爆发
② in advance 提前，预先
③ heel /hi:l/ *n.* 脚后跟

④ unharmed /ʌnˈhɑːmd/ *a.* 没有受伤的，无恙的
⑤ awful /ˈɔːful/ *a.* 糟糕的，可怕的

⑥ froze（freeze的过去式）freeze /friːz/ *v.* 冻结，冷冻

⑦ somewhat /ˈsʌmwɒt/ *ad.* 稍微，有些

there was little use in killing another. Then I remembered all at once that I had long wanted some **leather**① to make shoes of, and this old mother seemed so hard that I just made up my mind to stick her, and you see I've done it!"

"That you certainly have, Peterkin," said Jack, as he was examining the animal.

We now considered how we were to carry our meat home, for, although the distance was short, the pig was very heavy. **At length**② we hit on the plan of **tying**③ its four feet together, and passing the spear **handle**④ between them. Jack took one end on his shoulder, I took the other on mine, and Peterkin carried the small pig.

Thus we came back to our house, beating, as Peterkin said, the fruits of a noble hunt. As he afterwards spoke in the same warm terms of the supper that followed, there is every reason to believe that we retired that night to our leafy beds in a high state of satisfaction.

① leather /ˈleðə/ n. 皮革，皮制品

② at legth 终于，最后

③ tie /taɪ/ v. 系，打结，约束
④ handle /ˈhændl/ n. 把手，柄

说，"但是将来它跟我要穿的鞋关系可大了。拉尔夫，实际上我看到你那么准地打中了那头猪，突然想起来我们用不着再杀一头，但立刻又想到我一直都想要些皮子做鞋，这头老母猪的皮看起来很结实，因此我就决定用渔叉叉它，你们看我成功了！"

"你当然成功了，彼得金。"杰克一边查看那头猪一边说。

我们现在在想怎么把这些肉带回家，尽管路不远，但是这头猪太重了。我们终于想出了一个好办法，我们把猪的四条腿绑在一起，然后把渔叉的木柄从中间穿过去，我和杰克一人抬着一头，彼得金则扛着那头小猪。

就这样我们抬着彼得金称之为辉煌战果的猎物回了家。后来他又用同样令人兴奋的字眼谈论起随后的晚餐，毋庸置疑，那天晚上我们在铺着树叶子的床上睡得很香。

Chapter 13
We Build a Boat

For many days after this Jack applied himself to the making of our boat, which at length began to look somewhat like one. But those only who have had the thing to do can have a right idea of the difficulty of such a work, with no other tools than an axe, a bit of iron, a **sail-needle**①, and a broken knife. But Jack did it.

As this boat was interesting in its way, a few words here about the manner of its building may not be **out of place**②.

I have already mentioned the tree with its wonderful boards. This tree, then, **furnished**③ us with the chief part of our material. First of all, Jack **sought out**④ a **limb**⑤ of a tree of such a form and size as, while it should form the bottom, a bend at either end should form the back and front **posts**⑥. Such a piece, however, was not easy to obtain; but at last he got it, by rooting up a small tree which had a branch growing in the proper direction about ten feet up its stem, with two strong roots growing in such a form as **enabled**⑦ him to make a boat flat at the back. This placed, he took three branching roots, which he fitted to the bottom at equal distances, thus forming three strong supports.

Now the squaring and shaping of the roots, and the cutting of the

13
我们造了一条船

① sail-needle *n.* 制帆针

② out of place 不合适的（不相称的,不适合的）

③ furnish /ˈfɜːnɪʃ/ *v.* 供给，提供

④ sought out 搜寻出（挑出,竭力找出）

⑤ limb /lɪm/ *n.* 树枝

⑥ post /pəʊst/ *n.* 标竿,柱

⑦ enable /ɪˈneɪbl/ *v.* 使…能够

打猎回来后，杰克一连许多天专心致志地造我们的船，最后总算有些船的样子了。但是只有那些动手去做的人才能确切地知道这件工作的难度，因为我们除了一把斧子、一小块铁、一个制帆针，还有一把断了的刀子，什么都没有。但是杰克完成了。

造这条船的过程很有趣，这里不妨略微说上几句。

我前面已经讲过那种长着奇特板子的树。这种树成了我们主要的材料。首先杰克需要找到这样一种树枝，它的大小和形状不但可以用来制成船的底部，而且它两端的弯度恰好形成船的前后支柱。这样的材料十分难找，但他最终还是找到了。他将一棵小树连根拔起，小树主干上大约十英尺的地方长着一根角度合适的支干，还有两条粗大的根茎，形状恰好可以用来做一条底部扁平的船。这个问题解决了，他又找到三条根杈，把它们等距离地固定在底部，从而形成了三个结实的支座。

现在要把树根弄成直角形，从底部把不需要的

· 159 ·

places for them in the bottom was an easy enough matter, as it was all work for the axe, in the use of which Jack was become wonderfully good; but it was quite a different affair when he came to **nailing**① the supports to the bottom, for we had no tool for **boring**② a large hole, and no nails to fasten them with. We were, indeed, almost stopped here; but Jack at length made a tool that served very well. Two holes were bored in each support, about an inch and a half **apart**③, and also down into the bottom, but not quite through. Into these were placed strong pieces of wood from a tree called iron-wood; and, when they were hammered well home, the supports were as firmly fixed as if they had been nailed with iron. But, besides the wooden nails, the sides were firmly tied to the end posts and supports by means of a kind of rope which we had made out of the coconut cloth. When a number of the threads were joined together they formed excellent rope. At first we tied the different lengths together; but afterwards we managed to make good rope of any size or length we chose. Of course it cost us much time and **labour**④, but Jack **kept up**⑤ our spirits when we grew **weary**⑥, and so all that we required was at last made.

Boards were now cut off the trees of about all inch thick. These were dressed with the axe — but roughly, for an axe is ill-fitted for such work. Five of these boards on each side were enough; and we formed the boat in a very rounded shape, in order to have as little turning of the boards as possible, for although we could easily bend them, we could not easily turn them. Having no nails to fix the boards with, we threw aside the ordinary fashion of boat-building and made up one of our own. The boards were therefore placed on each other's edges, and **sewn**⑦ together with the rope already mentioned. They were also thus sewed to the front, the back, and the bottom.

① nail /neɪl/ v. 用钉钉牢，使固定
② bore /bɔː/ v. 钻，凿，挖

③ apart /əˈpɑːt/ ad. 分别地，分开地

④ labour /ˈleɪbə(r)/ n. 劳动力
⑤ keep up 保持，继续，维持
⑥ weary /ˈwɪərɪ/ a. 疲倦的，厌烦的

⑦ sew /səʊ/ v. 缝纫（缝补，缝上）

部分砍下来就很简单了。这些都是用斧子完成的，杰克现在成了用斧子的好手，但是他在把船底和支座钉在一起时，遇到了相当大的困难，因为我们没有工具来钻一个大洞，也没有钉子把它们钉到一起。我们真的几乎都要停工了。但是后来杰克还是做了一个很好用的工具。我们在每个支座上钻了两个孔，中间有一英寸半的距离，而且，在船底上也钻了孔，当然不能钻透。我们在这些孔里放了许多从一种叫作"铁树"上弄来的坚硬的木块。把这些木块锤进去之后，支座就像用铁钉钉的一样牢固了，但是除了用木钉以外，我们还用椰子皮制成的绳子将船帮紧紧绑在船尾的支柱和支座上，几股纤维拧在一起，就成了很好的绳子。开始的时候我们把不同长度的绳子系在一起，但是后来就能做我们所需要的各种尺寸的好绳子了。这当然消耗了我们大量的时间和体力，但是在我们开始厌倦的时候，杰克总是不断地鼓励我们，最后我们终于做出来我们所要的东西。

　　大约一英寸厚的木板从树上砍了下来，然后用斧子砍光滑，但是还是很粗糙，因为这种活用斧子干很不顺手。船的一侧只需要五块木板，为了尽可能减少木板的弯度，我们把船造成圆形，因为使木板弯曲不难，但弯得很大就不容易了。因为没有钉子把木板钉在一起，我们放弃了传统的造船方法，建立了一套适合自己的方式。我们将木板的边压着边，用先前提到的绳子将它们穿缝起来，船头、船尾和船底都是这样穿缝起来的。

　　除了这些以外，我们还在木板缝隙里塞上椰子皮。因为椰子皮湿了之后就会膨胀，我们希望它能

Besides this, we placed between the edges of the boards coconut cloth, which, as it **swelled**① when **wetted**②, would, we hoped, make our little **vessel**③ **watertight**④. Thus the inside was covered with a watertight material; while the outside, being uncovered so that the water would make it swell, was, we hoped, likely to keep the boat quite dry. I may add that our hopes were not **vain**⑤ ones.

Our Food

While Jack was thus at work, Peterkin and I sometimes assisted him; but as our **assistance**⑥ was not much required, we more frequently went a hunting on the wide **mud-flats**⑦ at the entrance of the long valley which lay nearest to our house. Here we found large flocks of ducks of various kinds, some of them being so much like the wild ducks of our own country that I think they must have been the same. On these occasions we took the bow and the sling, with both of which we were often successful, though I must say I was the **least**⑧ so. Our suppers were thus pleasantly different from each other, and sometimes we had such a large choice spread out before us that we frequently knew not with which food to begin.

The large flat stone, or rock of coral, which stood just in front of the entrance to our house, was our table. On this rock we had spread out the few articles we possessed the day the ship struck; and on the same rock during many a day afterwards, we spread out the rich supply with which we had been **blessed**⑨ on our Coral Island. Sometimes we sat down at this table to a **feast**⑩ consisting of hot rolls — as Peterkin called the newly **baked**⑪ bread-fruit — a roast pig, roast duck, boiled and roasted yams, coconuts, taro, and sweet potatoes; which we followed

① swell /swel/ v. 增大,使…膨胀
② wet /wet/ v. (使)弄湿
③ vessel /'vesl/ n. 船
④ watertight /'wɔ:tətaɪt/ a. 不漏水的

⑤ vain /veɪn/ a. 徒然的,空虚的

⑥ assistance /ə'sɪstəns/ n. 帮助,援助
⑦ mud-flat 淤泥滩

⑧ least /li:st/ a. 最少,最小

⑨ bless /bles/ v. 祝福,祈佑
⑩ feast /fi:st/ v. 宴会,酒席
⑪ bake /beɪk/ v. 烘焙,烤

让我们的小船不漏水。这样我们在船里铺上了防水材料,在外面因为没有涂层,所以海水能把椰子皮泡涨,我们想这样也许能使我们的船保持干燥。我想补充的是我们的愿望没有落空。

我们的食物

杰克埋头工作的时候我和彼得金有时去帮他,但是他在很多时候并不怎么需要帮忙,因此我们就越来越多地到离我们住处最近的那条长山谷入口处的淤泥滩去打猎。我们在那儿发现了一大群各种各样的野鸭子,其中有些很像我们家乡的鸭子,我想它们一定是那种鸭子。打猎时,我们带着弓和投石器,虽然我得说我的技术不好,但是这两样东西总能让我们得手。因此,令人高兴的是我们的晚饭顿顿都不重样,有时候,可选择的花样太多了,我们常常不知道先吃什么好。

就在我们房门口的前面立着一块平坦的大石头,或者说珊瑚礁,那是我们的饭桌。船触礁那天,我们在这块石头上摆过我们仅有的几样东西。在此后的许多天里,我们在同一块石头上又摆上了珊瑚岛赐给我们的丰盛的食物。有时我们坐在这张桌子旁边大吃一顿,食物包括:"热卷"——彼得金给刚烤好的面包果起的新名字——烤猪,烤鸭子,煮或烤的白薯,椰子,山药,还有甜土豆,我们还有水果吃。

up with fruit.

Occasionally[1] Peterkin tried to make some new **dishes**[2]; but these generally turned out so bad that in the end he gave up his **trials**[3] — not forgetting, however, to point out to Jack that his failure had proved the falseness of the saying which he, Jack, was constantly repeating — namely, that "where there's a will there's a way." For he had a great **will**[4] to become a cook, but could by no means find a way to become one.

One day, while Peterkin and I were seated beside our table, on which dinner was spread, Jack came up from the beach, and, throwing down his axe, cried:

The Boat Finished

"There, my boys, the boat's finished at last, so we've nothing to do now but shape two pairs of oars, and then we may put to sea as soon as we like."

This piece of news threw us into a state of great joy; for although we knew that the boat had been slowly getting near its completion, it had taken so long that we did not expect it to be quite ready for at least two or three weeks. But Jack had worked hard and said nothing, in order to surprise us.

"My dear fellow," cried Peterkin, "you're a perfect **angel**[5]. But why did you not tell us it was so nearly ready? Won't we have a fine sail tomorrow, eh?"

"Don't talk so much, Peterkin," said Jack; "and, pray, **hand**[6] me a bit of that pig."

"Certainly, my dear," cried Peterkin, seizing the axe. "What part will you have? A leg, or a **wing**[7], or a piece off the body — which?"

① occasionally /əˈkeɪʒənəli/ ad. 偶尔地
② dish /dɪʃ/ n. 一样菜，一道菜
③ trial /ˈtraɪəl/ n. 尝试，努力，试验
④ will /wɪl/ n. 意志，决心

⑤ angel /ˈeɪndʒəl/ n. 天使

⑥ hand /hænd/ v. 支持，交给

⑦ wing /wɪŋ/ n. 翅膀，翼，边沿部分

有时彼得金尝试着做一些新的菜式，但是菜通常做得很糟糕，结果他放弃了尝试——但他还是没忘记对杰克说，他的失败证明了杰克经常说的那句话是错的——那就是"有志者事竟成"。彼得金很想成为一名厨师，但是他根本没有办法去实现自己的愿望。

一天，我和彼得金坐在桌子旁，饭都摆好了，这时杰克从海滩回来了，他扔掉斧子喊道：

船做好了

"好啦，伙计们，船终于做好了，我们现在要做的就是做两对桨了，然后我们一想下海就可以下海了。"

这条消息让我们欣喜若狂，因为虽然我们知道这条船快要做好了，但是花的时间太长了，我们觉得至少在两三个星期内别想大功告成。但是杰克干得很卖力，而且一声不吭，他是想给我们一个惊喜。

"亲爱的朋友，"彼得金叫道，"你真是个天使啊。但是你为什么不告诉我们船马上就要做好了呢？明天我们来一次带劲儿的航海怎么样，啊？"

"别说个没完没了，彼得金，请你递给我一块猪肉，"杰克说。

"没问题，亲爱的，"彼得金叫着，拿起斧子，"你要什么部位？一条腿，一个前蹄，还是身上的

"A **hind**① leg, if you please," answered Jack; "and, pray, be so good as to include the tail."

"With all my heart," said Peterkin, **exchanging**② the axe for his iron knife, with which he cut off the desired portion.

"Well, 'but," continued Peterkin, "I was talking of a sail tomorrow. Can't we have one, Jack?"

"No," replied Jack, "we can't have a sail, but I hope we shall have a row, as I intend to work hard at the oars this afternoon, and, if we can't get them finished by sunset, we'll light our nuts, and finish before we turn into bed."

"Very good," said Peterkin. "I'll help you, if I can."

"Afterwards," continued Jack, "we will make a sail out of the coconut cloth, and **fix up**③ a mast, and then we shall be able to sail to some of the other islands, and visit our old friends the penguins."

The idea of being so quickly able to visit the other islands and enjoy a sail over the beautiful sea gave us much delight, and after dinner we set about making the oars in good **earnest**④. We worked hard and rapidly, so that when the sun went down, Jack and I came back to the house with four fine oars, which required little to be done to them save a **slight**⑤ shaping with the knife.

After supper we retired to rest and to dream of **wonderful**⑥ **adventures**⑦ in our little boat, and distant **voyages**⑧ upon the sea.

① hind /haɪnd/ a. 后部的

② exchange /ɪks'tʃeɪndʒ/ v. 交换

③ fix up 安排（安顿，决定，解决）

④ earnest /'ɜːnɪst/ n. 认真，诚挚
⑤ slight /slaɪt/ a. 轻微的，微小的
⑥ wonderful /'wʌndəfəl/ a. 精彩的，极好的
⑦ adventure /əb'ventʃə/ n. 冒险，奇遇
⑧ voyage /'vɒɪɪdʒ/ n. 航行，旅程

一块肉？哪块？"

"麻烦你给条后腿吧，如果能带着尾巴那就更好了。"杰克说。

"十分乐意效劳。"彼得金说着放下斧子换了把铁刀，切下了杰克想要的部分。

"好啦，"彼得金接着说，"我刚说到明天航海的事呢，我们能去吗，杰克？"

"不行，"杰克回答，"我们还不能去航海，但是我想我们能划划船，因为今天下午我想抓紧把桨做好，要是太阳落山了我们还没有做完，我们就点上坚果灯，睡觉前把它们做完。"

"好的，"彼得金说，"要是能帮忙，我会帮你的。"

"然后，"杰克接着说，"我们还要用椰子皮做一张帆，装上一根桅杆，这样我们就能划到其他一些岛上，还可以去看看我们的老朋友——企鹅。"

想到这么快就能去别的海岛看看，还能在美丽的海上愉快地航行，我们都非常高兴。吃完饭以后，我们开始很认真地做船桨。我们很卖力气，快手快脚地干着，在太阳下山的时候，我和杰克拿着四只很棒的船桨回到了家。现在只要用刀子在桨的外形上做一点小小的改进就可以了。

晚饭以后，我们躺下休息，梦想乘坐小船进行奇妙的探险和远程航海。

Chapter 14
We Examine the Lagoon

It was a bright, clear, beautiful morning, when we first put out our little boat and rowed out upon the calm waters of the lagoon. Not a breath of wind moved the surface of the sea. Not a cloud **spotted**① the deep blue sky. The sea was shining like a **sheet**② of glass, yet slowly rising and falling with the long deep **swell**③ that, all the world round, **indicates**④ the life of Ocean, and the bright seaweeds and corals were shining at the bottom of that clear water, as we rowed over it, like rare and precious **gems**⑤.

At first, in the strength of our delight, we rowed without aim or object. But after the first joy of our spirits died down, we began to look about us and to consider what we should do.

"I **vote**⑥ that we row to the reef," cried Peterkin.

"And I vote that we visit the islands within the lagoon," said I.

"And I vote we do both," cried Jack, "so **pull away**⑦, boys."

As I have already said, we had made four oars, but our boat was so small that only two were necessary. The second pair were kept in case anything should happen to the others. It was therefore only needful that two of us should row, while the third guided us, by means of an oar,

14
我们查看环礁湖

① spot /spɒt/ v. 装点
② sheet /ʃiːt/ n. 张,片
③ swell /swel/ n. 巨浪

④ indicate /ˈɪndɪkeɪt/ v. 显示,象征,指示

⑤ gem /dʒem/ n. 宝石

⑥ vote /vəʊt/ v. 投票拥护

⑦ pull away（把…）开走，（使）离开

　　这是一个明亮、晴朗、美丽的早晨，我们第一次把小船推下水，划到环礁湖平静的海面上。海面上没有一丝风，深蓝色的天空没有一点云彩，大海就像一块玻璃一样闪闪发亮，但随着又长又大的海涌慢慢起伏，周围的一切都显示着太平洋的勃勃生机。当我们划过水面时，色彩亮丽的水草和珊瑚在清澈的海底发着光，像是一些珍贵的宝石。

　　开始的时候，因为心里高兴，我们盲目地划着船。但是当最初的兴奋消失以后，我们开始环顾四周考虑一下该做什么。

　　"我提议划到那块礁石那边。"彼得金叫道。

　　"我提议去看看那些在环瞧湖里的岛。"我说。

　　"我说两个地方都去，"杰克叫道，"接着划吧，小伙子们！"

　　我前面说过，我们做了四只桨，但是船太小了，用两只桨已经足够了。另外一对放在那儿是为了应付可能发生的事情。因此现在只要两个人划船就行了，第三个人做向导，不时用桨指挥着

· 169 ·

and changed places with the **rowers**① occasionally.

On the Reef

First we landed on one of the small islands, and ran all over it, but saw nothing **worthy**② of particular notice. Then we landed on a larger island, on which were growing a few coconut trees. Not having eaten anything that morning, we gathered a few of the nuts and breakfasted. After this we pulled straight out to sea and landed on the coral reef.

This was indeed a new and interesting sight to us. We had now been so long on shore that we had almost forgotten the appearance of waves, for there were none within the lagoon. But now, all the joy of the sailor was awakened in our hearts, and as we gazed on the **widespread**③ **ruin**④ of that single huge wave that burst in **thunder**⑤ at our feet, we forgot the Coral Island behind us; we forgot our house and the calm rest of the quiet woods; we forgot all that had passed during the last few months, and remembered nothing but the storms, the calms, the fresh winds, and the ever moving waves of the open sea.

This huge, ceaseless wave, of which I have so often spoken, was a much larger and finer object than we had at all **imagined**⑥ it to be. It rose many yards above the level of the sea, and could be seen approaching at some distance from the reef. Slowly and calmly it came on, gaining greater volume and speed as it advanced, until it took the form of a clear watery **arch**⑦, which glanced in the bright sun. On it came — the upper edge lipped gently over, and it fell with a roar that seemed as though the heart of Ocean were broken in the noise of the water, while the coral reef appeared to tremble beneath the **mighty**⑧ shock!

① rower /'rəʊə(r)/ n. 划手

② worthy /'wɜːði/ a. 有价值的

③ widespread /'waɪdspred,-'spred/ a. 分布(或散布)广的，普遍的

④ ruin /rʊɪn;'ruːɪn/ n. (pl.) 毁灭

⑤ thunder /'θʌndə/ n. 雷电，雷声

⑥ imagine /ɪ'mædʒɪn/ v. 想像

⑦ arch /ɑːtʃ/ n. 拱

⑧ mighty /'maɪti/ a. 强有力的

划船的人改变方向。

在礁石上

  我们首先登上了一座小岛，匆匆忙忙地看了一遍，没有发现什么特别值得注意的东西，后来我们在一座长着几棵椰子树的大一点儿的岛上了岸。因为早上没吃东西，我们就摘了几个椰子做早餐。然后我们就直接划到大海上，爬上了彼得金说的那块珊瑚礁。

  这里的景象对我们来说才确实是既新鲜又有趣。我们在岸上待得太久，几乎忘记了海浪是什么样子的，因为岸边的环礁湖里是没有海浪的。但是现在作为一名水手的快乐在我们内心苏醒了。巨浪打来，在我们的脚下撞得粉身碎骨，发出雷鸣般的轰响，我们凝视着飞溅的浪花，忘记了身后的珊瑚岛，忘记了我们的家，忘记了在寂静的树林里的安静的歇息地，忘记了在过去几个月中发生的一切事情。我们现在只记得海上的风暴，海上的风平浪静，清新的海风，以及公海上不断涌动的波浪。

  我经常提到的这种巨大的咆哮不停的海浪，比我们想象的更大更壮观。它高出海平面很多很多，离开珊瑚礁很远都能看到，海水慢慢地平静地涌上来，向前涌动的时候体积和速度大大增加，最后形成一个清澈的拱形巨浪，一闪一闪地反射着太阳的光芒。当它冲过来的时候，浪头的边缘轻轻翻转过来，然后落下，发出震耳的呼啸，太平洋的心脏仿佛在这咆哮声中破碎了，珊瑚礁也仿佛在这巨大的

The Coral Island

We gazed long and **wonderingly**① at this great sight, and it was with difficulty we could tear ourselves **away**② from it. As I have once before mentioned, this wave broke in many places over the reef, and **scattered**③ some of its water into the lagoon, but in most places the reef was broad enough and high enough to receive and check its entire force. In many places the coral rocks were covered with plants — the beginning, as it appeared to us, of future islands.

Thus, on this reef, we came to see how most of the small islands of those seas are formed. On one part we saw the water from the wave washing over the rocks, and **millions**④ of little busy creatures continuing the work of building up this living wall. At another place, which was just a little too high for the waves to **wash over**⑤ it, the coral animals were all dead; for we found that they never did their work above water. Again, in other spots the **ceaseless**⑥ waves of the sea had broken the dead coral in pieces, and cast it up in the form of sand. Here seabirds had come to earth, little pieces of seaweed and bits of wood had been **washed up**⑦, seeds of plants had been carried by the wind, and a few lovely **blades**⑧ of bright green had already come up, which, when they died, would increase the size and richness of these gems of Ocean. At other places these little islands had grown greatly, and were shaded by one or two coconut trees, which grew in the sand, and were constantly washed by the water of the Ocean.

Having satisfied and enjoyed ourselves during the whole day, in our little boat, we rowed back, somewhat wearied, and rather hungry, to our house.

"Now," said Jack, "as our boat serves us so well, we will get a mast and sail made immediately."

"So we will," cried Peterkin, as we all helped to drag the boat

① wonderingly /ˈwʌndərɪŋlɪ/ ad. 觉得奇怪地
② tear away （使）勉强离去
③ scatter /ˈskætə/ v. 散开，散布，散播

④ million /ˈmɪljən/ n. 百万

⑤ wash over 溅泼

⑥ ceaseless /ˈsiːslɪs/ a. 不绝的，不停的

⑦ wash up 将…冲上岸
⑧ blade /bleɪd/ n. 叶片，刀刃

撞击之下颤抖了。

我们久久凝视着眼前壮观的景象，惊讶不已，简直是不忍离去。我前面提到过，海浪打在礁石的许多地方，一些海水溅到环礁湖里，但是大多数地方的礁石很宽很高，足以抵挡海水的全部威力。珊瑚礁有许多地方覆盖着植物——在我们看来，这是形成未来岛屿的开端。

因此，从这片礁石上，我们开始明白这片海域的大部分小岛是怎么形成的了。在一个地方我们看到海浪冲刷着礁石，无数忙碌的小珊瑚虫在不停地营造着这堵生命之墙。在另外一个地方，岩石的高度刚好让海浪够不到它，珊瑚虫全都死了，由此我们发现珊瑚虫离开水面就无法工作。在其他一些地方，海浪一次又一次地拍打着那些死了的珊瑚，把它们拍成碎片，冲沙似的把它们冲到岸上。海鸟飞来落脚，小海藻和小木块被冲上岸来，风把草木的种子带到这里，已经有几片鲜绿可爱的嫩叶长出来了，当它们消亡的时候，这些明珠般的海岛会变得更大、更富饶。另外一些小岛也生机勃勃，上面长着一两棵椰子树，椰子树长在沙子里，不断受到海浪的冲击。

整整一天我们很高兴，很知足。我们坐进小船向家划去，不仅感到有点儿累，还觉得很饿。

"嘿，"杰克说，"既然船的性能不错，那我们就应该马上把桅杆和船帆做好。"

"我们一定会做好的，"当我们都帮着把船拉上岸的时候彼得金叫道，"我们今晚就点上灯干，啊哈，使劲拉，伙计们！"

The Coral Island

above high-water mark; "we'll light our light and set about it this very night. Hurrah, my boys, pull away!"

As we dragged our boat, we observed that she rubbed heavily on her bottom, and as the sands were in this place **mixed with**[①] broken coral rocks, we saw portions of the wood being **rubbed off**[②].

"Hallo," cried Jack, on seeing this; "that won't do. The bottom will be **worn off**[③] in no time at this rate."

"So it will," said I, thinking deeply as to how this might be stopped. But I could think of no way out save that of putting a plate of iron on the bottom; but as we had no iron, I knew not what was to be done. "It seems to me, Jack," I added, "that it is impossible to stop the bottom being worn off thus."

"Impossible!" cried Peterkin. "My dear Ralph, you are **mistaken**[④]; there is nothing so easy."

"How?" I asked, in some surprise.

"Why, by not using the boat at all!" replied Peterkin.

We Make a Sail

"Be quiet, Peterkin," said Jack, as he **shouldered**[⑤] the oars; "come along with me and I'll give you work to do. In the first place, you will go and collect coconut cloth, and set to work to make **sewing**[⑥] thread with it —"

"Please, captain," cried Peterkin, "I've got lots of it made already — more than enough, as a little friend of mine used to be in the habit of saying every day after dinner."

"Very well," continued Jack; "then you'll help Ralph to get coconut cloth, and cut it into shape, after which we'll make a sail of it. I'll see

① mix with 与…混在一起
② rub off 擦掉

③ wear off 磨损（逐渐消失）

④ mistake /mɪsˈteɪk/ v. 犯错,误认

⑤ shoulder /ˈʃəʊldə/ v. 肩负,承担

⑥ sew /səʊ/ v. 缝合,缝纫

拖船的时候，我们发现这地方的沙滩上混杂着破碎的珊瑚石，船在上面拖过的时候，船底磨得很厉害。一些木屑被磨掉了。

"噢，"看到这种情况杰克叫道，"这样不行。照这么下去船底没几天就完蛋了。"

"肯定会的。"我一边说，一边绞尽脑汁想着怎么避免这种情况。但是我想除了在底下包上铁板之外，没有别的办法。可因为现在根本就没有铁，我也就无能为力了。"依我看，杰克，"我接着说，"要想不擦伤船底是不可能的。"

"不可能！"彼得金叫起来，"亲爱的拉尔夫，你错了，这事再简单不过了。"

"为什么？"我有点奇怪地问。

"嗨，我们不用它不就行了！"彼得金回答道。

我们做好了一张帆

"安静点儿，彼得金，"杰克说，他把桨扛在肩膀上，"跟我来，给你派点儿活干。你先去找点椰子皮，然后把它们搓成穿缝用的线绳——"

彼得金嚷道："哎哟，头儿，我已经搓了很多了，在我的小朋友晚饭后聊天的时候，我搓的绳子老多啦。"

"好，"杰克接着说，"那你就帮着拉尔夫去找些椰子皮吧，把它们裁下来，我们用它做张帆，我负责弄桅杆和绳子。好了，我们开始工作吧。"

我们立刻紧张地工作起来，仅用三天时间我们

to getting the mast and the ropes; so let's to work."

And to work we went right busily, so that in three days from that time we had set up a mast and sail, with the necessary ropes, in our little boat. The sail was not, indeed, very **handsome**① to look at, as it was formed of a number of pieces of **cloth**②, but we had sewed it well by means of our sail-needle, so that it was strong, which was the chief thing.

Jack had also overcome the difficulty about the bottom, by pinning to it a **false**③ bottom. This was a piece of wood as long and as wide as the real bottom, and about five inches deep. He made it of this thickness because the boat would be **thereby**④ made not only much more safe, but more able to make its way against the wind; which, in a sea where the strong winds blow so long and so hard in one direction, was a matter of great importance. This piece of wood was fixed very firmly to the bottom; and we now put our boat into the water with the comfort of knowing that when the false bottom should be worn off we could easily put on another; but, should the real bottom have been worn away, we could not have put on another without taking our boat to pieces.

The mast and sail served us excellently, and we now sailed about in the lagoon with great delight, and examined with much interest the appearance of our island from a distance. Also, we gazed into the water, and watched for hours the strange and bright-coloured fish among the corals and seaweed. Peterkin also made a fishing-line, and Jack made a number of **hooks**⑤, some of which were very good, others very bad. Some of these hooks were made of iron-wood, which did pretty well, the wood being extremely hard, and Jack made them very thick and large. Some of the bones in fish-heads also served this purpose **pretty**⑥ well. But that which formed our best and most **serviceable**⑦ hook was

① handsome /ˈhænsəm/ a. 英俊的
② cloth /klɒ(ː)θ/ n. 布

③ false /fɔːls/ a. 假的

④ thereby /ˈðeəˈbaɪ/ ad. 因此，从而

⑤ hook /hʊk/ n. 钩子

⑥ pretty /ˈprɪtɪ/ ad. 相当地
⑦ serviceable /ˈsɜːvɪsəbl/ a. 有用的，耐用的

就在小船上立起了根桅杆和一张帆，配上了要用的绳子。船帆实际上不是很好看，因为是用几块椰子皮做成的，我们用制帆针仔细地把它们缝在一起，因此帆很结实，这才是最重要的。

杰克也解决了船底的难题，他在上面钉了一个假底。这是一块长宽都和真底一样的木头，大约有五英寸厚，杰克把它做成那个厚度是因为船不仅因此变得更加安全，而且可以抗风。海上的狂风向一个方向吹的时间很长也很猛烈，船能抗风是件非常重要的事情。这块木头被结结实实地固定在船底，现在我们把船推进水里，一点儿也不用担心，因为我们知道如果这个假底磨坏了，可以很容易地装个新的，但是一旦那个真正的船底坏了，我们就只有把船拆了再造一只新的。

帆和桅杆都很好用，我们兴致勃勃地驾船在环礁湖里行驶，带着极大的兴趣在远处注视着我们的海岛。我们也一连几小时地注视着水里，看着各种奇特而色彩斑斓的鱼在珊瑚和水草间穿梭。彼得金还做了渔线，杰克做了许多渔钩，有些很好用，有些很糟糕。有些钩子是用铁木做的，非常棒。木头很硬，杰克把它们做得又大又厚。有些用鱼头上的骨头做的钩子也很好用，但是做得最好、用得最多的钩子取材于杰克的那个黄铜戒指。

如果让我描述日复一日我们用黄铜渔钩钓到的各种各样的鱼，那可是件费时费力的事。彼得金老是钓上鱼来——我们发现他从钓鱼中得到了很多的

The Coral Island

the brass finger-ring belonging to Jack.

It would be a matter of much time and labour to describe the appearance of the many fish that were day after day drawn into our boat by means of the brass hook. Peterkin always caught them — for we observed that he obtained much pleasure from fishing — while Jack and I found enough to interest us in looking on, also in gazing down at the coral **groves**①.

During these delightful fishing and boating journeys we caught many fish, which we found to be very good to eat. Moreover, we discovered many shell-fish, so that we had no **lack of**② change in our food; and, indeed, we never passed a week without making some new and interesting discovery of some **sort**③ or other, either on the land or in the sea.

乐趣。而我和杰克则发现坐在一旁观看，并且凝视水下的珊瑚丛是件很有意思的事。

在愉快的钓鱼和航海过程中，我们抓到了很多鱼，而且发现它们很好吃。此外我们还找到了许多贝类，因此我们的食物不断地改变花样。真的，我们每过一周，不是在陆地上就是在海里，总有这样或那样的有趣的新发现。

① grove /grəuv/ *n.* 小树林

② lack of 缺乏

③ sort /sɔːt/ *n.* 种类,样子

Chapter 15
Penguin Island

One day, not long after our little boat was finished, we were sitting on the rocks above Diamond Cave, and talking of a journey which we intended to make to Penguin Island the next day.

"You see," said Peterkin, "it might be all very well for a fellow like me to remain here and leave the penguins alone, but it would be quite against your **characters**① as clever fellows to remain any longer without knowing the **customs**② of these birds, so the quicker we go the better."

"Very true," said I, "There is nothing I desire so much as to have a closer **view**③ of them."

"And I think," said Jack, "that you had better remain at home, Peterkin."

"Stay at home!" cried Peterkin. "My dear fellow, you would certainly **lose** your **way**④, or **turn** the boat **over**⑤, if I were not there to take care of you."

"Ah, true," said Jack gravely; "that did not occur to me; no doubt you must go. Our boat does require a good deal of weight; and all that you say, Peterkin, carries so much weight with it, that we won't need

15
企鹅岛

  小船完工后不久，我们有一天坐在钻石洞上面的岩石上，谈论着打算次日开始的企鹅岛之行。

  "瞧，"彼得金说，"像我这样的人待在这儿，睬都不睬企鹅，可能是理所当然的，但是像你们这么聪明的人，却仍然不知道这些鸟儿的习性，就太不符合你们的特点了，所以我们还是尽快去比较好。"

  "说得对，"我说，"我太想到跟前看看它们了，没有什么愿望能和这个愿望相比。"

  "我想，"杰克说，"彼得金，你最好待在家里。"

  "待在家里！"彼得金叫了起来，"老朋友，如果我不在旁边关照你的话，你肯定会迷航，或者把船给弄翻了。"

  "噢，对呀，"杰克严肃地说，"我没想到这一点，你的确得去。我们的船真的需要很重的分量，彼得金，你说的这番话太有分量了，如果你去的

① character /ˈkærɪktə/ n. 个性
② custom /ˈkʌstəm/ n. 习惯，风俗
③ view /vjuː/ n. 观点，景色
④ lose way 迷路
⑤ turn over 翻过来，滚动

stones if you go."

We prepared a supply of food, for we intended to be away at least a night or two, perhaps longer. This took us some time to do, for while Jack was busy with the boat, Peterkin was sent into the woods to **spear**[1] a pig or two, and had to search long, sometimes, before he found them. Peterkin was usually sent, when we wanted a pig (which was often), because he could run so wonderfully fast that he found no difficulty in catching the pigs; but being **dreadfully**[2] careless, he almost always **fell over**[3] stones in the course of his wild **chase**[4], and usually came home with the skin off his legs. But although Peterkin was often **unfortunate**[5] in the way of getting falls, he was successful on the present occasion in hunting, and came back before evening with three very nice little pigs.

I also was successful in my visit to the mud-flats, where I killed several ducks. So that, when we loaded our boat at sunrise the following morning, we found our store of food to be more than enough. We thought that this supply would last us for several days; but we afterwards found that it was much more than we required, especially **in regard to**[6] the coconuts, of which we found large supplies wherever we went. However, as Peterkin said, it was better to have too much than too little, as we knew not what we might meet during our journey.

We Set Out[7]

It was a very calm, sunny morning when we **set forth**[8] and rowed over the lagoon towards the opening in the reef, and passed between the two green islands that guard the entrance. We met with some difficulty and no little danger in passing the big waves at the reef, and shipped a good deal of water; but, once past the wave, we found ourselves

① spear /spɪə/ v. 用矛刺

② dreadfully /ˈdredfəli/ ad. 可怕地,糟透地
③ fall over 跌倒,从…掉下来
④ chase /tʃeɪs/ n. 追求,狩猎
⑤ unfortunate /ʌnˈfɔːtʃənɪt/ a. 不幸的,令人遗憾的

⑥ in regard to /rɪˈɡɑːd/ 关于,至于

⑦ set out 动身,起程

⑧ set forth 出发

话,我们就用不着压石头了。"

我们打算在外面至少过一两个晚上,或许更长些,因此准备了食物。为此花了我们一些时间。因为杰克忙船上的活,彼得金就到树林里去叉一两头猪,他有时要花很长的时间才能找到猪群。我们想吃猪肉的时候(我们经常想吃),彼得金总是到林子里去,因为他跑得太快了,不费什么力气就能追上猪群。但是他太粗心了,在玩命追赶野猪的时候,几乎总是被石头绊倒,经常是两腿挂彩地回家。虽然彼得金很倒霉,总是摔跟头,但是他是个成功的猎手,天黑之前,他带着三头很不错的小猪回来了。

我在淤泥滩上的狩猎也很成功,在那儿我打到了几只鸭子。所以在第二天早上日出装船的时候,我们发现储备的食物太多了。我们想这些东西够我们吃几天的,但是后来发现用不了这么多,特别是椰子,因为无论到什么地方去,我们都能发现大量的椰子。但是就像彼得金说的,多了总比不够好,因为我们不知道途中会遇到什么事。

我们出发了

出发的时候是个风和日丽的早上,我们取道环礁湖,划向珊瑚礁的开口,然后从守卫在开口处的两座海岛中间穿过去。我们遇到了些麻烦,通过礁石边的大浪时很危险,船进了很多水,但大浪一过,我们就发现自己平静地漂浮在长而平滑的波涛

The Coral Island

floating calmly on the long oily swell that rose and fell slowly as it rolled over the wide ocean.

Penguin Island lay on the other side of our own island, at about a mile beyond the outer reef, and we thought that it must be at least twenty miles distant by the way we should have to go. We might, indeed, have shortened the way by coasting round our island inside of the lagoon, and going out at the opening in the reef nearly opposite to Penguin Island; but we preferred to go by the open sea — first, because it was a **bolder**① thing to do, and, secondly, because we should have the pleasure of again feeling the motion of the sea, which we all loved very much, not suffering from sea-sickness.

"I wish we had a wind," said Jack.

"So do I," cried Peterkin, resting on his oar and **wiping**② his heated brow; "pulling is hard work. Oh dear, if we could only catch a hundred or two of these sea-birds, tie them to the boat with long **strings**③, and make them fly as we want them, how fine it would be!"

"Or bore a hole through a shark's tail, and put a rope through it, eh?" remarked Jack. "But, I say, it seems that my wish is going to be **granted**④, for here comes a wind. Ship your oar, Peterkin. Up with the mast, Ralph; I'll see to the sail. Look out for **storms**⑤!"

This last speech was caused by the sudden appearance of a dark-blue line on the sky-line, which, in a short space of time, swept down on us, raising great waves as it went. We presented the back of the boat to its first force, and, in a few seconds, it **calmed down**⑥ into a good wind, before which we spread our sail and flew **swiftly**⑦ over the waves. Although the wind died away soon afterwards, it had been so **stiff**⑧ while it lasted that we were carried over the greater part of our way before it fell calm again; so that, when the noise of the sail against the mast told us that it was time to take up the oars again, we were not

① bolder /bəʊld/ a. 大胆的

② wipe /waɪp/ v. 擦,消除,拭去

③ string /strɪŋ/ n. 线

④ grant /grɑːnt/ v. 授予
⑤ storm /stɔːm/ n. 暴风雨

⑥ calm down 平静下来（镇定下来）
⑦ swiftly /ˈswɪftlɪ/ ad. 很快地,即刻
⑧ stiff /stɪf/ a. 严厉的

上了，波涛缓慢地起伏着，滚过宽阔的海面。

企鹅岛在我们这个岛的另一侧，离外侧的珊瑚礁大约有一英里远，按照现在要走的路线，我们觉得至少得走二十英里。实际上如果我们在环礁湖里绕着海岛环行，从那个几乎正对着企鹅岛的礁石开口出去，就可以近很多，但是我们还是宁愿走开阔的海面——因为，第一，这样做更能显示勇气；第二，重新感受大海的波动会给我们带来的欢乐，我们都非常喜欢大海的波动，且并不会遭受晕船之苦。

"我希望有风，"杰克说。

"我也希望，"彼得金放下桨擦着热腾腾的脑门叫道，"划船太辛苦了。哎呀，如果我们能抓住一两百只海鸟，用长绳子把它们拴在船上，让它们按着我们的意愿飞，那该有多美啊！"

"或者是在鲨鱼的尾巴上打个洞，把绳子穿过去，怎么样？"杰克回答，"可是听着，看起来我的愿望快要实现了，这儿来风了。彼得金，把桨放进船里，拉尔夫，竖起桅杆，我管船帆，小心大风！"

之所以说最后这句话，是因为在天边突然出现了一道发黑的蓝线。狂风很快朝我们猛袭过来，横扫洋面时掀起了巨大的海浪。风头扑来的时候我们躲在船尾，几秒钟以后，它就平静下来，变成徐徐微风。我们迎风展开了船帆，船飞快地穿过海浪。虽然这阵风很快就平息了，但是它刮得太猛了，在平息下来之前，我们被它向前吹了很长一段距离。所以当桅杆上的帆声告诉我们又得拿桨划船的时候，我们离企鹅岛只有一英里多了。

The Coral Island

much more than a mile from Penguin Island.

"There go the soldiers!" cried Peterkin, as we came in sight of it. "How clean their white trousers look this morning! I wonder if they will receive us kindly. D'you think they are kind, Jack?"

"Don't talk, Peterkin, but pull away and you shall see **shortly**①."

The Penguins

As we drew near to the island we found much to laugh at in the movements and appearance of these strange birds. Having approached to within a few yards of the island, which was a low rock, with no other plants on it than a few bushes, we lay on our oars and gazed at the birds with surprise and pleasure, they returning our gaze with interest.

We now saw that their soldier-like appearance was owing to the stiff, **erect**② manner in which they sat on their short legs — "bolt-upright," as Peterkin expressed it. They had black heads, long sharp beaks, white **chests**③, and dark-blue backs. Their wings were very short, and we soon saw that they used them for the purpose of swimming under water. There were no proper feathers on these wings, but a sort of **scales**④, which also thickly covered their bodies. Their legs were short, and placed so far back that the birds, while on land were obliged to **stand up**⑤ straight in order to **keep their balance**⑥, but in the water they **floated**⑦ like other water-birds. At first we were so surprised with the noise which they and other sea-birds kept up around us, that we knew not which way to look — for they covered the rocks in thousands; but, as we continued to gaze, we observed several four-legged animals (as we thought) walking in the middle of the penguins.

"Pull in a bit," cried Peterkin, "and let's see what these are. They must be fond of **noisy**⑧ company, to live with such creatures."

① shortly /ˈʃɔːtlɪ/ ad. 立刻，马上

② erect /ɪˈrekt/ a. 直立的，竖立的，笔直的

③ chest /tʃest/ n. 胸，胸部

④ scale /skeɪl/ n. 鳞

⑤ stand up 站立
⑥ keep balance 保持平衡
⑦ float /fləʊt/ v. 漂浮，浮现

⑧ noisy /ˈnɔɪzɪ/ a. 喧闹的，嘈杂的

"士兵在那儿！"我们看到它们时，彼得金叫起来，"今天早上它们的白裤子看起来真耀眼！我想知道它们是不是能友善地接待我们，杰克，你觉得它们会对我们好吗？"

"别讲话，彼得金。接着划，你马上就能见到它们了。"

企 鹅

当小船接近海岛的时候，我们发现这些怪鸟的动作和样子真是可笑。这个岛是一片低矮的礁石，除了些灌木没有别的植物，我们在靠近小岛大约几码的地方收起桨，又惊又喜地盯着这些鸟，它们也好奇地盯着我们。

我们现在才明白它们外表像士兵，是因为它们身子安在短腿上，姿态僵直，用彼得金的话来说是"笔杆条直"。它们长着黑色的脑袋，长长的尖嘴，白色的胸脯，还有深蓝色的后背。它们的翅膀很短，我们很快发现翅膀是用来游水的。翅膀上没有什么真正的羽毛，只有一种鳞状物，它们的身上也厚厚地披着这种东西。它们的腿很短，而且长得很靠后，在陆地上只有直立才能保持平衡，但是在水里它们也像其他水鸟一样漂游着。开始的时候，我们对周围此起彼伏的喧叫声感到非常惊讶，那是企鹅和其他海鸟发出的，我们都不知道朝哪儿看了——因为它们成千上万，岩石都给遮住了。但是接着看的时候，我们发现一些四条腿的动物（我们是这么想的）在企鹅中间漫步。

"划近点儿，"彼得金叫道，"让我们看看它们

The Coral Island

To our surprise we found that these were no other than penguins which had gone down on all-fours, and were walking among the bushes on their feet and wings. Suddenly one big old bird, that had been sitting on a point very near to us, gazing in silent surprise, became alarmed, and running down the rocks, fell, rather than ran, into the sea. It dived in a moment, and, a few seconds afterwards, came out of the water far ahead, with such a jump, and such a dive back into the sea again, that we could scarcely believe it was not a fish that had **leaped**① in sport.

"That beats everything," said Peterkin, robbing his nose, and putting on an expression of surprise and anger. "I've heard of a thing being neither fish, **flesh**②, nor bird, but I never did expect to live to see an animal that was all three together — at once — in one! But look there!" he continued, pointing with a tired look to the shore, "look there! there's no end to it. What has that bird got under its tail?"

We turned to look in the direction pointed out, and there saw a penguin walking slowly along the shore with an egg under its tail. There were several others, we observed, doing the same thing; and we found afterwards that these were a kind of penguins that always carried their eggs so. Indeed, they had a most useful pocket for the purpose, just between the tail and the legs. We were very much struck with the **regularity**③ and order of this **colony**④. The island seemed to be divided up into squares, of which each penguin possessed one, and sat in stiff **graveness**⑤ in the middle of it, or took a slow **march**⑥ up and down the spaces between. Some were sitting on their eggs, but others were **feeding**⑦ their young ones in a manner that caused us to laugh not a little. The mother stood on a raised rock, while the young one stood **patiently**⑧ below her on the ground. Suddenly the mother raised her head and uttered a number of loud, unpleasant noises.

"She's going to be ill," cried Peterkin.

是什么。它们一定是喜欢和吵吵闹闹的动物搭伴过日子。"

意想不到的是它们还是企鹅,只不过是匍匐在地上,用它们的脚和翅膀在灌木丛里行走。在离我们很近的地方有一只体形硕大的老企鹅,它正一声不吭地用惊奇的目光望着我们,突然,它不安起来,向岩石下跑去,然后跌进海里,而不是跑进海里。它潜了一会儿,几秒钟后,在远处露出水面,再一跳,又潜回到水里,我们差点以为它是一条活蹦乱跳的鱼。

"绝了,"彼得金说,他揉着鼻子,露出一种又惊又恼的神情,"我听说过一种既不是鱼,也不是走兽或飞禽的动物,但是我从没想到能活着见到同时集三种特点于一身的动物!看那儿!"他不耐烦地用手指着岸边,接着又说:"看那儿!这些东西没完没了。那只企鹅的尾巴底下有什么?"

我们转过身朝他指的方向望去,看到一只企鹅在尾巴底下带着个蛋,沿着海岸慢慢走着。我们看到其他一些企鹅也这么做。我们后来发现这种企鹅总是这样带着它们的蛋。实际上,为了装蛋,它们长了一个很有用的袋子,就在尾巴和两腿之间。我们被这个群体的井然有序深深地打动了。这个岛看来被划分成许多区域,每只企鹅都拥有一块领土,它们庄严而僵直地待在领地中间,或者在自己的领土下蹒跚而行。有的正坐在它们的蛋上,而另一些用一种令我们开怀大笑的姿势喂它们的孩子。母企鹅站在高处的石头上,而小企鹅则耐心地站在下面的地上,突然母企鹅抬起头,发出一阵很响很难听的叫声。

"它要生病了。"彼得金喊道。

---

① leap /liːp/ v. 跳跃

② flesh /fleʃ/ n. 肉,兽肉

③ regularity /ˌreɡjʊˈlærɪtɪ/ n. 有规则,匀整

④ colony /ˈkɒlənɪ/ n. 殖民地

⑤ graveness /ˈɡreɪvnɪs/ n. 重大,严重,认真

⑥ march /mɑːtʃ/ v. 行军,进军

⑦ feed /fiːd/ v. 喂养,饲养

⑧ patiently /ˈpeɪʃəntlɪ/ ad. 有耐心地

But this was not the case, although she looked like it. In a few seconds she put down her head and opened her mouth, into which the young one put its **beak**① and seemed to take something from her throat. Then the noise was repeated, the eating continued, and so the **operation**② of feeding was carried on till the young one was satisfied; but what she fed her little one with we could not tell.

"Now, just look over there!" said Peterkin, in an interested tone. "If that isn't the worst piece of **motherly**③ **conduct**④ I ever saw! That wicked old lady penguin had just thrown her young one into the sea, and there's another about to follow her example."

This indeed seemed to be the case, for on the top of a steep rock close to the edge of the sea we observed an old penguin trying to get her young one into the water; but the young one seemed very **unwilling**⑤ to go, and moved very slowly towards her. At last she went **gently**⑥ behind the young bird and pushed it a little towards the water, but with great **tenderness**⑦, as much as to say, "Don't be afraid, dear; I won't hurt you, my little one!" but no sooner did she get it to the edge of the rock, where it stood looking **thoughtfully**⑧ down at the sea, then she gave it a sudden, hard push, sending it head first down the **slope**⑨ into water, where its mother left it to swim to the shore as it best could. We observed many of them doing this, and we thus learnt that this is the way in which old penguins teach their children to swim.

Scarcely had we finished making our observations on this, when we were surprised by about a dozen of the old birds jumping in the most unsafe and funny manner towards the sea. The beach here was a sloping rock, and when they came to it some of them jumped down in safety, but others lost their balance, and rolled and fell down the slope in the most helpless manner. The instant they reached the water, however, they seemed to be in their proper place. They dived and **bounded**⑩ out of it

① beak /biːk/ n. 鸟嘴
② operation /ˌɒpəˈreɪʃn/ n. 行动,活动,操作

③ motherly /ˈmʌðəlɪ/ a. 母亲的
④ conduct /ˈkɒndʌkt, -dəkt/ 行为,举动,品行

⑤ unwilling /ˈʌnˈwɪlɪŋ/ a. 不愿意的
⑥ gently /ˈdʒentlɪ/ ad. 轻轻地,温柔地

⑦ tenderness /ˈtendənɪs/ n. 柔软,亲切,柔和

⑧ thoughtful /ˈθɔːtfəl/ a. 考虑周到的(思索的)
⑨ slope /sləʊp/ n. 倾斜,斜坡

⑩ bound /baʊnd/ v. 跳跃

虽然看起来是这样,但事实并非如此。母企鹅马上低下头,张开嘴,小企鹅把尖嘴伸进去,似乎从它的喉咙里吃了些东西。然后母企鹅又叫了起来,小企鹅又接着吃。喂食就这样持续着,直到小企鹅觉得饱了为止。但是它喂什么东西给它孩子吃我们就说不出来了。

"喂,看那边!"彼得金用一种关注的语调说,"那一定是我见过的最蹩脚的母亲!那个恶毒的母企鹅刚才把它的孩子扔进海里,那儿还有一只正在学它的样。"

这回看来确实是对的,在靠近海边的一块陡峭的岩石上,我们看见一只老企鹅正试图把它的孩子推进海里,那只小企鹅看起来非常不愿意,慢慢地挪向它的妈妈。最后老企鹅轻轻地走到小企鹅后面把它向水那边推了推。但是动作非常轻柔,仿佛在说:"别害怕,亲爱的,我不会伤害你的,我的小宝贝!"但是当它把小企鹅推到岩石边上的时候,小企鹅站在那儿若有所思地往海里看,老企鹅立即猛地用力一推,小企鹅头朝下滚过斜坡跌进水里,小企鹅的妈妈让掉进水里的孩子尽最大的努力游回岸边。我们发现许多企鹅都在这么做,我们这才明白这是老企鹅教孩子学游泳的办法。

还没有看完这边,我们又奇怪地发现许多只成年企鹅用一种极其不安全和可笑的姿势跳进海里。这里的海岸是一片有坡度的岩石,从那儿跳进海里时,有一些企鹅很安全,另一些则失去平衡,叽里咕噜地滚下了坡,姿态完全失去了控制。但是它们一到水里,就仿佛是如鱼得水。它们潜到水里,然后跃出水面,接着又潜下去,极其轻松自如。就这

The Coral Island

and into it again with the greatest ease; and so, diving and bounding — for they could not fly — they went rapidly out to sea.

On seeing this, Peterkin turned with a grave face to us and said, "It's my opinion that these birds are all completely and entirely mad, and that this is a **magic**① island. I therefore say that we should either put about ship and fly in **terror**② from the spot, or land bravely on the island, and fight as hard as we can."

"I vote for landing; so **pull in**③, lads," said Jack, giving a stroke with his oar that made the boat turn.

In a few seconds we ran the boat into a little bay, where we made her fast to a piece of coral, and running up the beach, entered the ranks of the penguins **armed**④ with our sticks and our spear. We were greatly surprised to find that, instead of **attacking**⑤ us or showing signs of fear at our approach, these strange birds did not move from their places until we took hold of them, and merely turned their eyes on us in wonder as we passed.

There was one old penguin, however, that began to walk slowly towards the sea, and Peterkin took it into his head that he would try to stop it, so he ran between it and the sea and waved his stick in its face. But this proved to be a **determined**⑥ old bird. It would not go back; in fact, it would not cease to advance, but **battled with**⑦ Peterkin bravely, and drove him before it until it reached the sea. Had Peterkin used his stick he could easily have killed it, no doubt; but as he had no wish to do so cruel an act merely out of sport, he let the bird escape.

We spent fully three hours on this island in watching these strange birds, and when we finally left them, we all three decided, after much talking, that they were the most wonderful creatures we had ever seen; and further, we thought it **probable**⑧ that they were the most wonderful creatures in the world!

珊瑚岛

样，它们潜下去又跃出来——因为不会飞——迅速地游向大海。

看到这些，彼得金转向我们一脸严肃地说："依我看这些鸟完完全全地疯了，这是个魔岛。因此我说我们要么调转船头，从这里仓皇逃跑，要么就勇敢地上岸。尽我们最大的努力战斗。"

"我赞成上岸，靠岸吧，伙计们。"杰克边说边划了一下桨，掉转了船头。

眨眼工夫我们就驾船驶进一个小海湾，我们把船拴在一块珊瑚上，然后跑上岸，用棍子和渔叉做武器走进企鹅的队伍里。令我们大吃一惊的是，我们发现这些奇怪的鸟不是向我们发起进攻，或是对我们的到来显出害怕的样子，而是连窝都不挪，直到我们抓住它们为止，我们走过的时候，它们只是转动眼珠，好奇地望着我们。

然而有一只老企鹅开始慢慢地走向海里，彼得金突然心血来潮想拦住它，他跑到大海和企鹅中间，冲着企鹅的脸挥舞着他的大棍子。这是一只意志坚定的老企鹅。它不肯往回走，实际上是勇往直前，和彼得金勇敢搏斗，在入海之前赶着彼得金往前走。毫无疑问，彼得金用他的棍子可以轻而易举地杀死企鹅，但是他不想仅仅是因为玩就做这么残忍的事，所以他放企鹅跑了。

我们在岛上花了整整三个小时的时间观察这些奇怪的鸟，不断地议论着它们。当我们最后离开它们的时候，我们三个都认为，它们是我们所见过的最奇妙的动物，而且我们觉得企鹅可能也是世界上最奇妙的动物。

---

① magic /ˈmædʒɪk/ *a.* 有魔力的
② terror /ˈterə/ *n.* 恐怖
③ pull in 拉入（同步引入）
④ arm /ɑːm/ *v.* 武装，装备
⑤ attack /əˈtæk/ *v.* 攻击
⑥ determine /dɪˈtɜːmɪn/ *v.* 决定，决心要
⑦ battle with 与…战斗
⑧ probable /ˈprɒbəbl/ *a.* 很可能的

Chapter 16
Another Storm

It was evening before we left the island of the penguins. As we had made up our minds to camp for the night on a small island, on which grew a few coconut trees, about two miles off. we used our oars with some **energy**①. But a danger was **in store**② for us which we had not expected. The wind, which had carried us so quickly to Penguin Island, increased as evening **drew on**③, and before we had gone half the distance to the small island, it became a bad storm. Although it was not so directly against us as to **prevent**④ our rowing in the course we wished to go, yet it checked us very much. And although the force of the sea was somewhat broken by the island, the waves soon began to rise, and to roll their broken heads against our small boat, so that she began to take in water, and we had much difficulty in keeping our boat from going down. At last the wind and sea together became so **terrible**⑤ that we found it impossible to reach the island, so Jack suddenly put the head of the boat round and ordered Peterkin and me to set a **corner**⑥ of the sail, intending to turn back to Penguin Island.

"We shall at least have the shelter of the bushes," he said, as the

16
另一场暴风雨

① energy /ˈenədʒɪ/ n. 精力，能量
② in store 必将到来，快要发生
③ draw on 临近

④ prevent /prɪˈvent/ v. 预防，防止

⑤ terrible /ˈterəbl/ a. 可怕的，糟糕的
⑥ corner /ˈkɔːnə/ n. 角落，转角

　　我们离开企鹅岛的时候，天色已经变暗了。我们打定主意到大约两英里以外的一个小岛上过夜，于是就起劲地朝着长着几棵椰子树的小岛划去。但是意想不到的危险正在等着我们。风，就是那阵眨眼工夫就把我们吹到企鹅岛的强风，在夜幕降临的时候变大了。我们刚走到半路，风就变成了一场可怕的风暴。虽然风没有正对着我们吹，使我们偏离预定的航向，但是还是让我们每划一下都很困难。尽管海岛抵消了一些海水的冲击力，海浪还是很快变高，翻滚的浪尖砸向我们的小船，这样一来小船开始进水了，防止船往下沉真是难啊。后来狂风卷起巨浪，骇人极了，我们发现要想到达那个海岛是不可能的了，杰克突然掉转了船头，命令我和彼得金改变帆的角度，打算返回企鹅岛。

　　"我们至少能在灌木丛里找个安身之处，"当我们的船被风吹得飞奔时杰克说，"企鹅会和我们做伴的。"

The Coral Island

boat flew before the wind, "and the penguins will **keep us company**①."

As Jack spoke, the wind suddenly changed and began to blow so much against us that we were forced to put up more of the sail in order to reach the island, being by this change thrown much to the side of it. What made matters worse was, that the storm came in bursts, so that we were more than once nearly **upset**②.

"**Stand by**③, both of you," Cried Jack, in a quick, earnest tone; "be ready to let down the sail. I very much fear we won't make the island after all."

Peterkin and I were so much used to trusting everything to Jack that we had fallen into the way of not considering things, especially such things as were under Jack's care. We had, therefore, never doubted for a moment that all was going well, so that it was with no little fear that we heard him make the above **statement**④. However, we had no time for question, for at the moment he spoke a heavy burst of wind was coming towards us, and as we were then flying with one side going **occasionally**⑤ under the waves, it was clear that we should have to lower our sail **altogether**⑥.

In a few seconds the storm struck the boat, but Peterkin and I had the sail down in a moment, so that it did not turn us over; but when it was past we were more than half full of water. This I soon threw out, while Peterkin again put up a corner of the sail; but the **evil**⑦ which Jack had feared came upon us. We found it quite impossible to make Penguin Island. The storm carried us quickly past it towards the open sea, and the terrible truth came to us that we should be carried out and left to die slowly in a small boat in the middle of the wide ocean.

This idea was forced very strongly upon us, because we saw nothing in the direction in which the wind was blowing us save the fierce waves

① keep company 结交(和…交往)

② upset /ʌp'set/ v. 颠覆，推翻
③ stand by 准备行动，坚持

④ statement /'steɪtmənt/ n. 陈述，声明
⑤ occasionally /ə'keɪʒənəlɪ/ ad. 偶尔地

⑥ altogether /ɔ:ltə'ɡeðə/ ad. 总共

⑦ evil /'i:vl/ n. 邪恶，罪恶

　　杰克正说着，风突然改变了方向，开始猛烈地对着我们吹。为了到达海岛，我们不得不升高船帆。风向的改变实际上把我们抛向了海岛的侧面，更糟糕的是，风暴更猛烈了，我们好几次差点儿翻船。

　　"准备好，你们两个，"杰克喊道，语气急促而严肃，"准备放下船帆。我担心我们根本上不了这个岛。"

　　无论什么事，我和彼得金一向都非常信任杰克，已经到了不肯思考的地步了，特别是这种应当由杰克操心的事。我们丝毫不怀疑过一会儿就会没事，所以听到杰克说上面的那番话，心里一个劲儿打鼓。但是我们没有时间询问了，因为这时候杰克说一阵狂风正向我们袭来，届时船速很快，一侧船舷有时会被浪头压住，事情明摆着，我们得把帆全部降下来。

　　狂风很快就向小船扑来，但是我和彼得金已经放下了船帆，这样风暴才没有把船掀翻。但是当风暴过去之后，船里进了大半船的水。我很快地把水排净，彼得金又把帆升起了一点儿。杰克担心的事情终于发生了。我们发现到企鹅岛去是完全不可能了。风暴带着我们飞快地从它旁边驶过，直奔大洋而去。一个可怕的事实摆在我们面前：我们将被带到汪洋大海之中，在小船上慢慢死去。

　　这个念头死死地压着我们，因为狂风正吹着我们飞跑，前面的大海上除了惊涛骇浪什么也看不

· 197 ·

of the sea; and, indeed, we were afraid as we gazed round us, for we were now beyond the shelter of the islands, and it seemed as though any of the huge waves, which **curled**① over in masses of angry water might swallow us up in a moment. The water, also, began to wash in over our sides, and I had to keep constantly throwing it out, for Jack had to guide the boat, and Peterkin could not **quit**② the sail for an instant without putting our lives in **danger**③ Suddenly Jack uttered a cry of hope, and pointed towards a low island or rock which lay directly in front. We had not seen it before, owing to the dark clouds in the sky and the **blinding**④ drops of water that seemed to fill the whole air.

As we neared this rock we observed that there were no trees or other plants on it, and that it was so low that the sea broke completely over it. In fact, it was nothing more than the top of one of the coral rocks, which rose only a few feet above the level of the water, and, in **stormy**⑤ weather, could only just be seen. Over this island the waves were breaking with great force, and our hearts were filled with fear as we saw that there was not a spot where we could put our little boat without its being dashed to pieces.

"Show a little bit more sail," cried Jack, as we were **sweeping**⑥ past the weather side of the rock with fearful speed.

Peterkin put up about a foot more of our sail. Little though the addition was, it caused the boat to **lie over**⑦ so much, as we rushed through the angry waves, that I expected it to turn over every instant; and I **blamed**⑧ Jack in my heart for his **boldness**⑨. But I did him **injustice**⑩, for although during two seconds the water rushed into the boat in a river, he succeeded in guiding us sharply round to the sheltered side of the rock, where the water was calmer and the force of the wind broken.

"Out your oars now, boys! That's well done. Row!"

① curl /kɜːl/ v. 弄卷，卷曲，弯曲

② quit /kwɪt/ v. 离开，辞职，停止
③ in danger 在危险中
④ blinding /'blaɪndɪŋ/ a. 使盲的

⑤ stormy /'stɔːmi/ a. 暴风雨的，粗暴的

⑥ sweep /swiːp/ v. 掠过

⑦ lie over 延期，搁延

⑧ blame /bleɪm/ v. 责备
⑨ boldness /'bəʊldnɪs/ n. 大胆，冒失
⑩ injustice /ɪn'dʒʌstɪs/ n. 不公正

见。事实上，我们环顾四周时感到心惊胆战，现在我们失去了海岛的庇护，那些翻卷怒吼的冲天巨浪似乎马上就要吞掉我们。海水从四面八方涌进船来，我得不停地把水淘掉。杰克得驾船，彼得金得时刻操纵船帆，否则我们就有生命危险。突然杰克指着正前方的一个低矮的小岛（也可能是一片岩石）充满希望地叫了一声。由于满天乌云，铺天盖地的水滴使人睁不开眼睛，所以先前我们没有看见它。

当我们靠近这块岩石的时候，我们发现这上面既没有树也没有草，它很低，海水从四周涌上来撞击着它。实际上它只是一块珊瑚礁的顶部，仅仅高出海平面几英尺，在暴风雨的天气里，只能勉强看到。海浪疯狂地冲击着这个小岛，我们没有找到一块能让船停靠，而又不被撞成碎片的地方，内心不禁充满了恐惧。

"帆升高一点儿，"当我们以可怕的速度掠过礁石向风侧的时候杰克叫道。

彼得金把帆升起了大约一英尺多。虽然只是升高了一点点，当我们冲过怒涛时，帆几乎让船停下来，我感到每时每刻都有翻船的危险。我在心里暗暗责备杰克的大胆。很快我就发现这对他是不公平的，虽然有两秒钟海浪涌进船里成了河，但是他成功地操纵着小船敏捷地绕到岩石避风的这面，这里的水相对平静一些，风势也较弱。

"现在把桨伸出去，伙计们！好极了，划！"

The Cave

We obeyed instantly. The oars went into the waves together. One good hard pull, and we were floating in a calm opening that was so narrow as to be just able to admit our boat. Here we were in perfect safety, and as we leaped on shore and fastened our rope to the rocks, I thanked God in my heart for our **deliverance**① from so great danger.

But although I have said we were now in safety, I think that few of my readers would have liked to be in our place. It is true we had no lack of food, but we were wet to the skin; the sea was beating round us and the water flying over our heads, so that we were completely clothed, as it were, in water. The spot on which we had landed was not more than twelve yards across, and from this spot we could not move without the chance of being carried away by the storm. At the upper end of the bay was a small **hollow**② or cave in the rock, which sheltered us from the force of the winds and waves; and as the rock **extended**③ over our heads, it prevented the drops of water from falling upon us.

"Why," said Peterkin, beginning to feel cheerful again, "it seems to me that we have got into a fish's cave, for there is nothing but water all round us; and as for earth or sky, they are things of the past."

Peterkin's idea was more than a fancy, for what with the sea **roaring**④ in white waves up to our very feet, and the water flying in white sheets **continually**⑤ over our heads, and more water dropping heavily from the rock above like a **curtain**⑥ in front of our cave, it did seem to us very much more like being below than above water.

"Now, boys," cried Jack, "let's make ourselves comfortable. Toss out our food, Peterkin; and here, Ralph, help me to pull up the boat.

岩 洞

我们立刻照着命令去做。几条桨一齐伸进波涛里。我们用力一划就漂到一个平静的开口上了,那开口很窄,刚好能容得下我们的小船。这里非常安全,我们跳上岸,把小船用绳子系在岩石上的时候,我从心里感谢上帝,他把我们从极其危险的境地解救出来。

虽然我说我们现在已经安全了,但是我想没有人愿意处在我们现在的境地。是的,我们不缺吃的,但是我们浑身上下都湿透了。大海在我们身边沸腾着,海浪从我们头上掠过,可以说,我们浑身上下都是水。我们上岸的地方不到十二码宽,在这地方只要一动就会被风暴带进海里。在小海湾上部的礁石里有一个小洞,它使我们躲避了狂风恶浪的淫威,一块岩石从我们头上伸出来,挡住了落在我们身上的水珠。

"啊哈,"彼得金说,他又开始高兴起来,"我觉得我们好像进了一个鱼洞。这儿除了水没有别的东西,至于天和地嘛,那都是过去的事情了。"

彼得金的想法可不是幻想。因为大海咆哮着,白色的浪花直扑我们的脚下,铺天盖地的白色浪头不断从我们头上飞过,大量海水从头顶的岩石上哗哗流下,好像在我们的洞前挂了一条水帘,我们真的觉得这更像在水下而不是在水上。

"喂,伙计们,"杰克叫着,"我们还是把自己弄得舒服一点。彼得金,从船上把食物弄下来。

① deliverance /dɪˈlɪvərəns/ n. 救出,救助,释放

② hollow /ˈhɒləʊ/ n. 洞穴
③ extend /ɪkˈstend/ v. 扩充,延伸,伸展,扩展

④ roar /rɔː/ v. 吼叫,咆哮
⑤ continually /kənˈtɪnjʊəlɪ/ ad. 不断地,频繁地
⑥ curtain /ˈkɜːtn/ n. 窗帘,门帘

The Coral Island

Make haste."

We were much cheered by the cheerful manner of our companion. Fortunately the cave, although not very deep, was quite dry, so that we succeeded in making ourselves much more comfortable than could have been expected. We landed our food, dried our garments, spread our sail below us, and after having eaten a good meal, began to feel quite cheerful. But as night drew on our spirits went down again, for with the daylight all **proof**① of our **security**② disappeared. We could no longer see the firm rock on which we lay, while the storm roared loudly round us.

The night grew perfectly dark as it advanced, so that we could not see our hands when we held them up before our eyes, and were obliged to feel each other occasionally to make sure that we were safe, for the storm at last became so terrible that it was difficult to make our voices heard. A slight change of the wind, as we supposed, caused a few drops of water ever and again to blow into our faces; and the sea, in its mad boiling, washed up into our little bay until it reached our feet and threatened to **tear away**③ our boat. In order to prevent this latter **misfortune**④, we pulled the boat farther up and held the rope in our hands.

Occasional **flashes**⑤ of lightning showed us the fearful **scene**⑥ all round us. Yet we **longed for**⑦ those flashes, for they were less terrible than the thick blackness that succeeded them. The thunder seemed to tear the skies in two, and fell upon our ears through the wild shouting of the storm as if it had been but a gentle summer wind; while the waves burst upon the weather side of the island until we fancied that the rock was giving way, and in our terror we held on to the bare ground, expecting every moment to be carried away into the black sea. Oh, it was a night of terrible fear! And no one can **imagine**⑧ the feelings of joy with which we at last saw the **dawn**⑨ of day break through the clouds round us.

① proof /pru:f/ *n.* 证据,证明
② security /sɪˈkjʊərɪtɪ/ *n.* 安全

③ tear away (使)勉强离去
④ misfortune /mɪsˈfɔːtʃən/ *n.* 不幸,灾祸
⑤ flashe /flæʃ/ *n.* 光芒
⑥ scene /siːn/ *n.* 场,景,情景
⑦ long for 渴望

⑧ imagine /ɪˈmædʒɪn/ *v.* 想象
⑨ dawn /dɔːn/ *n.* 黎明,曙光

嘿,拉尔夫,帮我把船拉过来,赶快。"

我们被同伴的乐观态度鼓舞着。幸运的是,虽然这个洞不很深,但是很干燥,因此我们可以让自己很舒服,起码比想象的要好。我们把食物拿上岸,弄干衣服,把船帆铺在地上,在美美地吃了一顿之后,开始感觉很不错了。但是入夜时我们又精神不振了,我们平安无事的所有证据都和白天一道消失了。暴风雨在我们身边发出震耳的呼啸,我们已经看不到躺在身下的坚固的石头了。

夜越来越深,天越来越黑,伸手不见五指,我们不得不不时地摸摸对方,来确定我们都还活着,这时候暴风雨变得可怕之极,听到对方的声音都很困难,我们感觉到风起了一点变化,不时有些水滴被吹落到我们脸上。大海疯狂地翻腾着,冲上那个小小的海湾直抵我们脚下,威胁着要把船夺走。为了不让这种倒霉的事发生,我们把船又向上拉了拉,把绳子攥在手里。

我们不时借闪电的亮光看清了周围的可怕景象,但是我们还是渴望闪电再次出现,因为紧接在后面的黑暗比闪电更令人害怕。霹雳好像要把天空撕成两半,雷声穿过暴风雨的怒吼传到我们的耳边,仿佛只是一阵夏日的和风。海浪猛烈袭击小岛向风的一侧,我们觉得那边的岩石就要塌掉了,因为害怕,我们紧紧抓住裸露的地面,觉得每时每刻都有可能被冲进黑暗的大海。噢,这真是一个恐怖之夜!没有人能想象得到当我们终于看到曙光冲破四周云层时的那份快乐。

The Coral Island

For three days and three nights we remained on this rock, while the storm continued. On the morning of the fourth day it suddenly ceased, and the wind fell completely, but the waves still ran so high that we did not dare to **put off**① in our boat. During the greater part of this **period**②, we had scarcely gone to sleep for more than a few minutes **at a time**③, but on the third night we were soon asleep. Early on the fourth morning, we found the sea very much down, and the sun shining brightly again in the clear blue sky.

We Return

It was with light hearts that we set forth once more in our little boat, and rowed away for our island home, which, we were happy to find, was in sight in the distance, for we had feared that we had been blown entirely out of sight of it. As it was perfectly calm, we had to row during the greater part of the day; but towards the afternoon a fair wind came on, which allowed us to put up our sail. We soon passed Penguin Island, and the other island which we had failed to reach on the day the storm **commenced**④. But as we had still enough food, and were anxious to get home, we did not land, to the great **sorrow**⑤ of Peterkin, who seemed to be very fond of the penguins.

Although the wind was pretty fresh for several hours, we did not reach the outer reef of our island till **nightfall**⑥, and before we had sailed more than a hundred yards into the lagoon, the wind **died away**⑦ altogether, so that we had to take to our oars again. It was late, and the moon and stars were shining brightly when we arrived opposite the house and leaped upon the shore. So glad were we to be safe back again on our island, that we scarcely took time to drag the boat a short way up the

① put off 不安,摆脱,延期
② period /ˈpɪəriəd/ n. 一段时间,时期
③ at a time 每次,一次

④ commence /kəˈmens/ v. 开始
⑤ sorrow /ˈsɒrəʊ/ n. 悲伤,懊悔
⑥ nightfall /ˈnaɪtfɔːl/ n. 傍晚,黄昏
⑦ die away 减弱,消失

我们在岩石上已经三天三夜了,暴风雨还在继续。在第四天的早上雨突然停了,风也大大减弱了,但海浪仍旧很高,我们不敢乘船离开。在这期间的绝大部分时间里,我们睡觉几乎没有一次超过几分钟的,但是在第三天晚上,我们很快睡着了。第四天一大早,我们发现大海平静了许多,太阳又明晃晃地照耀在蔚蓝的天空上。

回　家

又一次坐在小船上起航,向海岛上的家划过去,心情格外轻松。我们高兴地发现在远处可以看到海岛,我们还担心我们被风吹到了根本见不到它的地方了呢。因为几乎没有风,在一天中的大部分时间里我们不得不划船。但是接近下午的时候,一阵畅快的海风吹来,我们又可以升起帆了。我们很快经过了企鹅岛,还有那座在暴风雨骤起那天没有上去的岛。但是因为我们还有足够的食物,又都渴望回家,所以我们没有上岸,这让彼得金很遗憾,他看起来非常喜欢企鹅。

虽然风强劲地吹了几个小时,但是在傍晚时分我们还没有到达海岛外面的珊瑚礁。我们在环礁湖里航行了还不到一百多码,风就完全停了,我们又得操起桨来。我们在靠近房子的岸边登陆时,天已经很晚了,星星和月亮都亮闪闪的。能安全地回到我们的岛,真让人高兴。我们匆忙把船拖到离水不

The Coral Island

beach, and then ran up to see that all was right at the house. I must say, however, that my joy was mixed with a sort of fear in case our home had been visited and **destroyed**[①] while we were away; but on reaching it we found everything just as it had been left.

① destroy /dɪˈstrɔɪ/ v. 破坏，毁坏

远的岸上，就跑去看我们的家是否一切都好。然而我必须说，我欢乐的心情里还夹着一丝忧虑，说不定我们不在的时候，有人到过我们的小屋还把它给毁了，但是我们回到屋子里，发现所有东西都和我们离开时一样。

Chapter 17
A Battle

For many months after this we continued to live on our island in great peace and happiness. Sometimes we went out fishing in the lagoon, and sometimes went hunting in the woods, or climbed to the mountain-top, by way of a change, although Peterkin always said that we went for the purpose of calling to any ship that might chance to come in sight. But I am certain that none of us wished to be taken out of our **prison**①, for we were extremely happy, and Peterkin used to say that as we were very young we should not feel the loss of a year or two. Peterkin, as I have said before, was fourteen years of age, Jack eighteen, and I fifteen. But Jack was very tall, strong, and **manly**② for his age, and might easily have been mistaken for twenty.

Our Employments③

The weather was beautiful, and as many of the fruit-trees continued to bear fruit and **blossom**④ all the year round, we never wanted for a **plentiful**⑤ supply of food. The pigs, too, seemed rather to increase than

17
一场战斗

暴风雨过后，我们在海岛上又安宁快活地住了好几个月。有时我们到环礁湖里钓鱼，有时我们去树林里打猎，或者爬上山顶换换口味，然而彼得金总是说我们之所以上山，是为了呼叫可能碰巧从附近经过的船只。但是我确信没人想离开这个樊笼，因为我们在这儿过得非常快乐，彼得金常说我们还非常年轻，浪费一两年时间没有关系。我从前说过，彼得金十四岁，杰克十八岁，我十五岁。但是杰克就其年龄来说，又高大，又强壮，像个大男人，很容易被误认为有二十岁了。

我们的活动

这里的气候宜人，岛上许多果树一年四季都开花结果，因此我们从来不用担心我们的食物供应。虽然彼得金经常用他的渔叉去袭击猪群，但是看起来猪的数目是增多了，而不是减少了，如果我们没

① prison /ˈprɪzn/ *n.* 监狱

② manly /ˈmænlɪ/ *a.* 像男人的,强壮的

③ employment /ɪmˈplɔɪmənt/ *n.* 工作

④ blossom /ˈblɒsəm/ *v.* 开花

⑤ plentiful /ˈplentɪfʊl/ *a.* 多的,丰富的

·209·

The Coral Island

become fewer, although Peterkin was very frequent in his attacks on them with his spear. If at any time we failed in finding a herd, we had only to pay a visit to the tree under which we first saw them, where we always found a large family of them asleep under its branches.

We employed ourselves very busily during this time in making various garments of coconut cloth, as those with which we had landed were beginning to be very **worn**①. Peterkin also made excellent shoes out of the skin of the old pig, in the following manner: — He first cut a piece of the **hide**② a few inches longer than his foot. This he left for some time in water, and while it was wet he sewed up one end of it, so as to form a rough back to a shoe. This done, he bored a row of holes all round the edge of the piece of skin, through which a line was passed. Into the sewed-up part of this shoe he pushed his **heel**③. Then drawing the string tight, the edges rose up and came over his foot all round. It is true there were a great many **ill-looking**④ places in these shoes, but we found them very **serviceable**⑤, all the same, and Jack came at last to prefer them to his long boots.

We also made various other useful articles, which added to our comfort, and once or twice spoke of building us a big house. But we liked our present one so much, and found it so serviceable, that we determined not to leave it, nor to attempt the building of another house, which in such a country might turn out to be rather unpleasant than useful.

Diving in the Water Garden also still gave us as much pleasure as ever; and Peterkin began to be a little more used to the water from constant practice. As for Jack and me, we began to feel as if water were our **native**⑥ place, and spent so much time in it that Peterkin said he feared we would turn into fish some day, and swim off and leave him;

① worn /wɔːn/ *a.* 用旧的，穿坏的

② hide /haɪd/ *n.* 兽皮

③ heel /hiːl/ *n.* 脚后跟

④ ill-looking /ˈɪlˈlʊkɪŋ/ *a.* 丑陋的

⑤ serviceable /ˈsɜːvɪsəbl/ *a.* 可用的，耐用的

⑥ native /ˈneɪtɪv/ *a.* 出生地的

能找到猪群，不管是什么时候，只要去我们第一次发现它们的那棵大树底下，就总能看到一大群躺在树底下睡觉。

这段时间里我们忙着用椰子皮做各种衣服，我们上岛时穿的衣服已经开始变得破烂不堪了。彼得金还用那头老猪的皮做了些很不错的鞋子，方法如下：首先，他剪下一块比他脚大几英寸的皮子。然后把它放在水里一段时间，等它泡湿之后，把皮子的一边缝起来，就成了一个简陋的鞋后跟。做完这个之后，他在这块皮子的两边各打上一排孔眼，把绳子从孔眼中穿过去。他把脚后跟放进皮子缝合的部分里，然后把绳子系紧，这样皮子的两边向上包过来把他的脚全部包住。尽管这些鞋子的确在很多地方还存在着缺陷，但是我们发现它们还是非常实用，结果杰克觉得和他的长筒靴相比，还是猪皮鞋更可取。

我们还做了其他各种有用的东西，过得更舒服了一些，有时还谈到建一所大房子的事。但是我们非常喜欢现在住的房子，觉得它很实用，所以决定不搬家。也不想再另建一所房子，在这种地方盖大房子，结果很可能是招人烦而不是实用。

在"水底花园"里的潜水仍像从前一样带给我们极大的快乐。由于经常练习，彼得金开始有点适应水了。至于我和杰克，则开始觉得水好像是我们的出生地，我们花很长时间泡在水里，彼得金说他害怕有一天我们会变成鱼，甩下他游走了。

adding that he had been for a long time observing that Jack was becoming more and more like a shark every day. **Whereupon**[①] Jack replied that if he, Peterkin, were changed into a fish, he would certainly turn into nothing better or bigger than a crab.

Poor Peterkin was not so sad at being unable to come with us in our delightful dives under water, except, indeed, when Jack would dive down to the bottom of the Water Garden, sit down on a rock and look up and make faces at him. Peterkin did then often say he would give anything to be able to do that. I laughed when Peterkin said this; for if he could only have seen his own face when he happened to take a short dive, he would have seen that Jack's was easily beaten by it; the great difference being, however, that Jack made faces on purpose — Peterkin couldn't help it!

Now, while we were **engaged with**[②] these **occupations**[③], an event occurred one day which was as unexpected as it was alarming and **horrible**[④].

Canoes[⑤] **Appear**

Jack and I were sitting, as we often used to do, on the rocks above Diamond Cave. Peterkin was getting the water from his garments, having just fallen into the sea — a thing he was constantly doing — when our attention was suddenly drawn to two objects which appeared on the sky-line.

"What are they; do you know?" I said, **addressing**[⑥] Jack.

"I can't think," answered he. "I've noticed them for some time, and fancied they were black sea-birds, but the more I look at them the more I feel **convinced**[⑦] they are much larger than birds."

① whereupon /(h)weərəˈpɒn/ conj. 然后,于是

② engage with 与…开战,从事
③ occupation /ˌɒkjʊˈpeɪʃən/ n. 职业
④ horrible /ˈhɒrəbl/ a. 可怕的

⑤ canoe /kəˈnuː/ n. 独木舟,轻舟

⑥ address /əˈdres/ v. 发表演说,讨论

⑦ convince /kənˈvɪns/ v. 说服,使…相信

他还说，很长时间以来他发现杰克一天天变得越来越像鲨鱼了。于是杰克回答说如果彼得金变成鱼，也肯定不会变成一条好鱼，比螃蟹好不了多少。

实际上对于不能和我们一起愉快地潜水，可怜的彼得金已经不那么伤心了，除了在杰克能够潜到水底，坐在岩石上冲岸上的彼得金做鬼脸的时候。此时彼得金总是说他愿付任何代价学会这招。每到这时我就会发笑。要是彼得金入水以后马上就能看到自己的脸，那该多好啊，他会发现杰克的鬼脸太逊色了。但是两者之间有明显的不同。杰克的鬼脸是故意做的，而彼得金则是不由自主。

正当我们忙于这些活动的时候，有一天，突如其来地发生了一件非常可怕的事情。

出现独木舟

我和杰克像往常一样坐在"钻石洞"上面的岩石上，彼得金正在把刚刚掉进海里的衣服拧干，他老是干这种事，这时我们的注意力突然被天边出现的两件东西吸引过去。

"那是什么？你知道吗？"我对杰克说。

"不知道，"杰克回答，"我已经注意它们一段时间了，开始我觉得它们是黑色的水鸟，但是我越看越坚信它们比鸟大多了。"

· 213 ·

The Coral Island

"They seem to be coming towards us," said I.

"Hallo! What's wrong?" asked Peterkin, coming up.

"Look there," said Jack.

"Fish!" cried Peterkin, **shading**[①] his eyes with his hand. "No — eh —*can* they be boats, Jack?"

Our hearts beat with joy at the very thought of seeing human faces again.

"I think you are about right, Peterkin. But they seem to me to move strangely for boats," said Jack, in a low **tone**[②], as if he were talking to himself.

I noticed that a shade of alarm crossed Jack's face as he gazed long at the two **objects**[③], which were now nearing us fast. At last he jumped to his feet.

"They are canoes, Ralph! Whether war-canoes or not I cannot tell; but this I know, that all the natives of the South Sea Islands are **fierce**[④] man-eaters, and they have little respect for strangers. We must hide if they land here, which I **earnestly**[⑤] hope they will not do."

We Hide

I was greatly alarmed at Jack's speech, but I thought less of what he said than of the earnest, anxious manner in which he said it, and it was with very uncomfortable feelings that Peterkin and I followed him quickly into the woods.

"What a pity," said I, as we gained the shelter of the bushes, "that we have forgotten our arms!"

"It doesn't matter," said Jack. "Here are sticks enough and to **spare**[⑥]."

As he spoke he laid his hand on a number of thick poles of various

① shade /ʃeɪd/ v. 遮蔽

② tone /təʊn/ n. 语气,音调

③ object /ˈɒbdʒɪkt/ n. 物体,目标

④ fierce /fɪəs/ a. 猛烈的,残忍的,狂暴的,强烈的

⑤ earnestly /ˈɜːnɪstlɪ/ ad. 认真地,热心地

⑥ spare /speə/ n. 剩余,备用 a. 多余的 v. 剩下的

"它们好像朝我们这边来了。"我说。

"嘿！怎么啦？"彼得金爬上来问。

"瞧那边。"杰克说。

"鱼！"彼得金手搭凉棚叫道，"噢，不！能是船吗？杰克？"

一想到又可以见到人的面孔了，我们的心都高兴得嘣蹦直跳。

"我想你差不多说对了，彼得金。可要说是船嘛，我又觉得它们动得有些怪。"杰克说，他的声音很低，仿佛是在自言自语。

杰克紧盯着那两件东西时，我发现他脸上掠过一道恐怖的阴影，那两件东西正飞快地向我们靠近。最后他跳了起来：

"那是独木舟，拉尔夫！我不知道它们是不是作战用的，但是我知道，南海诸岛的土著人都是凶残的食人族，而且他们对陌生人一点也不客气。如果他们在这儿上岸，我们必须躲藏起来。我打心眼里希望他们别来。"

藏　身

听了杰克的话，我感到非常害怕，但是让我更揪心的不是这番话本身，而是他讲话时那种严肃而焦急的神态，我和彼得金跟着杰克急忙躲进树林，心里忐忑不安。

"真可惜，"我们在灌木林里藏起来的时候我说，"我们忘了拿武器了。"

"没关系，"杰克说，"这里有的是棍子用。"

The Coral Island

sizes, which Peterkin's ever-busy hands had formed during our **frequent**① visits to the place, for no other purpose, it would seem, than that of having something to do.

We each selected a thick stick according to our several tastes, and lay down behind a rock, whence we could see the canoes **approach**②, without ourselves being seen. At first we said a word or two now and then on their appearance, but after they entered the lagoon, and drew near the beach, we ceased to speak, and gazed with the greatest interest at the scene before us.

We now observed that the first canoe was being chased by the other, and that it contained a few women and children, as well as men — perhaps forty **souls**③ in all; while the boat which pursued it contained only men. They seemed to be about the same in number, but were better armed, and had the appearance of being a **war-party**④. Both **crews**⑤ were **paddling**⑥ with all their might, and it seemed as if the men behind paddled hard themselves to catch the others before they could land. In this, however, they failed.

The first canoe made for the beach close beneath the rocks behind which we were hidden. Their short oars flashed in the water, and sent up a constant shower of drops. The water **curled**⑦ from the front, and the eyes of the rowers were shining in their black faces as they rowed with all their force; nor did they stop till the canoe struck the beach with a shock. Then with a shout the whole party jumped, as if by magic, from the canoe to the shore. Three women, two of whom carried babies in their arms, rushed into the woods; and the men **crowded**⑧ to the water's edge, with stones in their hands, spears and sticks raised, to prevent their enemies from coming on shore.

The distance between the two canoes had been about half a mile,

① frequent /ˈfriːkwənt/ a. 频繁的,经常的

② approach /əˈprəʊtʃ/ v. 靠近,接近

③ soul /səʊl/ n. 人,精髓

④ war party n. 主战派
⑤ crew /kruː/ n. 全体船员
⑥ paddle /ˈpædl/ v. 划动

⑦ curl /kɜːl/ v. 弄卷,使弯曲

⑧ crowd /kraʊd/ v. 拥挤,挤满,挤进

说着他把手放在一大堆大小不一的粗棍子上。这些棍子是在我们多次光顾这儿的时候,彼得金用那双闲不住的手做的。在当时看来做这些东西只是想找点事干,没有其他的目的。

根据个人的喜好,我们每人挑了一根粗棍子放在岩石后面,从那儿我们能看到独木舟正在逼近,而对方却看不到我们。开始我们还不时地谈论上一两句,但是后来他们进到了环礁湖里,靠近岸边,我们就闭上了嘴,怀着极大的兴趣注视着眼前的一幕。

这时我们发现第一艘独木舟是被第二艘追赶着的,上面装着男人,还有几个妇女和儿童,总共大约有四十人。追赶着他们的那艘船上都是男人。他们差不多也有四十人,但全副武装,看上去是一个作战团伙。两伙人都在拼命划桨。后面的那些人使劲地划,似乎想在前面的人上岸之前抓住他们,但是他们的目的没有达到。

第一艘独木舟靠近我们藏身的岩石下面的海滩了。他们的短桨在水里闪着光,不断扬起阵阵水花。海水在船头翻卷着,划船的人拼尽全力划,眼睛在黝黑的脸膛上闪闪发光。等船撞到了岸上,他们才停下桨来。然后,随着一声叫喊船上的人全都跳了起来,就像变魔术一样从独木舟一下子到了岸上。有三个妇女,其中有两个抱着她们的孩子,冲进了树林里。男人们聚集在岸边,手里拿着石头,举着梭镖和木棒,阻止敌人上岸。

两艘独木舟相距大约只有半英里,因为速度很

and, at the great speed they were going, this was soon passed. As the second boat neared the shore, no sign of fear could be noticed. On they came like a wild horse — received but took no notice of a shower of stones. The canoe struck, and with a shout they leaped into the water, and drove their enemies up the beach.

The Battle

The battle that immediately took place was frightful to behold. Most of the men used sticks of huge size and strange shapes, with which they beat in each other's heads. As they wore almost no clothes, and had to bound, leap, and run in their terrible **hand-to-hand**① fights, they looked more like **devils**② than human beings. I felt my heart grow sick at the sight of this **bloody**③ battle, and would have liked to have turned away, but something seemed to hold me down and keep my eyes upon the fighting men. I observed that the attacking party was led by a most strange being, who, from his size and strangeness, I thought was a **chief**④. His hair stood out, so that it looked like a large hat. It was a light yellow colour, which surprised me much, for the man's body was as black as coal, and I felt certain that the hair must have been coloured. He was painted from head to foot. With his yellow hair, his huge black **frame**⑤, his shining eyes and white teeth, he seemed the most terrible **monster**⑥ I ever saw. He was very terrible in the fight, and had already killed four men.

Suddenly the yellow-haired chief was attacked by a man quite as strong and large as himself. He waved a heavy club something like an **eagle's**⑦ beak at the point. For a second or two these huge men watched one another, moving round and round as if to gain an **advantage**⑧, but

快，后面的人很快就赶上来了。当第二艘独木舟靠近岸边的时候，上面的人显得无所畏惧。他们满不在乎地迎着雨点一般的石头像野马一样冲过来。独木舟触礁了，他们大叫一声跳进水里，上岸追赶敌人去了。

战 斗

随即爆发的战斗看上去太可怕了。大多数男人都拿着奇形怪状的大棍子，抢打对方的头部。因为他们几乎没穿衣服，所以他们在这场可怕的肉搏战中必须连跑带跳，看上去不像人而更像魔鬼。看着这场血腥的战斗我觉得恶心，真想背过身去，但是似乎有什么东西吸引着我，我的眼睛一直盯着那些人。我发现一个十分强壮的人指挥着进攻的这队人。从他的个头和古怪的样子来看，我想他是个首领。他的头发支棱着，看起来就像一顶大帽子。头发是浅黄色的，这让我们感到很奇怪，因为这人的身体像炭一样黑，我肯定他的头发一定是染成那样的。他从头到脚都绘着图案。他长着黄色的头发，巨大的黑色身躯，炯炯有神的大眼睛和白色的牙齿，我觉得他是我见过的最可怕的妖怪。在战斗中他很厉害，已经杀死了四个人了。

突然这个黄头发首领受到了一个和他同样强壮同样高大的男人的进攻。他挥舞着一根头上像鹰嘴的大棒子。两个巨人对视了一两秒钟，同时转着圈

---

① hand-to-hand *a.* 极接近的，白刃战的
② devil /ˈdevl/ *n.* 魔鬼，恶魔
③ bloody /ˈblʌdɪ/ *a.* 血腥的，嗜杀的

④ chief /tʃiːf/ *n.* 首领

⑤ frame /freɪm/ *n.* 框，结构，骨架
⑥ monster /ˈmɒnstə/ *n.* 怪物，恶人，巨物

⑦ eagle /ˈiːgl/ *n.* 鹰
⑧ advantage /ədˈvɑːntɪdʒ/ *n.* 优势，有利条件

seeing that nothing was to be gained by this, and that the loss of time might turn the **tide**① of battle either way, they made up their minds to attack at the same instant, for, with a wild shout and jump, I saw them **swing**② their heavy sticks, which met with a loud report. Suddenly the yellow-haired native **tripped**③, his enemy jumped forward, the great stick went up, but it did not come down, for at that moment the man was knocked down by a stone from the hand of one who had **witnessed**④ his chief's danger.

This was the end of the battle. The natives who landed first turned and ran towards the bush, on seeing the fall of their chief. But not one escaped. They were all caught and knocked over. I saw, however, that they were not all killed. Indeed, their enemies, now that they were **conquered**⑤, seemed anxious to take them alive; and they succeeded in securing fifteen, whom they bound hand and foot with ropes, and carrying them up into the woods, laid them down among the bushes. Here they left them, for what purpose I knew not, and came back to the scene of the late battle, where the rest of the party were washing their **wounds**⑥.

Out of the forty blacks that made up the attacking party, only twenty-eight remained alive, two of whom were sent into the bush to hunt for the women and children. Of the other party, as I have said, only fifteen were left, and these were lying bound and helpless on the grass.

Jack and Peterkin and I now looked at each other, and whispered our fears that the natives might climb up the rocks to **search for**⑦ fresh water, and so discover the place where we were hiding; but we were so much interested in watching their movements that we agreed to remain where we were — and, indeed, we could not easily have risen without

① tide /taɪd/ *n.* 潮，趋势，潮流

② swing /swɪŋ/ *v.* 摇摆，使…旋转

③ trip /trɪp/ *v.* 跌倒

④ witness /ˈwɪtnɪs/ *v.* 目击

⑤ conquer /ˈkɒŋkə/ *v.* 克服，征服,战胜

⑥ wound /wuːnd/ *n.* 创伤

⑦ search for 找寻（探索，探求）

子好像想从气势上压倒对方。但是看到谁都没有占到便宜，而且浪费了各自改变战局的时间，他们同时决定发起进攻，我看到他们疯狂地又跳又叫，挥动着手里的大棍子，棍子碰到一起时砰砰作。突然那个黄头发土著人绊倒了，他的对手向前跳了几步，大棍子举起来了，却没有落下去，就在这时，有个土著人看到主子处境危险，用石头把他砸倒在地了。

于是战斗结束了，看到自己的头领倒了下去，首先上岸的那些土著人向灌木丛跑去。但是没有人能逃脱，他们全都被抓住打倒在地上。然而我看到他们没有都被杀死。既然他们被打败了，他们的敌人当然很想活捉他们了。他们抓住了十五个人，这十五个人先是被绳索捆住手脚，然后被带进树林，按倒在灌木丛里。不知出于什么目的胜者走开了，回到了刚才的战场，这一拨其余的人正在那儿清洗伤口。

攻方的四十个黑人中，只剩下二十八个人还活着，其中两个人被派到灌木丛里搜寻妇女和孩子。另一拨人，我已经说过，只有十五个人还活着，他们被捆着手脚，孤立无援地躺在草地上。

我，杰克和彼得金你看着我，我看着你，小声地谈论我们担心的事情，土著人有可能爬上岩石找淡水喝，从而发现我们的藏身之处，但是我们对他们的所作所为实在太感兴趣了，所以决定留在原地不动，而且实际上我们很难站起来而不被发现。有一个土著人走到树林里，又很快拿着木头走出来。我们对他生火的办法感到十分意外，他也用弓钻取火，和杰克为我们生起第一堆火的

The Coral Island

showing ourselves. One of the natives now went up to the wood, and soon came with wood, and we were not a little surprised to see him set fire to it in the very same way as Jack had done the time we made our first fire — with the bow and **drill**①.

When the fire was burning, two of the party went again to the woods and came back with one of the bound men. A terrible feeling began to **creep**② over my heart as the thought flashed upon me that they were going to burn their enemies. As they bore him to the fire my feelings were almost too much for me. I breathed deeply, and seizing my stick, tried to jump to my feet; but Jack's **powerful**③ arm held me to the earth. Next moment one of the natives raised his club, and beat in the unhappy creature's head. He must have died instantly; and strange though it may seem, I had a feeling of pleasure when the deed was done, because I now knew that the poor man could not be burned alive. Scarcely had his limbs ceased to move when the natives cut pieces of flesh from his body, and, after roasting them slightly over the fire, ate them.

Prisoners④

Suddenly there came a cry from the woods, and in a few seconds the two natives hastened towards the fire dragging the three women and their two babies along with them. One of those women was much younger than her companions, and we were struck with the gentle look on her face, which, although she had the flat nose and thick lips of the others, was of a light **brown**⑤ colour, and we thought that she must be of a different **race**⑥. She and her companions wore short skirts. Their hair was **perfectly**⑦ black, but instead of being long, was short and **curly**⑧ — though not **woolly**⑨ — somewhat like the hair of a young boy.

① drill /drɪl/ n. 钻

② creep /kriːp/ v. 爬，蔓延

③ powerful /ˈpaʊəfʊl/ a. 强有力的

办法完全一样。

　　火在燃烧的时候，又有两个人走到了树林里带回了一个被绑着的男人。我忽然想到这些人是要把他们的敌人烧熟，一种可怕的感觉渐渐逼上心来。他们赶着俘虏走向火堆的时候，我的愤怒几乎按捺不住了。我喘着粗气，紧紧地抓住我的木棒，想一跃而起，但是杰克那有力的臂膀把我压在地上。接着一个土著人抡起大头棒，朝那个可怜的俘虏头上打去。俘虏一定是马上就死掉了，看到人死了，我反倒感到欣慰，这看起来可能很奇怪，但这是因为我知道这个可怜的人不会被活活烧死了。他的身躯刚刚停止抽搐，那些土人就从尸体上割下肉来，稍微在火上烤了烤就吃下去。

④ prisoner /ˈprɪznə/ n. 囚犯

俘　虏

⑤ brown /braʊn/ a. 褐色的，棕色的
⑥ race /reɪs/ n. 种族
⑦ perfectly /ˈpɜːfɪktlɪ/ ad. 完全地，无瑕疵地，完整地
⑧ curly /ˈkɜːlɪ/ a. 卷曲的
⑨ woolly /ˈwʊlɪ/ a. 羊毛制的，似羊毛的

　　突然从树林里传出一声尖叫，一会儿那两个土著人拖着三个妇女和她们的两个孩子匆忙地朝火堆走来。其中一个妇女要比两个同伴年轻很多，她脸上的那种温柔的神态深深地打动了我们。虽然她和其他人一样，鼻子扁扁的，嘴唇厚厚的，但是她的皮肤是浅棕色的，因此我们想她同这些人肯定不是一个种族。她和她的同伴都穿着短裙子。她们的头发油黑发亮，但是不长，是很短很卷曲的那种，但也不是羊毛卷，有些像小男孩的头发。

　　正当我们有点紧张地关注着这些可怜的俘虏的

The Coral Island

While we gazed with interest and some **anxiety**① at these poor creatures, the big chief advanced to one of the elder women and laid his hand upon the child. But the mother drew back from him, and holding the little one to her bosom, uttered a cry of fear. With a creel laugh, the chief tore the child from her arms and tossed it into the sea. A low sound burst from Jack's lips as he witnessed this wicked act and heard the mother's cry, as she fell fainting on the sand. The little waves rolled the child on the beach, as if they refused to be a party in such a wicked act, and we could observe that the little one still lived.

The young girl was now brought forward, and the chief addressed her; but although we heard his voice and even the words clearly, of course we could not understand what he said. The girl made no answer to his fierce questions, and we saw by the way in which he pointed to the fire that he **threatened**② her life.

"Peterkin," said Jack, in a whisper, "have you got your knife?"

"Yes," replied Peterkin, whose face was pale as death.

"That will do. Listen to me, and obey my orders quickly. Here is the small knife, Ralph, Fly, both of you, through the bush, cut the ropes that **bind**③ the prisoners, and set them free. There, quick, before it is too late." Jack jumped up, and **seized**④ a heavy but short stick, while his strong frame trembled with anger, and large drops rolled down his face.

To the Rescue⑤

At this moment the man who had killed the native a few minutes before advanced towards the girl with his heavy stick. Jack uttered a shout that **rang**⑥ like a death-cry among the rocks. With one bound he leaped over a side of the rock full fifteen feet high, and before the

① anxiety /æŋˈzaɪətɪ/ n. 焦虑,挂念,担心

② threaten /ˈθretn/ v. 威胁;恐吓

③ bind /baɪnd/ v. 绑,约束

④ seize /siːz/ v. 抓住,夺取

⑤ rescue /ˈreskjuː/ n. 救援

⑥ ring /rɪŋ/ v. 包围,环境

时候,那个大个子首领来到一个年长的妇女跟前,把手放在她孩子身上,那妇女急忙收回孩子,把他紧紧地抱在怀里,因为害怕尖叫了一声。随着一阵野蛮的大笑,那首领从她的怀里夺过孩子扔进海里。看到首领的暴行,听到孩子母亲昏倒在沙滩前发出的哭喊,杰克的嘴里迸发出一种低沉的吼声。轻柔的波浪把孩子卷到了海滩上,好像拒绝参与这种罪恶的谋杀似的,我们能看到那小家伙儿还活着。

那个年轻的女孩被带到前面来,首领在对她说话,当然啦,虽然他的声音甚至每个字我们都能听清楚,却听不懂他在说什么。女孩没有回答他令人厌恶的提问,我们看到他指着火堆,威胁要杀了她。

"彼得金,"杰克低声问,"你带刀子了么?"

"带了。"彼得金答道,他的脸像死人一样苍白。

"那好。听我说,赶快按我说的去做。拉尔夫,这儿有一把小刀。你们俩跑进灌木丛,割断那些俘虏身上的绳子,把他们放了。好啦,快跑,趁着还不算太晚。"杰克跳起来,拿起一根短粗的棍子。他那健壮的身躯因愤怒而颤抖着,大滴的泪水从脸上滑落下来。

营 救

这时候几分钟前杀死土著人的那个男人提着大头棒向那个女孩走去。杰克大吼一声,杀气腾腾的声音在岩石间回荡。他噌地一下从高达十五英尺的岩石边上跳了出来,趁土著人目瞪口呆,还没有回

natives had **recovered**① from their surprise, was in the middle of them; while Peterkin and I **dashed**② through the bushes towards the prisoners. With one blow of his stick Jack felled the man with the **club**③, then turning round with a look of terrible anger, he rushed upon the big chief with the yellow hair. If the blow which Jack aimed at his head had taken effect, the huge native would have needed no second stroke; but he was quick as a cat, and **avoided**④ it by jumping to one side, at the same time swinging his heavy stick at the head of his **foe**⑤.

It was now Jack's turn to leap away, and well was it for him that the first burst of his blind anger was over, else he had been an easy foe for his huge enemy; but Jack was cool now. He made his blows rapidly and well, and the great value of his light stick was proved in this fight; for while he could easily avoid the blows of the chief's heavy stick, the chief could not so easily avoid those of his light one. But he was so quick, and his stick was so frightful, that although Jack struck him almost every blow, the strokes had to be **delivered**⑥ so quickly that they wanted force.

It was a good thing for Jack that the other natives considered the success of their chief in this fight to be so certain that they did not come to his help. Had they doubted it, they would have probably ended the matter at once by felling him. But they contented themselves with waiting to see what happened.

The force which the chief had to spend in using his stick now began to be clear. He moved more slowly, he breathed hard, and the surprised natives drew nearer in order to assist him. Jack observed this. He felt that his **fate**⑦ was certain, and decided to cast his life upon the next blow. The chief's club was again about to descend on his head. He might have avoided it easily, but instead of doing so, he suddenly shortened his hold

① recover /rɪˈkʌvə/ v. 恢复,复原,补偿
② dash /dæʃ/ v. 猛冲,猛掷
③ club /klʌb/ n. 大头棒,棍棒

④ avoid /əˈvɔɪd/ v. 避免
⑤ foe /fəʊ/ n. 敌人,仇敌

⑥ deliver /dɪˈlɪvə/ v. 递送,交付

⑦ fate /feɪt/ n. 命运

过神儿来,一下子冲进他们中间,这时候我和彼得金冲进灌木丛朝那些俘虏跑去。杰克一棍子将手提大头棒的土著人打倒在地,然后满面怒容地转过身来,朝高大的黄毛首领冲去。如果杰克照头打的那下没有落空,大个子首领就用不着挨第二下了,但是他像猫一样敏捷,向旁边一跳就避开了杰克的进攻,同时挥舞大棒朝杰克头上打来。

现在轮到杰克跳开了,幸运的是杰克最初爆发出来的无名怒火已经平息了,不然的话,就他那庞大的敌人而言,他太容易对付了。但是杰克现在已经冷静下来了。他的进攻快速而有效,事实证明他那根分量不重的棍子在格斗中太有用了,他可以很容易地避开首领重棒的攻击,而那首领躲开他的进攻就不大容易了。但是他很敏捷,棒子也很有威力,虽然杰克几乎每下都击中了,但是由于出棍必须很快,所以力量就不够了。

其他土著人认为他们的首领肯定能在搏斗中取胜,因此没有上来帮忙,这对杰克来讲是件好事。要是他们心存疑虑,就很可能立刻把杰克打倒,结束这场战斗,但是他们只是满足于袖手旁观。

现在可以看清那个大个子首领挥舞大棒耗费气力了,他的动作慢多了,嘴里喘着粗气。那些大吃一惊的土著人围拢上来想帮首领一把,杰克察觉到了这一点,他觉得命运已定,是死是活就看下一棒了。首领的大棒又要落到他的头上了,他可以很容易地避开这一击,但是他没这么做,而是突然把棍子向上握了握,迎着大棒冲了上去,用尽全身力气击中了敌人两眼之间的部位,然后倒在地上,被首

The Coral Island

of his own club, rushed in under the blow, struck his enemy right between the eyes with all his force, and fell to the earth, crushed beneath the body of the chief.

A dozen clubs flew high in air, ready to descend on the head of Jack; but they waited a moment, for the huge body of the chief completely covered him. That moment saved his life. Before the natives could **tear**[1] the chief's body away, seven of their number fell beneath the clubs of the prisoners whom Peterkin and I had **set free**[2], and two others fell under our own hands. We could never have done this had not our enemies been so taken up with the fight between Jack and their chief that they had failed to observe us until we were upon them. They still had three more men than we had; but we were **joyful**[3] with **victory**[4], while they were taken by surprise and shocked by the fall of their chief. Besides, they were surprised by the **sweeping**[5] anger of Jack, who seemed to have lost his senses completely, and had no sooner shaken himself free of the chief's body than he rushed into the middle of them, and with three blows our numbers were equal. Peterkin and I flew to help him, the natives followed us, and in less than ten minutes the whole of our enemies were **knocked down**[6] or made prisoners, bound hand and foot, and stretched out side by side upon the seashore.

① tear /tɪə/ v. 撕破,夺走
② set free 释放

③ joyful /ˈdʒɔɪfʊl/ a. 欢喜的
④ victory /ˈvɪktərɪ/ n. 胜利
⑤ sweeping /ˈswiːpɪŋ/ a. 规模(或范围)大的

⑥ knock down 击倒,撞倒

领的身躯压在底下。

许多棍棒举到空中,准备猛打杰克的脑袋,但是却停留了片刻,因为首领硕大的身躯完完全全把杰克盖住了,这一时机救了他的命。那些土著人还没能把主子的尸体拖开,就有七人死在被我和彼得金解救的俘虏的棍棒之下,有两人死在我俩手里。要不是敌人全身心地关注杰克和他们主子之间的战斗,在我们袭击之前没有发现我们,我们绝不可能得手。他们比我们还多三五个人,但是我们正因为胜利而欢欣鼓舞,他们却因主子的死亡陷入震惊之中。另外,杰克的震怒使他们颇感意外,杰克看起来完全失去了理智,他扭动身子刚从首领身下挣脱出来,就冲到敌人中间,三棍过后,我们的人数就和敌人一样多了。我和彼得金飞跑着过去帮他,土著人也跟着我们。不到十分钟的功夫,所有的敌人不是被杀死了就是成了俘虏,他们手足被缚,直挺挺地并排躺在海滩上。

Chapter 18
Alone Again

After the battle was over, the natives crowded round us and gazed at us in surprise, while they continued to **pour**① upon us **a flood of**② questions, which of course we could not answer. However, by way of putting an end to it, Jack took the chief (who had recovered from the effects of his wound) by the hand and **shook**③ it **warmly**④. No sooner did the blacks see that this was meant to express our good wishes than they shook hands with us all round. After this was gone through Jack went up to the girl, who had never once moved from the rock where she had been left, but had continued **eagerly**⑤ watching all that had passed. He made signs to her to follow him, and then, taking the chief by the hand, was about to **conduct**⑥ him to the house, when his eye fell on the poor baby which had been thrown into the sea and was still lying on the shore. Dropping the chief's hand he **hastened**⑦ towards it, and to his great joy found it to be still alive. We also found that the mother was beginning to recover slowly.

"Here, get out of the way," said Jack, pushing us on one side, as we bent over the poor woman and tried to **restore**⑧ her. "I'll soon bring her round."

18
再陷孤独

① pour /pɔː, pʊə/ v. 倒,倾泻,蜂涌而来
② a flood of 一群

③ shake /ʃeɪk/ v. 摇动,握手
④ warmly /ˈwɔːmlɪ/ ad. 亲切地,温暖地,热心地

⑤ eagerly /ˈiːgəlɪ/ ad. 渴望地

⑥ conduct /ˈkɒndʌkt, -dəkt/ v. 引导,指挥,管理
⑦ hasten /ˈheɪsn/ v. 催促,赶快

⑧ restore /rɪsˈtɔː/ v. 回复,恢复,归还

战斗结束之后,土著人簇拥在我们身边,好奇地看着我们,同时提出了一连串的问题,当然我们没法回答这些问题。杰克握着他们首领的手(他已经从昏迷中苏醒过来)热烈地摇动着,才算结束了提问。这些黑人一看到我们用这种方式表达良好的愿望就立刻同我们每个人握手。握完手以后,杰克走到那个女孩面前,她还留在岩石边那儿一动不动,一直密切地关注着发生的一切。杰克示意她跟他走,然后拉着首领的手想把他带回家里去,这时他的目光落到那个被扔进海里,这会儿仍然躺在海滩上的可怜的孩子身上。他放下首领的手立刻冲过去,令他高兴万分的是他发现孩子还活着。我们还发现那位母亲也开始慢慢苏醒过来。

"嘿,让开,"杰克说着把我们推到一边,当时我们弯下了腰想弄醒这可怜的女人,"我很快就会把她救醒的。"

The Coral Island

So saying, he placed the baby on her bosom, and laid its warm cheek on hers. The effect was wonderful. The woman opened her eyes, felt the child, looked at it, and with a cry of joy took it in her arms, at the same time trying to rise, for the purpose, it would seem, of rushing into the woods.

"There, that's all right," said Jack, once more taking the chief by the hand. "Now, Ralph and Peterkin, make the women and these fellows follow me to the house. We'll feed them as well as we can."

In a few minutes the natives were all **seated**① on the ground in front of the house making a good meal off a cold roast pig, several ducks, and cold fish, together with a large supply of coconuts, bread-fruits, yams, taro, and fruit; with all of which they seemed to be quite **familiar**② and perfectly satisfied.

While they were eating, we three, being **thoroughly**③ tired with our day's work, took a good drink from a coconut, and throwing ourselves in our beds, fell fast asleep. The natives, it seems, did so too, and in half an hour the whole camp was sleeping.

How long we slept I cannot tell, but this I know, that when we lay down the sun was setting, and when we awoke it was high in the **heavens**④. I awakened Jack, who jumped up in surprise, and could not at first understand our **situation**⑤.

"Now, then," said he, "let's see after breakfast. Hallo, Peterkin, lazy fellow! How long do you mean to lie there?"

Peterkin rubbed his eyes. "Well," said he, looking up after some trouble, "if it isn't tomorrow morning, and me thinking it was to-day all this time! Hallo, beauty! Where did you come from? You seem quite at home, anyhow. Bah! might as well speak to a cat as to you."

This was **called forth**⑥ by the sight of one of the elderly women,

① seat /si:t/ v. 坐

② familiar /fəˈmɪljə/ a. 熟悉的
③ thoroughly /ˈθʌrəlɪ/ ad. 彻底地

④ heaven /ˈhevən/ n. 天空,天堂
⑤ situation /ˌsɪtjʊˈeɪʃən/ n. 形势,局面,处境

⑥ call forth 唤起,引起

说着,杰克把孩子放入她怀里,让孩子温暖的面颊贴着她。效果好极了。那女人睁开眼睛,发觉了孩子,看着他,然后高兴地叫了一声,把孩子搂在怀里,同时试图站起来,似乎是想冲进树林里去。

"你看,平安无事了。"杰克说,他又拉起了首领的手,"喂,拉尔夫,彼得金,让这些女人和男人跟我们回家去。我们要尽可能好好招待他们。"

几分钟以后,这些土著人全都坐在我们房前的地上,尽情地享用一只冷烤猪、几只鸭子和冷鱼,还有大量的椰子、面包果、甘薯、芋头和水果,所有这些东西他们看来都很熟悉,吃得心满意足。

在他们吃饭的时候,我们三个人痛痛快快地喝了些椰子汁,白天的事真把我们累垮了,然后我们就一头倒在床上,很快睡着了,那些土著人看起来也一样,半个小时之内,整个营地都入睡了。

我不知道我们睡了多长时间,我只知道我们躺下去的时候太阳正在西沉,当我们醒来的时候它又高高地挂在天上了。我叫醒杰克,他吃惊地跳起来,开头还弄不清是怎么回事。

"好啦,"他说,"让我们吃完早饭再想吧。哎,彼得金,懒虫!你打算在这儿躺多久?"

彼得金揉了揉眼睛,困惑地抬起头说:"哦,是今天早晨啦,我一直还以为是昨天呢。哎!美人儿!你从哪儿来?无论怎么看,你都像在家一样无拘无束啊。呸!跟你说话可能还不如跟猫说呢。"

· 233 ·

who had seated herself on the rock in front of the house, and, having placed her child at her feet, was busily engaged in eating the remains of a roast pig.

By this time the natives outside were all up, and breakfast nearly ready. During the course of it we several times tried to speak with the natives by signs, but without effect. At last we hit upon a plan of discovering their names. Jack pointed to his **chest**[①] and said "Jack" very clearly; then he pointed to Peterkin and to me, repeating our names at the same time. Then he pointed to himself again, and said "Jack," and laying his finger on the chest of the chief, looked clearly into his face. The chief **instantly**[②] understood him, and said "Tararo" twice clearly. Jack repeated it after him, and the chief, **nodding**[③] his head, said "Chuck." On hearing which Peterkin **burst out**[④] laughing; but Jack turned, and said, "I must look even more angry than I feel, Peterkin, for these fellows don't like to be laughed at." Then turning towards the youngest of the women, who was seated at the door of the house, he pointed to her; at which the chief said "Avatea."

Jack now made signs to the natives to follow him, and taking up his axe, he led them to the place where the battle had been fought. Here we found the prisoners, who had passed the night on the beach, having been completely forgotten by us, as our minds had been full of our guests, until we went to sleep. They did not seem the worse for their night on the beach, however, as we **judged**[⑤] by the way in which they ate the breakfast that was soon after given to them.

Jack then began to make a hole in the sand, and after working a few seconds, he pointed to it, and to the dead bodies that lay on the beach. The natives immediately saw what he wanted, and running for their **paddles**[⑥], made a hole in the course of half an hour that was quite large

① chest /tʃest/ n. 胸部

② instantly /ˈɪnstəntlɪ/ ad. 立即地,即刻地
③ nod /nɒd/ v. 点头
④ burst out 大声喊叫,突然发生

⑤ judge /dʒʌdʒ/ v. 断定,判断

⑥ paddle /ˈpædl/ n. 桨

  他说这番话是因为看见一个年纪大一点的妇女,坐在房子前的石头上,把孩子放在脚下,正起劲地吃剩下的烤猪肉。

  这时屋外的土著人全都起来了,早饭也差不多准备好了,这期间我们好几次试着用手势同他们交谈,但是都失败了。后来我们想出了一个办法来知道他们的名字。杰克指着自己的胸口清清楚楚地说:"杰克。"又指着我和彼得金,同时说出我们的名字,接着他又指着自己说:"杰克。"然后把他的手指放在首领的胸口上,一直看着他的脸。首领立即明白了他的意思,很清楚地说了两遍:"塔拉罗。"杰克跟着首领说他的名字,首领点点头说:"查克。"听见这话,彼得金哈哈大笑起来。杰克回过头说:"我的外表肯定比内心更生气,彼得金,这些人是不喜欢被嘲笑的。"然后转向那个最年轻的女孩,她正坐在屋子门口,杰克指着她,首领说:"阿瓦蒂亚。"

  杰克拿起他的斧子,示意那些土著人跟着他走,把他们带到了昨天打仗的地方。我们这才发现在海滩上过夜的那些俘虏已经被我们忘得一干二净,我们在睡觉之前把心思全都放在客人身上了,但是看起来他们夜里在海滩上过得还不算糟,我们根据他们吃早饭的情况做出了上述判断,早饭随后就发给他们了。

  接着杰克开始在沙滩上挖坑,挖了几下以后,他指了指坑,又指了指卧在海滩上的尸体。土著人立刻明白了杰克的意思,跑过去拿起他们的桨,挖起坑来,半个小时之内就挖好了一个够把所有尸体

enough to contain all the bodies of the dead. When it was finished they tossed their dead enemies into it with so little feeling that we felt certain they would not have put themselves to this trouble if we had not asked them to do so. The body of the yellow-haired chief was the last thrown in. This poor man would have recovered from the blow with which Jack knocked him down, and indeed he did try to rise during the fight that followed his fall; but one of his enemies, happening to notice the action, gave him a blow with his stick that killed him on the spot.

The Natives Depart①

When the boat was ready, we assisted the natives to carry the prisoners into it, and helped them to load it with food. Peterkin also went into the woods for the purpose of making a special attack upon the pigs, and killed no less than six of them. These we baked and **presented**② to our friends on the day that they went away. On that day Tararo made a great many signs to us, which, after much talking, we came to understand were to ask us to go away with him to his island; but having no **desire**③ to do so, we shook our heads very **decidedly**④. We gave him a piece of wood with our names cut on it, and a piece of **string**⑤ to hang it round his neck.

In a few minutes more we were all on the beach. Being unable to speak to the natives, we shook hands with them, and expected they would depart; but before doing so, Tararo went up to Jack and robbed noses with him, after which he did the same with Peterkin and me! Seeing that this was their way of saying **farewell**⑥, we determined to use their **custom**⑦, so we robbed noses with the whole party, women and all! Avatea was the last to take leave of us, and we felt a feeling of

都装进去的坑。坑挖完之后，他们带着一丝不易察觉的情绪把敌人的尸体扔进坑里，我们觉得如果不是我们让他们这么做，他们肯定不会找这个麻烦的。黄毛首领的尸体是最后一个抛下去的，这个可怜的人在杰克把他击倒之后会苏醒过来的。实际上他在摔倒之后，战斗仍在进行时确实想爬起来，但是正好被一个对手看到了，他给了他一棍子，当场把他打死了。

土著人走了

　　船准备好了，我们帮着土著人把俘虏带上船，又帮着把食物装好。彼得金还去了树林，专门是为了打野猪，他杀死了不下六头猪。我们把这些猪烤熟，在他们走的那天送给了他们。那天，塔拉罗冲我们打了很多的手势，比画了半天我们才明白了他是想请我们一起走，到他的岛上去，但是因为不想去，我们十分坚决地摇了头。我们送给他一块刻着我们名字的木片，还有一截绳子，好把木片挂在脖子上。

　　过了一会儿我们都来到了海边，因为无法用语言同他们交流，我们就同他们握手告别，以为他们要走了。但是在离去之前，塔拉罗走到杰克面前和他碰了碰鼻子，然后也同我和彼得金碰了鼻子！看到这是他们告别的方式，我们决定利用他们的风俗，于是同所有的人都碰了鼻子，男人、女人和孩子！阿瓦蒂亚是最后一个和我们告别的人，在她走近我们向我们告别的时候，我们真的感到很伤心。除了神态温柔，她是这些人当中惟一一个在与我们

① depart /diːpaːt/ v. 离开

② present /ˈpreznt/ v. 赠送，提出

③ desire /dɪˈzaɪə/ n. 愿望，欲望

④ decidedly /dɪˈsaɪdɪdlɪ/ ad. 断然地，果断地

⑤ string /strɪŋ/ n. 线，弦

⑥ farewell /fɛəˈwel/ n. 告别

⑦ custom /ˈkʌstəm/ n. 习惯，风俗

real sorrow when she approached to **bid**① us farewell. Besides her gentle manners, she was the only one of the party who showed the smallest sign of sadness at parting from us. Going up to Jack, she put out her flat little nose to be rubbed, and after that did the same to Peterkin and me.

An hour later the canoe was out of sight, and we, with a feeling of sadness creeping round our hearts, were seated in **silence**② beneath the shadow of our house, thinking of the wonderful doings of the last few days.

① bid /bɪd/ v. 命令，吩咐

② in silence 沉默地（无声地）

分别之际微露伤感的人。她走到杰克面前，伸出她那扁平的小鼻子和杰克碰了碰，然后跟我和彼得金碰了鼻子。

　　一个小时以后独木舟在视野里消失了。伤感悄悄爬满心头，我们无声地坐在房子的阴影下，想着几天来发生的种种令人惊叹的事情。

Chapter 19
Good-bye to the Coral Island

One day we were all enjoying ourselves in the Water Garden before going fishing; for Peterkin had kept us in such constant supply of pigs that we had become quite tired of them, and **desired**① a change. Peterkin was sitting on the rock, while we were **creeping**② among the rocks under the water. Happening to look up, I observed Peterkin making signs for us to come up, so I gave Jack a push and rose immediately.

"A sail! A sail! Ralph, look! Jack, away on the **sky-line**③ there, just over the entrance to the lagoon!" cried Peterkin, as we climbed up the rocks.

"So it is, a ship!" said Jack, as he began to dress **in haste**④.

Our hearts were thrown into a terrible state by this **discovery**⑤, for if it should touch at our island we had no doubt the captain would be happy to take us to some of the other islands, where we could find a ship sailing for England or some other part of Europe. Home, with all that it meant, **rushed**⑥ in upon my heart like a flood, and much though I loved the Coral Island and the house which had now been our home so long, I felt that I could have quitted all at that moment without a sigh. With hope and joy we hastened to the highest point of rock near our house,

19
告别珊瑚岛

① desire /dɪˈzɪə/ v. 渴望，向往
② creep /kriːp/ v. 爬，蹑手蹑脚地走

③ sky-line n. 水天交界线

④ in haste 急速地
⑤ discovery /dɪsˈkʌvərɪ/ n. 发现，发现物

⑥ rush /rʌʃ/ v. 冲，奔，仓促行事

一天，我们都在"水中花园"里尽情玩耍，然后要去钓鱼，彼得金总是让我们吃猪肉，我们都吃腻了，因而想换个花样。彼得金坐在岩石上。我们则在水底的岩石中爬行，我碰巧一抬头，发现彼得金正示意让我们上来，我推了杰克一下，立刻浮了上去。

"帆！帆！拉尔夫，看！杰克，在地平线那儿，就在环礁湖的开口上！"我们爬上岩石时彼得金大叫。

"对，是条船！"杰克边说边急忙动手穿衣服。

这个发现使我们的心顿时陷入了翻江倒海的状态。如果船能到达我们的岛，我们觉得船长一定乐意把我们带到其他一些岛上，在那里我们可以搭上去英国的或者是到欧洲其他地方的船。家，以及家的全部含义像潮水一样涌上心头。虽然我非常喜欢珊瑚岛，和那座许久以来一直是我们的家的小房子，但是我觉得那时我能毫不惋惜地放弃所有这一切。现在我们能看到那条船被一股强风吹着，正径

· 241 ·

and waited for the vessel, for we now saw that she was making straight for the island, under a strong wind.

In less than an hour she was close to the reef, where she rounded to, and stopped in order to look at the coast. Seeing this, and fearing that they might not see us, we all three waved pieces of coconut cloth in the air, and soon saw them beginning to get a boat into the water and run busily about the decks as if they meant to land.

Our Farewell Visits

Next day we paid a farewell visit to the different familiar spots where most of our time had been spent. We climbed the mountain-top, and gazed for the last time at the rich green trees in the valleys, the white sandy beach, the calm lagoon, and the coral reef with its great waves. Then we descended to the rocks above Diamond Cave, and looked down at the pale green animal which we had made such vain efforts to spear in days gone by. From this we hurried to the Water Garden, and took a last dive into its clear waters, and played for the last time among its corals. I hurried out before my companions, and dressed in haste, in order to have a long look at my hole in the rock. It was in fine **condition**① — the water perfectly clear; the red and green seaweed of the brightest colours; the red, **purple**②, yellow and green flower-animals with their arms fully **spread out**③, and stretched as if to welcome their former **master**④; and the shell-fish, as Peterkin said, looking as fine as ever. It was indeed so lovely and so interesting that I would scarcely allow myself to be torn away from it.

Last of all, we came back to the house and collected the few **articles**⑤ we **possessed**⑥. These we took on board in our little boat, after

直朝珊瑚岛驶来。满怀喜悦和希望我们爬到了屋子旁边最高的一块岩石上面,等着这条船。

不到一个小时这条船就靠近了珊瑚礁,它绕着珊瑚礁航行,为了看看海岸而停了下来。看到这些,因为害怕他们可能看不到我们,我们三个在空中挥舞着椰子皮,很快就看到他们开始放一条小船下水,并忙碌地在甲板上跑着,他们好像要登陆了。

最后一次环游海岛

第二天我们来到曾经度过大部分时间的各个熟悉的地方,向它们告别。我们爬上了山顶,最后一次注视着山谷里郁郁葱葱的树木,注视着白色的沙滩,平静的环礁湖和巨浪拍打的珊瑚礁。然后,我们下到"钻石洞"上面的岩石上,向水中望着那个淡绿色的"动物",在过去的日子里,我们白白费了很多力气想要叉住它。从这儿我们又匆忙赶到"水中花园",最后一次潜入清澈的水中,最后一次在珊瑚丛里嬉戏。我赶在同伴前面上岸,匆匆忙忙穿上衣服,为的是好好看看在岩石上的那个小洞。它的状况很好——水很清,红的、绿的水草颜色亮丽;红的、紫的、黄的和绿色的海葵,尽情地伸展着它们的触须,好像是在张开手臂欢迎它们先前的主人。还有那些牡蛎,就像彼得金说的,看来和以前一样好。小洞真是太可爱了,太有趣了,我几乎不能允许自己离它而去。

最后,我们回到屋里收拾了仅有的几样东西,带着它们登上小船,上船之前我们在一块铁木上刻

① condition /kən'dɪʃən/ n. 条件,情况
② purple /'pɜːpl/ a. 紫色的
③ spread out 伸张
④ master /'mɑːstə/ n. 主人
⑤ article /'ɑːtɪkəl/ n. 物品
⑥ possess /pə'zes/ v. 占有,拥有

The Coral Island

having cut our names on a piece of iron-wood, thus:

JACK MARTIN

RALPH ROVER

PETERKIN GAY

which we fixed up inside the house. The boat was then taken on board and the ship **moved off**[①]. A strong wind was blowing off shore when we set sail, at a little before sunset. It swept us quickly past the reef and out to sea. The shore quickly grew more faint as the shades of evening fell, while our ship bounded lightly over the waves. Slowly the mountain-top went down on the sky-line, until it became a mere spot. In another moment the sun and the Coral Island **faded away**[②] together into the broad bosom of the Pacific.

下了我们的名字：

> 杰克·马丁
> 拉尔夫·罗佛
> 彼得金·盖伊

  我们把铁木安顿在屋子里。小船被提到甲板上之后，大船就起航了。我们起航的时候太阳就要落山了，一股强风正从岸上吹来。风吹着我们飞快地经过珊瑚礁来到外面的大海。在暮色笼罩之际，海岸很快就变得模糊不清了，我们的船在苍茫中轻快地跃过海浪。山尖在地平线上慢慢下沉，最后变成了一个小点。转眼之间太阳和珊瑚岛一同消失在太平洋广阔的怀抱里。

① move off 离去，出发

② fade away 逐渐消失